ABRAHAM LINCOLN POLONSKY

AND THE

HOLLYWOOD LEFT

A VERY DANGEROUS CITIZEN

Paul Buhle

and

Dave Wagner

UNIVERSITY OF CALIFORNIA PRESS
Berkeley · Los Angeles · London

University of California Press
Berkeley and Los Angeles, California

University of California Press, Ltd.
London, England

© 2001 by the Regents of the University of
California

Library of Congress Cataloging-in-Publication Data

Buhle, Paul, 1944–.
    A very dangerous citizen : Abraham Lincoln
Polonsky and the Hollywood left / Paul Buhle
and Dave Wagner.
      p .   cm .
    Includes bibliographical references and index.
    ISBN 0-520-22383-7 (alk. paper)
    1. Polonsky, Abraham.   2. Blacklisting
of authors—California—Los Angeles.
3. Polonsky, Abraham—Political and social
views.   4. Authors, American—20th century—
Biography.   5. Hollywood (Los Angeles,
Calif.)—Biography.   6. Screenwriters—United
States—Biography.   7. Politics in motion pictures.   8. Motion picture authorship.
I. Wagner, David.   II. Title.
    PS3531.O377 Z59 2001
    791.43'0233'092—dc21   00-028692

Manufactured in Canada
9 8 7 6 5 4 3 2 1 0
10 9 8 7 6 5 4 3 2 1

To the Memory of the Blacklisted Generation

CONTENTS

Illustrations follow pages 86 and 182

ACKNOWLEDGMENTS

In examining Abraham Polonsky's work and that of his artistic milieu we begin to measure the earlier body of American film's cutting edge and to discern what it offers those of us who come so long after. Subsequent volumes by the same authors will examine the broader artistic and political issues at length and survey the many films that make up the American left wing's cinematic canon. Most of the debts owed for this book have been built up to friends and friendly institutions concerned with the larger issues of the blacklistees.

We wish first to thank the Harburg Foundation for support that made possible several interview trips to Los Angeles and the purchase of videos of dozens of rare films written or directed by blacklistees. Second, we wish to acknowledge the invaluable assistance of the late Marvin Goldsmith (and of his widow, Muriel Goldsmith) in locating and reaching the blacklist survivors across the Los Angeles area, including the earliest interview with a buoyant and bon mottish Abraham Polonsky in 1992. John Schultheiss not only has coproduced three annotated volumes of Polonsky's screenplays and teleplays but has offered us (and Polonsky himself) assistance in all kinds of helpful ways.

Next, we offer our heartfelt thanks to our blacklistee friends—Robert Lees, Walter Bernstein, Jean Butler, Anne Froelick, Wilma Shore Solomon, Ring Lardner, Jr., Alfred Lewis Levitt, and Joan Scott, among others, as well as acknowledging the late Frank Tarloff, Leonardo Bercovici, Millard Lampell, Carlton Moss, and Paul Jarrico—all of whom granted us interviews and told us much about Abraham Polonsky, affirming their admiration for him. John Weber, closest of Polonsky's friends among this circle, read the manuscript and gave us many useful suggestions along the way. Taylor Stoehr, literary executor for the estate of Paul Goodman, generously offered documents from the 1930s and many useful insights about the City College scene of those days. Robert Hethmon, responsible in part for the State Historical Society of Wisconsin's initial acquisition of the Polonsky Papers, kindly loaned us tapes made with Polonsky about John Howard Lawson.

Special thanks to Grace Wagner, Marion Coffey, and Kirsten Ostherr, who assisted in many research tasks along the way. Harold L. Miller and the archivists of the State Historical Society of Wisconsin extended every assistance (Allen Ruff also put in a day's work quickly making available material from the Polonsky Collection that we otherwise would have missed), as did Barbara Dunlap, archivist at the Special Collections of the City College of New York. We are in debt also to Syracuse University Special Collections for supplying an episode of *The Goldbergs*. Edward Portnoy hastily made available a copy of a Yiddish novelette by Joseph Opatoshu. Larry Ceplair lent his expert advice and encouragement, and Nora Sayre offered us a notebook of conversations that she had conducted with the Polonskys in 1980. Thom Andersen, another early scholar of the field, lent us copies of unpublished manuscripts and a video of his important documentary film, *Red Hollywood*. Great thanks to the staff of the Southern California Library for Research and Social Change, especially to Sara Cooper, whose work with the extended circle among Hollywood old-timers made the project possible. Final thanks to Eric Smoodin, our editor at the University of California Press, for his encouragement, his scholarly acumen, and his good humor.

INTRODUCTION

ABRAHAM LINCOLN POLONSKY is surely one of twentieth-century American culture's most intriguing personalities. The sometime noir master Polonsky was "discovered" by Hollywood, publicly praised yet privately viewed as a troublemaker, suspected of monstrous conspiracies, cast out, and finally "rediscovered" decades later. His life as a modernist fiction writer, realistic novelist, union educator, radio—and later, television—scriptwriter, wartime intelligence operative, and full-time radical romantic would be revealing even had he never turned to films. A *New York Times* reviewer noting Polonsky's return from the blacklist hailed him as American film's greatest single loss to McCarthyism.[1] Martin Scorsese echoed this judgment, personally rereleasing Polonsky's *Force of Evil* in 1996 and introducing it on-screen as the gem of neglected 1940s art cinema and a major influence on his own work.[2] Still spry and exceptionally witty in his late eighties, Polonsky the personality had come back into the picture. A series of appearances on National Public Radio and at screenings of his work at the Lincoln Center and assorted film festivals, then his role as Elia Kazan's bête noire, along with a flock of interviews in newspapers and on CNN and *Nightline* around the time of the 1999 Academy Awards ceremony, all rendered the ex-blacklistee a remarkable survivor of America's cultural cold war. The wry figure on the losing side of history in the second half of a disappointing century was reaching out to those who would make politics and culture in the new millennium.[3]

Polonsky's mark on American culture is indelible. Those raised on 1950s mass culture almost surely recall Walter Cronkite's memorably spoken catch lines for *You Are There* (1953–57): "What kind of day was it? A day like all days, with the events that alter and illuminate our time—AND YOU WERE THERE!" Conducting what he called "guerrilla warfare" against McCarthyism under a pseudonym, Polonsky delivered that series' most challenging scripts. Avid movie-watchers of all ages remember *Body and Soul,* arguably the greatest boxing film of all time, as well as John Garfield's personal best; *Tell Them Willie Boy Is Here,* widely hailed (and cursed) as the ultimate cinematic critique of American western mythology; or even *Romance of a Horsethief,* very possibly the spiritually most Yiddish film ever shot in English.

In recent years, once-blacklisted screenwriters have begun to reclaim their "missing" credits, although more often than not posthumously. A growing number of scholars and devotees of all kinds and in all parts of the globe are reassessing the artistic issues of the cold-war era. Rather than sputtering out, the attendant controversies give every indication of burning well beyond the lives of those who were directly affected, and for good reasons. Even though a recent American Film Institute poll was weighted heavily against pre-1950 movies, blacklistees either wrote, directed, or contributed to the scripts of five (arguably, six) of the first thirteen all-time best American movies. (A conspicuous "friendly witness" who learned his political aesthetics on the Left became the director of yet another of those first thirteen.) The blacklistees' credits appeared on eight or nine more of the first thirty-six films in the list.[4] Without the banished Left, Hollywood's canon would be both thinner and poorer by far.

None of Polonsky's features made the AFI list: a fair indication, perhaps, of how films like *The Unforgiven, Rocky, American Graffiti, Dances with Wolves, Forrest Gump,* and *Silence of the Lambs* crowded out many an older favorite. But among Hollywoodites themselves, he continued to loom large as the last of the serious 1940s Marxist thinkers and the finest aesthetician among the disappearing circle of Golden Age activists. In October 1997, when the talent guilds hosted a fifty-year remembrance of the blacklist at the Motion Picture Academy on Wilshire Boulevard, Billy Crystal, John Lithgow, and Kevin Spacey rose to dramatize testimony compelled by the House Committee on Un-American Activities. Polonsky, the last surviving blacklisted director and the wittiest of the interviewees in the American Movie Channel's award-winning documentary *Hollywood Remembers the Blacklist,* shared the stage with actress Marsha Hunt, writer-producer Paul Jarrico, and the current president of the Writers Guild, Daniel Petrie.

The moment was ironic, not only because the then Screen Writers Guild had blacklisted its own members during the McCarthy era but because many of the cinematic *objets d'art* now greatly admired in classrooms and film festivals a half-century later had been anything but premier productions. Such key films of the 1940s as Polonsky's *Force of Evil,* acknowledged precursors of the art cinema in Europe and Japan as well as later dark and moody trends within American film, had been B features in every production sense, generally run at the bottom of any given evening's local double-bill. The aesthetic vein mined by filmmakers and relished by audiences then and now, ostensibly narrow and commonplace, judged by its intended market niche, had somehow proved extraordinarily original and inventive.

Polonsky and the other artists working this vein, which admiring French critics designated *film noir,* made their names in assorted established and highly defined popular genres, from the action melodrama to the musical comedy. Except for a half-dozen years after the Second World War, they never escaped the rigid political and aesthetic controls of the commercial studios and (at closer range) the producers. Nonetheless, the quality and sheer scale of their work before they found themselves ejected from film paradise survive among Hollywood's most remarkable achievements.

The left-wingers around Polonsky—many of whom admired him as their foremost artistic figure—collectively wrote, directed, or provided the original stories for well over a thousand movies. Their credits could easily fill a film encyclopedia. Beginning with the dawn of sound pictures, their accomplishments include the first gangster films of note (*The Public Enemy, Little Caesar, Angels with Dirty Faces*); some of the outstanding early horror films (*Frankenstein, The Devil-Doll, The Raven*); most of the interesting Katharine Hepburn films (*The Little Minister, Holiday, The Philadelphia Story, Woman of the Year,* among others) and many other memorable women's films (*Kitty Foyle, The Bishop's Wife, Forever Amber*); classic literary adaptations (*Becky Sharp, The House of the Seven Gables, A Christmas Carol, A Place in the Sun*); many of the award-winning and box office bonanza war films (not only *Casablanca* but *Destination Tokyo, Pride of the Marines, Hitler's Children,* and *Objective Burma,* among others); political shockers like *Mr. Smith Goes to Washington, Watch on the Rhine, Talk of the Town,* and *All the King's Men;* not to mention Abbott and Costello's biggest hits, a large number of the acknowledged children's classics (*Adventures of Huckleberry Finn; Young Tom Edison; National Velvet; Lassie, Come Home;* and *My Friend Flicka*), the first sympathetic lesbian film (*These Three,* later remade as *The Children's Hour*), most of the early outstanding films about anti-Semitism (*Gentleman's Agreement, Crossfire*) and race (*Intruder in the Dust, Home of the Brave, Pinky, Cry, the Beloved Country,* and *Broken Arrow,* along with the "book" for *Stormy Weather*) made before the cultural Iron Curtain fell in America.

This short list excludes dozens of lively Left-written or Left-directed musicals starring Fred Astaire, Gene Kelly, and Lucille Ball, among others less famous; more than a hundred westerns, ranging from *High Noon* to Cisco Kid nonclassics; several slapstick comedies of Laurel and Hardy, not to mention several of Bob Hope's, Olson and Johnson's, or Judy Canova's. Nor does it enumerate the searing treatments of corrupted capital, tortured masculinity, and psychic crisis, filmic moments immortalized by the likes of Kirk Douglas, Burt Lancaster, and Susan Hayward in movies like *The Strange Love of Martha Ivers, The Champion,* and *Kiss the Blood off My Hands,* and several dozen other highly regarded noirs.

The enduring tragedy of Hollywood is the blacklisting of writers and directors (also some outstanding actors, Oscar-winner Anne Revere, Marsha Hunt, Zero Mostel, Howard Da Silva, Jeff Corey, and J. Edward Bromberg, to name a few of the dozens banned) at their moment of creative maturity; and the near-total absence of their artistic and political influence during the McCarthy era to follow, when only a small handful managed to continue working, mostly under pseudonyms. Their staggered return in relatively small numbers afterward essentially dramatized the large majority's absence.[5]

That a few artists like Carl Foreman, Joseph Losey, and Jules Dassin managed to build impressive careers abroad, that others wrote biblical and slave-theme classics like *The Robe, Spartacus,* and *Cleopatra* as well as dozens of nonclassics during the 1950s and 1960s, and that some blacklisted actors managed to continue on Broadway, could never be fair compensation for the loss. Everyone in Hollywood who was well informed suspected that banned Reds had to have scripted the Oscar-winning race and ethnicity films *The Brave One* and *The Defiant Ones.* Regaining these all-too-obvious credits took decades. Likewise the cinematic symptoms of recovery, which at least demonstrated the silenced generation's denied talent: *The Bridge on the River Kwai, Lawrence of Arabia* (both written under pseudonyms but awarded big-screen treatment), later *Planet of the Apes, The Long Hot Summer, Hud, Exodus, Fail-Safe, The Spy Who Came in from the Cold, Yanks, M*A*S*H, Phaedra, Never on Sunday, Julia, The Children's Hour, The Molly Maguires, The Front, The Great White Hope, Norma Rae, Cross Creek, Nuts, The Group, Midnight Cowboy, Zulu, The Servant, Coming Home, Serpico, The Accident,* and *The Romantic Englishwoman.*

Among the famed (and banned) writers and directors—Donald Ogden Stewart, Sidney Buchman, Waldo Salt, Martin Ritt, Lillian Hellman, and Dashiell Hammett, along with Foreman, Losey, and Dassin—Abraham Polonsky remained sui generis in a number of interesting ways. Nearly all of this group, unusually educated by the standards of the blacklisted Hollywood writers at large, nevertheless lacked Polonsky's formal intellectual background, which he had acquired as a radical-minded college English instructor. Nor did any of them have anything approaching Polonsky's background in labor as educational director of a district CIO unit, an experience particularly valuable to the self-confidence required for brushing aside logic-chopping Communist Party criticisms.

Polonsky's greatest weakness was also the source of his strengths: because he came to Hollywood late, past the age of thirty-five, he never regarded movies as his calling. When the blacklist struck, he made a living for more than a decade quietly doctoring films pseudonymously while others fled or despaired. He had hardly begun a renewed life in films under his own name when heart problems foreclosed on his opportunities as a director, the real creative role for him as an intellectual. His output, while vastly interesting, is also comparatively slight.

Often described as an existentialist, Polonsky was in his own mind a Marxist, not a socialist or a communist. By his own account, the difference was important, though it may seem curious after a century that saw so many defeats of movements calling themselves socialist or communist. With an intellectual self-assurance that was not arrogant, Polonsky insisted that his blacklistee compeers were essentially craftsmen working within the fixed framework of Hollywood filmmaking, men and women of good will who (with few exceptions) lacked any serious notion of the philosophical underpinnings and possible aesthetic implications of a materialist and dialectical view of history or of psychology. Not that he condemned them for it. As he once recalled observing to Albert Maltz, one of the Hollywood Ten, "you don't have to understand religion in order for it to have an effect on you." To believe is enough. Up to a point, that is.

Members of the Hollywood Left unquestionably believed, not excluding quite a number of those who later became friendly witnesses. They believed in unionism for themselves and others in Hollywood. They believed in defeating fascism, racism, and anti-Semitism. They believed in the Soviet Union, even if most believed in Franklin Roosevelt and the New Deal almost as strongly and as far more appropriate for America. They believed that global socialism was, barring catastrophe, probably inevitable, including the United States sometime in the future. But for them, as artists, for the most part as Jews in a world of pervasive anti-Semitism, and as successful American professionals, millenarianism mainly offered a necessary, ethical conclusion to history, a redemption of the materialistic wickedness and needless cruelty always evident in class society but especially so in the era of capitalist mass-production.

This subject has long been difficult or perhaps impossible to approach successfully. That Michael Denning's sweeping survey, *The Cultural Front*, allotted only two precisely chiseled chapters to film (one on Orson Welles, the other on Disney animators) testifies to the depth and complexity of the problem confronting scholars of film, the most influential form of popular culture.[6] In a melancholy afterword to their authoritative 1980 study of the Hollywood blacklist's historical context, Larry Ceplair and Steven Englund reflected that the survivors had determinedly and repeatedly refused to discuss their politics.[7] The further passage of time, the disappearance of most of a generation, and the collapse of the Soviet Union prompted a serious rethinking, as *Tender Comrades: A Backstory of the Hollywood Blacklist*, a volume of interviews, demonstrated.[8] Within the dwindling survivors' community in and around Los Angeles, the cerebral Polonsky was properly regarded as a key to grasping these politics and political aesthetics.

In any case, nearly everything in which the overwhelming majority of the blacklistees strongly believed lay outside filmmaking itself, save their understandable concern for their own working conditions and their flagging hopes for better movies. Generalizations are dangerous here, because the same screenwriters and directors were thoughtful and intelligent, as well as talented. In fact, they were among the most thoughtful people in Hollywood or American intellectual life at large. Nevertheless, for the overwhelming majority "film art" remained an oxymoron, at least in Hollywood. The bitter personal experience of seeing their best work ignored or destroyed reinforced the basic insights that serious writing almost never got translated onto the screen and that film's main potential consisted in plot, dialogue, and character development.

Those who analyzed Russian films knew that artistic visual experimentation had lapsed there after the 1920s, despite technological advances. But even without knowing of or agreeing with the dreadful precedent of artistic regression under Stalin, radicals could see that Hollywood offered visual sensation (Busby Berkeley, special effects) mainly as background for drama. Movies were in fact *moving pictures* of drama, and to a lesser extent vaudeville, transferred from the stage to the screen, with other elements plugged in. Like film music, added during post-production and beyond the director's creative control (or, to say the least, the screenwriter's), visual effect constituted one more element in the assembly-line Hollywood production model, often rendered at the end of the line by the unsung craftsmen of the cutting trade. Not so unlike Stalinist Russia in effect if not cause, little within the profit-making logic of the studio system offered any prospect of change until the system itself could be challenged.

One of the abiding ironies of the McCarthy period in Hollywood is the commonplace assertion that the corporate and collaborative nature of the medium effectively barred threatening material or radical approaches to the film narrative. From the 1940s on, only conservative critics insisted that the blacklisted filmmakers had somehow managed to get a message across to the movie-going public. Answering this charge in an authoritative Fund for the Republic report (1956), liberal but firmly anticommunist supporters of Hollywood criticized the blacklist as unnecessary because an impermeable line of defense already existed in the producers who, along with top studio executives, retained ultimate control of the medium. Even if a rogue director had managed to acquire enough power to push through an unacceptable political message, the study concluded, the protectors of the self-censoring Production Code would catch the corporate error.[9] The blacklist's victims, discouraged by the degree of censorship they had suffered and desperate to continue their careers, readily agreed with this judgment, adamantly refusing to acknowledge any radical aspect in their work.

Investigating committees did find one source of concern: not film plots (with the notable exception of the propagandistic *Mission to Moscow*, informally ordered by Washington, perhaps even by Roosevelt himself), not even characters, but wartime throwaway lines about then-ally Russia, its smiling faces, its dames, and its steadfastness in the face of Nazism. This later inquisitorial wisdom accurately reflected the fallback position of lesser writers who despaired of real influence on film but occasionally sneaked political angles into the margins, especially during songs and ostensibly pure entertainment.

From the perspective of time, however, a comparative study of the films on which the Hollywood Left worked from the early 1930s to their moment of exile reveals a very different picture. What if "subversion" (or radicalism) had less to do with international policies than the grinding effects on the postwar American character of increasing commercialization and the cash nexus? Or still worse, what if it had more to do with that hard-driving, myth-fed American character itself as seen through the thinking and actions of women who challenged the gender basis of the social pyramid? What if the solutions to modern dilemmas were not as simple as a new New Deal (let alone American soviets) but required a fundamental change of heart? And what if the subversion operated more deeply through the art form itself?

More than any other art, the cinema under the studio system transparently reflected the country's social organization. Vast sums of capital were required for labor, equipment, and distribution, and studio owners and their managers vigilantly prevented anything of real social significance from slipping through. But precisely because of this organizational structure, the industry's "literary" workers were able to apply pressure to get something through, not propaganda but a few shards of life recognizable to themselves and to their popular audiences.

Not only the Hollywood Left but independent-minded directors, producers, and stars all saw a chance in the later 1940s to break away from studio domination. In the most primitive Marxist terms, it could be described as an attempt to seize the means of production, but only the most literal or most visionary would have taken such a term seriously. What the insurgents really wanted was to secede from the existing means of production and set themselves up independently, with distribution by the major studios where necessary or desirable. In 1948, the Supreme Court decision against studio ownership of theater chains greatly reinforced this impulse. The prospective sharp decline of movie-going, however, undercut the small-budget operations' potential and, therefore, the viability of wide-scale independence, especially for the low-budget B film genres, where television had its sharpest effect. The new independent American production companies upon which so many hopes for the future were pinned had hardly begun to have an impact when the blacklist swept away Hollywood's most controversial and interesting filmmakers, Polonsky among them.

More than anyone else in the major studios or the independents during this unique moment of mass-culture creativity, Polonsky managed to develop a style of heightened dialogue, stylized camerawork, and forceful characterization that transcended genre. In these films, whose remaining prints might have been lost in some studio vault, can be found the kernel of some of the best films ever produced in the United States, right up to the beginning of the new century.

It could be argued that the movies of the 1960s, including Polonsky's own later films, realized at least some of the early promise of 1940s genre films. But, of course, the particular postwar social forces of class, gender, race, and culture that combined to make the earlier films possible could not be replicated.[10] Filmmaking would grow more demographically diverse, but likely never again would writers and directors come from blue-collar Jewish backgrounds where radical ideas were common and where a New Deal had semiofficially validated social art as no future patronage of the avant-garde by the National Endowment of the Arts possibly could. No generation of writers and directors would know anything quite like the further spiritual uplift of a world crusade against fascism (and anti-Semitism) or the colossal disappointment that followed in McCarthyism and its Russian counterpart.

As the credits roll in *Guilty by Suspicion,* the roughly autobiographical 1991 HBO movie originally scripted by Polonsky, a lean and intense Robert De Niro, returning from France, is picked up at the Los Angeles airport by his determinedly cheerful friend, played by George Wendt. We are in a fictional 1950. That evening, dozens of Hollywood intellectuals, screenwriters, and others gather at a surprise party honoring the returnee, where they reveal their panic and despair. The key scene is a chillingly realistic book-burning incident that is taken from Polonsky's 1956 novel about the blacklist, *A Season of Fear.* At certain moments De Niro even looks passably like a forty-year-old Polonsky, if never so obviously witty or cerebral in his dialogue.

Guilty by Suspicion as shot, however, deleted a crucial episode from Polonsky's original screenplay. Back in France, the real-life Polonsky had mulled whether to remain in Europe or to return to the United States. Virtually every Hollywood blacklistee who fled to Mexico, London, Paris, or Athens, days, weeks, or months ahead of a subpoena, nurtured the idea of an ultimate American vindication. Yet Polonsky alone abandoned a safe haven and probable success to return to the movie-making capital at the height of McCarthyism. Unlike colleagues who soon made Paris a second home, Polonsky already possessed a solid command of French and a world of contacts. Friends he had made during the Resistance and the Liberation were emerging in French politics, and many in the French film industry admired him for *Body and Soul* and *Force of Evil*. His family (contrary to the rewritten story line in *Guilty by Suspicion*, which found De Niro divorced and alone) remained happily by his side. Why in the world would he want to return to a situation that would almost certainly lead to a congressional subpoena, attacks from the press, and long-term unemployment?

Typical of his generation of Jews who personally endured (and saw in their extended families' lives) far worse than loss of profession and artistic expression, Polonsky shrugged when asked about this decision. The United States, even in bad times, could hardly avoid the status of chosen country for someone whose first two names were Abraham Lincoln. He was not about to be run out, not by the Dixiecrats and anti-Semites who ran the House Committee on Un-American Activities and not by sophisticated liberals such as Arthur Schlesinger, Jr., who congratulated the studios for the blacklist. True, the Left had been reduced to shambles and Hollywood would lose much of its creativity for the foreseeable future, ruling out the kind of art films that Polonsky most desired to make. But someone has to fight the losing battles. Entirely aside from his standing as an artist and an intellectual and his willingness to run to the sound of the guns, Polonsky also represented a collective artistic-political past both older and greater than his own.

The real-life antagonists had already made their stage entrances when Polonsky reappeared in 1950, larger in life and far more interesting than in *Guilty by Suspicion*. In the film, actor Sam Wanamaker (exiled to London in real life, and the driving force behind the rebuilding of Shakespeare's Globe Theater) plays the sleazy Hollywood lawyer who unsuccessfully works on De Niro to collaborate with the FBI. The hapless director refuses and the FBI pursues him across the rest of the film. Martin Gang, the Hollywood personality who successfully wheedled confessions from others, never would have bothered trying to cadge the real Polonsky. The alternative story line, revealed only with the release of FBI documents in the 1990s, topped that one by a mile.

Several years earlier, Los Angeles Bureau Special Agent R. B. Hood had identified Polonsky as a "dangerous" filmmaker. Hood himself had taken the time to write a careful thematic analysis of *Force of Evil*, textually supported by phone wiretaps made expressly for Chief J. Edgar Hoover. The Hon. Harold Velde of Illinois, a conservative Republican who chaired the House Committee on Un-American Activities, had concluded for other reasons that the writer-director threatened the national security.

On his return from France, Polonsky (not unlike De Niro in this case) immediately focused on his own professional concerns. He had already signed to write and direct a film for Darryl Zanuck, one of the most skilled and independent-minded producers in Hollywood. Zanuck quickly learned, however, that he could not continue to protect anyone who had not been "cleared." With Hollywood's rumor mill reporting that Polonsky was about to be named as a Communist, Zanuck advised him to work at home and keep a low profile. But when future *Rockford Files* scripter Meta Reis Rosenberg (who knew Polonsky well), mildly talented screenwriter Richard Collins (who barely knew him), and handsome actor Sterling Hayden (who knew him not in the least) all named Polonsky on cue from the committee, an early subpoena became inevitable. For a few weeks before his committee appearance, the studio faithfully kept Polonsky on the payroll. Then, without ceremony, they dropped him. Fifteen years passed before he was allowed again to work under his own name in Hollywood.

In most respects, Polonsky's actual appearance before the committee on April 25, 1951, proved totally predictable. Using his Fifth Amendment privilege, he refused to cooperate when asked about himself and his associates, and he was dismissed after relatively brief questioning. Neither side had anticipated anything different. But in one important respect, Polonsky was different. His service in the Office of Strategic Services hinted at possible intelligence knowledge, perhaps even espionage. As the questioning commenced, an unidentified figure (presumably from the United States intelligence services) approached Velde and whispered something to him. A few moments later, Velde dubbed the witness "a very dangerous citizen." Asked by friends about this characterization, the wry Sylvia Polonsky quipped, "Only to himself!" It must have been hard to laugh, however, at a moment when Congressman Richard Nixon could describe the "Pumpkin Papers" (later the damning microfilm proved to be merely Bureau of Standards data, readily available in public libraries) as evidence of a Soviet spy ring turning over vital secrets to the enemy and when deportations, jailings, and the firings of thousands of public employees took place amid similarly wild accusations.[11]

Moving from life to art, Polonsky's original script for *Guilty by Suspicion* had foregrounded the moment of confrontation—in which a brave if rather confused De Niro also refuses to testify—to the very beginning of the film, an approach that French director Bertrand Tavernier rejected early on as making the rest of the story anticlimactic. Perhaps an even more personal approach, again with the bizarre elements of literal McCarthyism, might have been perfect. The notion that his past as an admired antifascist radio dramatist in the OSS had led Polonsky into some conspiracy of almost unimaginable magnitude was extravagant, to put it mildly. From another angle, however, the charges might be seen as a measure of the high regard for Polonsky among his enemies in Hollywood and the intelligence community. Apart from scientists working on the Manhattan Project and high-ranking New Deal administrators, scarcely anyone, certainly no one in the entertainment world, earned such careful attention. Among the tens of thousands of pages of FBI files on Hollywoodites surveilled or otherwise investigated and released on microfilm in 1991, the tap on Polonsky's phone and transcriptions of selected conversations are unique, suggesting the special attention he received.

The FBI's interest in Polonsky began with scattered references in the year or two after the war and ultimately developed into a rapt attention bordering on obsession. Perhaps his station as secretary of a Hollywood Writers Mobilization subgroup that agitated against restricted-covenant housing in Los Angeles caught Hoover's imagination. The FBI director was compulsively interested in all movements of "Negro Equality," the specter of which disturbed him more continuously than either organized crime or communism.[12] At any rate, by 1947–49 Polonsky's profile had sharpened astonishingly. An informer's report characterized him as "one of the really brilliant men in the [Left] movement," full of "brilliant ideas," and evidently "headed for a very successful future as a screen writer and possibly as a director." Another report, describing him from the standpoint of certain studio executives, went on to call him an "arrogant, difficult man who is disliked by many people in the motion picture industry. According to T-1, POLONSKY feels that capitalism and the capitalistic system is the thing that killed his father who was a small druggist who died at an early age."[13]

Asked about these allegations a half-century later, Polonsky nodded, "About right!"—especially in contrast to the frightened (or paid) informers' usual misjudgments about purported conspiracies of left-wing activities and the political logic of Communist-written films.

One unusually astute FBI report focused on the single issue that might credibly have made Polonsky "a very dangerous citizen," at least for those rare FBI staffers who believed in the creative power of nonpropagandistic art. The long struggle of screenwriters and directors to acquire artistic autonomy from studio dictates had become Polonsky's particular story. Special Agent Hood grew increasingly less preoccupied with Polonsky's labor activities or his participation in subversive campus or public organizations. The danger lay rather in Polonsky's abilities as a filmmaker and equally in his influence on other filmmakers.

Hood evidently had been trying for years to alarm Washington about the subtle influence of movies that questioned the morality of American capitalism. Now he apparently was convinced that he had hit pay dirt. Photostats of the transcribed phone conversations between Polonsky and Ira Wolfert (the author of the novel *Tucker's People,* upon which the film *Force of Evil* was based) highlighted Polonsky's remarks about passing over MGM. "We had a bad reaction [from MGM] to the script on the grounds that, 'What are you trying to do, overturn the system?' So we dropped them like a hot potato."[14]

As a casual remark, this sounds innocuous enough, but not to those who feared that left-wingers' and Jews' iconoclastic and accusatory films had begun to exert wide influence over the popular mind. Emerging from the war stronger than before, these dissidents had gained the self-confidence, and perhaps the clout, to proceed with an openly anticapitalist program. Hood noted that Polonsky's previous film, *Body and Soul,* made between three and four million dollars and had stirred great interest among the major studios. Enterprise, the independent studio that produced *Body and Soul* and gave Polonsky a flattering if nominal vice presidency, had even surmounted opposition from Hollywood's internal censor, the Breen Office, and thereby had begun to chip away at the system protecting public decency. Who knew what they could or would do next?

The sad irony of *Guilty by Suspicion* (which did not prevent the acute Roger Ebert from praising it as "one of the best Hollywood movies I've seen")[15] lay in its treatment of the De Niro character's artistic aspirations. If he ever had any, they were lost in the victimization narrative. Agent Hood may well have been going out on a limb, although in those days no accusation was too far-fetched for serious consideration. Hollywood left-wingers had certainly made films far more didactic than Polonsky's, especially on the acceptable themes of war, fascism, and anti-Semitism. But *Body and Soul, Force of Evil,* and even *I Can Get It for You Wholesale* (the last scripted by Polonsky but produced without giving him any creative control) were far subtler, a different kind of art film as well as a different kind of political film. Polonsky, the most intense of the FBI informers suggested, could be described as the coming figure within the Hollywood Left, a model for the future radical filmmaker. Agent Hood was not so wrong after all: from the Greek theater to Shakespeare to modern film, effective and popular art was always the real danger. And always would be.

ADVENTURES OF THE
ARTIST AS INTELLECTUAL

ABRAHAM POLONSKY LIKED TO DATE his artistic perceptions and the beginnings of his political life to his childhood in the 1910s. The legends and legacies that subtly primed the cultural politics of the 1930s and '40s began with the bohemian innocence and proletarian verve of those years before the First World War. Europe had already seen the night-blooming flowers of decadence in the fin de siècle, and the avant-garde theater of Strindberg, Wedekind, and Ibsen had flourished in Paris, London, Berlin, and Rome at the turn of the century. Sophisticated classes there talked about free love and practiced it. America, meanwhile, was breeding a distinctly vernacular modern culture, from Tin Pan Alley and the Yellow Kid to Model-T Fords. After 1910, modernism dominated the public imagination in an urban America where the Industrial Workers of the World, jazz dancing, Charlie Chaplin, constructivism, and Margaret Sanger all seemed to career together toward the future.

Radicalism, for the moment, looked like a happy extension of the Progressive Era that swept the country. Left-leaning intellectuals and artists, who could rightly claim to have pioneered journalistic muckraking and aesthetic experiments such as Ashcan art and cubism, envisioned themselves leading the awakened masses into the promised land.

The real future, however, lay in a war that would swiftly encompass everything. Wild hopes inspired by foreign revolutions and domestic socialist expectations that had been decades in the making were wiped out during the Palmer Raids and the associated repression of Woodrow

Wilson's outspokenly liberal (as well as deeply racist) administration. Across the Atlantic, European socialism also collapsed, and after the war's smoke cleared, only a haggard Communist regime remained in power on the other side of the world, overburdened with a starving population, a broken economy, a host of international enemies, and a bureaucracy borrowed from czarism. Those who saw the future without illusions about either bolshevism or aspirin-age capitalism knew that it did not work, at least not in the humane sense imagined for "socialism" or "democracy" during more innocent times. Something had slipped away, and nothing was likely to make up for the loss. But the work of the artist's imagination might sustain hope as it realized the individual's and even the civilization's undestroyed possibilities.

The same sense that prevented Polonsky from wildly embracing the Russian-sounding slogans common among intellectuals during the early 1930s prepared him for the complex and difficult times ahead. He would be an artist within the life of the nation and beyond, bearing all the political obligations of the age but also holding back a part of himself for work that politicians of every shade considered neither necessary nor valuable.

1

Abraham Lincoln Polonsky, nine-year-old son of free-thinking radicals, caught an early glimpse of America's scary possibilities when officers from the new Bureau of Investigation closed in on a Bronx neighbor with (in Hollywood talk) "guns blazing." The raid did not drive Polonsky either to reclusiveness or to hunger for revenge. But the incident punctuated the childhood of the boy who loved both his neighborhood and the world opening to him. He understood the Red scare's significance for Jews as well as for radicals.[1]

Perhaps the best entry into Polonsky's life during this era is the novel he described as the closest thing to autobiography he would ever choose to write, Zenia's Way (1980). The world of the boy, Ram, is more or less transparently Polonsky's own childhood world of East 180th Street in the Bronx, close to the Bronx Zoo, Bronx Lake, Bronx River, and the Botanical Gardens. Although the area was on the verge of becoming a vast housing tract, "miles and miles of empty lots where once there had been farms" remained empty during the late 1910s and early 1920s, not only near real working farms but easily accessible to wilder countryside by way of trolleys. Polonsky begins, identifying his childhood almost taxonomically:

> In those days on hot summer nights the mothers used to call their children home across the empty lots. Names mingled with meteors, with lilies, with the perfume of flowering burdock. . . . Where the lots were deep and rich, it grew more than eight feet tall, with wide foot-long leaves, coarse up close but beautiful as the weed spread for the sun, loaded with twigs of burrs whose purple sticky flowers besieged our whole neighborhood with their fragrance. . . .
>
> We lived and played in a landscape of lots, old neighborhoods with older villages tucked within them . . . where still a farmhouse stood isolated among the flowering weeds with the trim garden, grape arbors or wisteria vines.[2]

Other slightly transformed memories, recorded later in an unpublished short story, recall a "tall, wide-eyed boy, with a pale face in which glimmered an ambiguous smile," a boy running through the weeds or heading off to the movie serial "seen weekly at the Mosque Theater." He played in cowboy games, the evil Black Riders against the good White Rider, who (with a secret message on a slip of paper stuffed into his mouth) endured torture rather than put at risk the mythical village. Another favorite narrative featured "the girl and her poor old father" in need of the hero's aid. These, of course, were standard themes of the early film western. Was the boy only playing a game, Polonsky mused later, or was he experiencing "suffering in the profound sense of the word, a knowledge and appropriate choreography in the presence of an idea worth every tribute," something far beyond the serial adventure actor's role on the silent screen?[3] The memories of B movies and of play remained a vital part of Polonsky's feeling for genres and for the craving for entertainment that haunts ordinary people.

Zenia's Way offers even more insight when read as autobiography, its fictionalized details of daily life so closely observed that even the made-up characters give important clues about Polonsky as a child. The boy soon learned about all sorts of real-life mysteries, including love for Laura, a little Italian American who lives a few apartment houses away. According to this fictional account, Laura is that rare girl who plays as an equal in boys' games just as long as they permit her to do so and who refuses to confine her reading to stereotyped "girls' stories" during the schoolchildren's collective library visits. Perhaps because her father is an anarchist, Laura knows more about life than Ram, having "secretly observed, in the darkness of the dark, the motion and the passion" of her parents' lovemaking, an experience that "brought into her life an exquis-

ite tenderness toward her father and a gentleness toward her mother."[4]
On rainy summer afternoons, he in her parents' apartment or she in his,
the two listen to the only other adults of the neighborhood who talk
openly about sexual matters; that listening creates a bond between the
two children, an opening to wonder rather than an invitation to shame.

The children's relationship intensifies when her uncle is gunned down
by the Red Squad, and her father disappears. Ram and Laura race away
together, through the Bronx Zoo, making themselves at home among the
"kidnapped" creatures, finally huddling under a canvas in the barn. Ram
recalls, "We both felt this park of wild beasts was safer than the world."[5]
Later, as he sleeps, Laura leaves him. After a brief reunion, Laura is
placed on a train to distant Minnesota for her own safety. Thus ends the
boy's first romance. Yet he sees Laura's physical leanness and her sturdy
character matched in the novel's philosopher, his father's sister, Zenia. In
moments of excitement, with "arched eyebrows, strange beautiful arches
of black," Zenia's eyes have an "electric light in them at night that
glowed in a kind of wet hardness . . . hiding their radiance of gold"
above a body "graceful and beautiful . . . and filled with authority which
she exercised because of her lively spirit and general sense of command-
ing the universe to obey and show itself for what it was."[6]

Whether Polonsky really fell in love with a little Italian girl or shared
intimate emotional moments with an aunt is not nearly as important as
his vivid awareness of the life around him. This awareness would later
make his art possible. Even favorable critics complained that Aunt Zenia
was too finished, too wise—and they had a point. Like Laura, Zenia was
an invention, even though Polonsky in fact slightly knew a real aunt
who took a medical degree in New York and returned to Russia to join
the Revolution. Just as the fictional Laura was Polonsky's imagining a
love like that for the ballerina whom he would eventually marry, the fictional Zenia was Polonsky's recreation of his family, with its radical
Jewish immigrant sensibility.

The women of Polonsky's fictional world—so unlike I. B. Singer's or
Philip Roth's unpleasant characterizations or the etched proletarian
superhero women of Old Left iconography—were the wise ones, especially in matters of personal life. Even Ram's fictional mother (drawn,
Polonsky insisted, directly from his own mother, Rebecca Rosoff
Polonsky), constrained to limit the boy's behavior, delivered an occasional warning slap, not only to protect him but to civilize him in ways
that the neighbors could not have imagined. These female companions
were, in fact, preparing the child for a unique cultural role.

Male bonding offered no comparison, at least until his college days. Boys seemed to come and go, without leaving a mark. But love also brings loss. Ram's childhood, so full of sacred memory, closes when Laura is shipped off to relatives. Likewise his youth closes with Zenia's departure, a fiction that corresponds with a stonier family reality and Polonsky's own adolescence in 1920s America, where grandiose visions (or illusions) of world transformation would disappear into art and private pleasures.[7]

Above all loomed the dark reality of his father's frustrated and difficult life. Born during the 1880s in the pale where most Russian Jews lived, Henry Polonsky was the son and nephew of pedagogues, himself well educated. En route to the United States early in the century, the elder Polonsky (according to family legend) hopped off a freighter in Palermo and stayed to learn the language, one of a half-dozen that he could read and in which he proudly owned books. Soon moving on to New York, he worked and married a woman from a devoutly religious but also upward-bound family. He urgently wanted to become a doctor, perhaps as distinguished as his brother-in-law, dentist Max Rosoff, who taught at Columbia Medical School. But a medical education was a long haul, at heavy odds, for a young, married Jew in Progressive Era America. Instead, Henry entered pharmacy training in 1909 and regretted it the rest of his life. Faced with heavy financial obligations—a daughter born nine years after Abraham, and a son after that—he dreamed hopelessly of returning to school; meanwhile, he clung to health made precarious by diabetes and grudgingly accepted his fate. Polonsky describes him literally in *Zenia's Way*:

> My father was slight . . . although not small. He had . . . warm or passionate eyes. He was good-looking but his face always seemed a little drawn. He was warm, temperamental, witty. . . . [W]hen he didn't own drugstores which he couldn't afford to keep, he used to work for Eimer and Amend, the chemical manufacturers downtown. Mostly, though, he seemed to be wanting to have a different profession entirely and often spoke of it as if it were still possible. Anyway he was clever and witty about it.[8]

Like so many Jews of his time, Henry was both a socialist and a skeptic. As recalled in *Zenia's Way*, his actions sometimes reveal "someone who has for too long wondered that perhaps the life he had chosen was not the one he might have preferred to live."[9] He had, in short, been compromised in too many different ways. Typical for an educated Russian immigrant, he considered his own world of business and his son's world of school and neighborhood friends full of "backward people," outsiders to the family's educated, sophisticated circle. All the more, then, he loved literature, especially the Russian writers and George Eliot, his absolute favorite. He kept an expansive personal library of many literary and some scientific classics. Not drawn to political activity in the United States himself, he directed his legacy to the son born in 1910, whom he named, with pride and expectation, Abraham Lincoln.

If Polonsky's father never ceased to feel Jewish in every secular drop of his cultivated European blood, that feeling in no way extended to religion. When the family on both sides pressed him to have Abraham barmitzvahed, he relented only so far as to have a Protestant seminary student teach him the Hebrew phrases to be memorized for the ceremony. He never even considered the alternative, the *cheder* teachers notorious for their slaps and insults. The famed realist Yiddish writer Joseph Opatoshu, upon whose short stories the film *Romance of a Horsethief* was based, devoted an entire novel, *Hibru*, to describing the stifling atmosphere of the cheder. It was published in 1918, just a few years before Polonsky would have been sent to one of those infamous sites of rote memorization.

In one of the dozens of closely written notebooks that Polonsky deposited with his private papers, he envisions a dialogue in which a grandfather insists that God sent him to America "to civilize it." When the grandmother insists that there is no god, the grandfather answers curtly, "It's too soon to tell that to the Americans!"[10] The passage never made it into print, but the mentality did: America was not a country to be civilized at will or perhaps at all. This conversation could not have been taken from real life, because Polonsky's own paternal grandfather remained in the Old Country, and his mother's father spent his days davening, as Polonsky said, "in murmured dialogue with God." But the point holds for left-wing Jewish culture then and for a generation or two to come. Not that all or even most Jews ever fit this mentality, but as Woody Allen quipped about Manhattan, the world's premier Jewish city, other Americans were convinced that Manhattanites (by which he meant Jews) were a bunch of atheist-communist homosexuals and, relatively speaking, they were right. In short, the Polonsky family constituted proud disbelievers (or believers in un-Americanisms), a people apart.

Polonsky's maternal grandmother *(bobbe)*, an avid storyteller, read to him endlessly in Yiddish from the fiction of the *Jewish Daily Forward*, transposing historical characters rather than just translating the language. For her (and for the credulous boy), in a story that Polonsky recalled repeatedly, Huck and Tom in that most famous of all American adventure stories were actually Jewish boys rafting the Volga, and Jim was a muzhik, a runaway serf whom they assisted in his escape! Polonsky swears that the world of the *shtetl* that he sought many decades later to reconstruct in *Romance of a Horsethief* was dictated by Bobbe's voice. She had, in his vivid memories, remained with him at every moment. When Polonsky also swore that she gave him all the stories that he would ever need, we can take him at his metaphorical word: she bestowed upon him a literary way of looking at the world. He would become many things but would remain always a storyteller.[11]

Yiddish literature was not just a literature of storytellers. From its rise during the later nineteenth century to its slow fade during the 1930s to the 1960s, it was a literature of a particular kind of storyteller. The first popular Yiddish fiction writer, pen-named Mendele Mokhir Sforim (literally "Mendele the Bookseller"), already demonstrated in his satirical shtetl parables the simple, radical technique of ridiculing the existing authorities—religion and business—by drawing upon a counterculture, or counterauthority, of what Yiddish savant Aaron Lansky has called "redemption in the everyday."[12] Social discontent, a sense of solidarity with the poor, and an overwhelming sense of emerging crisis for the Jewish community (threatened, by the 1880s, with new pogroms) flowed easily into socialist movements, especially the Jewish Labor Bund, toward the end of the century. But they also flowed into the folk art of a displaced petit bourgeoisie.

The output of Sholem Aleichem, I. L. Peretz, and hundreds of other feuilletonists, poets, playwrights, and novelists quickly filled new periodicals in Yiddish-speaking communities around the globe, especially in Eastern Europe, Paris, London, and New York. These writers resisted bourgeois versions of Enlightenment (the Jewish *Haskalah,* which sought to eradicate Yiddish as a "mongrel" language, in the Jewish wealthy classes' upward climb) with nearly the same vigor that they resisted organized anti-Semitism. Moreover, they viewed both as products of an ugly capitalism. In the United States, Yiddish was inherently linked with the Left, its rise in the 1890s a part of the first wave of Jewish socialism and labor activity. Twenty years later the pioneer generation had become more bourgeois, but the "1905ers," tempered by pogroms and simultaneously shaped by the first Russian Revolution, brought new political vigor and a new taste for Yiddish culture.

Yiddish, inherently a fusion language (drawn from High Middle German with doses of Hebrew, French, and Slavic), was a sort of living catalog of Jewish experience and occupied an even more curious space in vaudeville-era America. Yiddish books sold in the thousands, while Yiddish theater, the so-called Second Avenue Broadway, drew some of the biggest crowds (and best-paid actors, thanks to unionization) in New York. Even silent films with Yiddish subtitles—Jewish theater restaged for the camera—began to occupy a niche. This was only a spectacular sideline, however, to the role of Yiddish speakers and their children in popular culture at large.

Yiddishkayt, an ambiance of ironic humor, storytelling, and a marked musical adaptiveness, provided the force and spirit behind a thousand popular culture gestures that went to the heart of goyish America and the world. Often enough its native speakers, like George Burns, learned how to play seamlessly to the gentiles without a hint of contradiction (as *The Burns and Allen Show*'s suburban house and perfectly assimilated son demonstrated on television decades later). But for the close observer a feeling of being outsiders always lingered—even if it was more and more just a memory—and it linked the Jew to other outsiders, to working people, to nonwhites, and even to the stubborn hope for capitalism's end. As the most popular Yiddish novelist, Sholem Asch (father to Moses Asch, founder of Folkways Records), put it simply, "We must work out a world order which shall rest upon equal distribution of labor and rewards."[13]

Art historian Avram Kampf adds that progressive Jewish artists of the 1910s and '20s, from Max Weber to Marc Chagall, often sought to reenergize the old symbols of Jewishness in the times' modernist terms.[14] Popular artists likewise responded to the same impulses, although drawing still more from vernacular Yiddishkayt than from religious Judaism. The beloved cartoonists of the ghetto weekly *Groysser Kundes* (the Big Stick) depicted Marx as Moses leading the Jewish children across the Red Sea of capitalism and with biting satire made out contemporary Jewish intellectuals as Old Testament figures in modern clothes. Yiddish stage actor Muni Weisenfreund translated the old symbols into new media, becoming the movies' Paul Muni, playing idealists as well as gangsters from the classic stock of character types. So did future director Sidney Lumet, a child actor on the Yiddish stage; so did E. Y. "Yip" Harburg, writer of 1930s America's favorite protest and fantasy music, from "Brother, Can You Spare a Dime?" to "We're Off to See the Wizard"; and so did Abraham Polonsky, who spoke Yiddish only in joking phrases but understood it perfectly well—right down to Yiddishkayt's emotional core.

Like many other universalist intellectuals of Jewish origin (Lewis

Mumford, the illegitimate son of a Jewish businessman and his German maid, immediately comes to mind), Polonsky had one other major source of childhood enlightenment: the New York Public Library system. At age ten he wrote a paper on fire prevention that won a grade-school essay contest and flattering comments from his teacher, Mrs. Bronstein. When the same teacher asked each student to write an in-class essay describing himself or herself as a particular inanimate object, Polonsky chose Mambrino's helmet (the barber's bowl that poor Don Quixote took to be a noble warrior's headgear) and briefly related how the novel had made such an impression upon him. A surprised Mrs. Bronstein made an appointment with Polonsky's parents and warned them not to discourage him from becoming a writer, something they had no intention of doing. (In another version of this story, the son announces to his parents that he has decided to become a novelist.)

Mrs. Bronstein also wrote an official letter recommending that her precocious student use the adult section of the then-grand public library branch a block south of Sutton Place at 185th Street. He already had been to the children's section many Saturdays; this time he went as an adult, even a would-be writer.[15] But young Polonsky still looked the part of a bothersome boy. Brushed off by a librarian who would not take seriously a child his age, he pulled from the shelf almost at random Dimitri Merejkovsky's *The Romance of Leonardo da Vinci* and checked it out for home reading. The day was memorable in other ways: rather than taking a bus, he walked to the library and back, each way saving a nickel that his mother gave him but arriving home hours late and worrying her terribly. When he tried to claim the dime she slapped him, but the library visit would still be a positive experience. Like the pictures in his father's medical books (*Pathogenic Microorganisms* was the boy's favorite), the biography of da Vinci left a lasting impression of the connection between art and suffering. Specifics he could learn later. For now the library signified his expanded literary world, an opening to authors with whom, he began more and more to think, he had a definite affinity. Meanwhile, still reading from his father's collection, he ranked *The Collected Works of Edgar Allan Poe* near the top of his list, as had several generations of Americans from all social classes. Polonsky personally paid homage to the master of the weird by visiting the Poe Cottage in the Bronx. So he grew.

The years of his adolescence in the 1920s were an especially apt time for men (and a few women) from socialist families to envision becoming writers and artists precisely because they had been practically excluded from every other radical activity. The wartime strike wave climaxed in 1919 with the Seattle General Strike. In the shadow of the consolidating Russian Revolution, the strikes had at first promised some great radical compensation for the recently spilled ocean of blood. But facing an exhausted Europe as the most powerful nation on earth, bourgeois America was not going to permit any revolution in the foreseeable future. Young women, Floyd Dell lamented, "wanted babies" and the solidity of conventional middle-class life rather than the free life imagined beforehand. (So did Dell himself.)[16] And as Dell also might have lamented, the Sheridan Square subway stop opened and the upper middle class rushed to suddenly fashionable Greenwich Village, which daily became more expensive and less quaint. The revolution was definitely over and preserved behind glass when the Museum of Modern Art opened, transforming the once radical avant-garde into the eminently collectible.

Artistic revolutionaries—at least the lucky ones—headed abroad, as did some political revolutionaries. Polonsky's real-life aunt, his father's sister, upon whom he would model the idealized Zenia, postponed her return to Russia until she had become a physician armed with the skills to help a suffering population. Along with her went several thousand other professionals and proletarians, abandoning fat America to help the lean young Revolution. Among those radicals who stayed behind, the least compromised were the Jewish garment workers, especially the miserably exploited young ones, recently arrived from Europe with the fire of Red Russia still in their eyes. They easily could imagine capitalism's sudden collapse, especially because the garment industry was itself collapsing; waves of violent strikes reminded everyone that the class struggle had survived. Jewish intellectuals connected with the Left clung to the young and fanatic communist movement. Or they suspended all direct political engagement as they continued to write political novels or poetry or plays in English or Yiddish. All of them wondered, what next? Socialism was not a vocation, even for a socialist; not, at least, in America.

A thousand years seemed to pass, including huge moral defeats to communism as untainted idealism. Then came the stock market crash of 1929, when Polonsky was just nineteen. For a long moment following the crash, the thirties threatened a resurgence of an unfinished radicalism that had not reached the masses only because capitalism had maintained "illusions" now evidently shattered. But neither radicalism nor the masses could return to 1919 or 1917 or even 1912. The shadow of fascism had wiped away the optimism, the American Communist Party had become grimly undemocratic as well as bombastic. Memories of war and of the public rush toward the 1920s' materialist possibilities had transformed the psychic landscape. In a memorable novel, *Haunch, Paunch and Jowl* (1926), Polonsky's future comrade and screenwriting colleague Samuel Ornitz beautifully depicted the corruption of Jewish dreams in America, updating and broadening Abraham Cahan's unloving and perhaps unintentional self-portrait in *The Rise of David Levinsky* (1917) from a decade earlier.

These details all help explain the limits on Abraham Polonsky's generation of radical intellectuals. But they do not explain the vigor, the brilliance, and the inclination toward popular culture that they instinctively exploited with a radical edge unlike any generation before or since.

In 1923, during his early adolescence, Polonsky's family moved from the Bronx to Manhattan to be closer to his father's drugstore on Second Avenue near Bowery, in the depths of the old Lower East Side. Interestingly, the autobiographical details cast so artistically in *Zenia's Way* disappear here. The future screenwriter might capture Manhattan in the films *Force of Evil* or *I Can Get It for You Wholesale,* but he would not depict the downtown scenes in fiction save in a few unpublished short stories.

Before the move, young Abe had brought his father special food all the way from the Bronx on the old Third Avenue Elevated, getting off at Houston Street and Third Avenue. (He frequently stopped at a used book store where, at seventeen, he bought an instructive volume on the nature of literary symbolism that would become a lifelong treasured possession.) As the father's health sagged, the son opened and usually closed the family drugstore, seven days a week, sweeping and washing the floors, learning the trade of deciphering formulas, measuring powders, reading scales, and making pills. He took no salary because he knew his father struggled just to make ends meet. He continued that work into the early thirties, operating the soda fountain and sandwich bar until his father bought into a Bronx store on the Grand Concourse.

Some nights, Polonsky made deliveries along Second Avenue, then glowing with the theatrical "Yiddish Renaissance"; he also delivered "shmink" (make-up) to the Winter Garden, one of the most famous burlesque houses in the world. His father sagely advised, "It's natural to be curious but don't spend too much time around the dressing room." Abe first learned about the city, he said, by looking out the window of the Third Ave. Elevated. He learned important human lessons from talking to stage girls five to fifteen years or more older than he, dames who liked to have a sturdily built, cute young fellow around for any number of reasons. From these women unread in any philosophical work, he claims to have gained a philosophy of life and love. For Polonsky, they were not bimbos but vital human beings whose woes and pleasures gained the future writer's ready ear.[17]

Polonsky claimed to have been only a year or so older, thirteen or fourteen, when a traveling businessman's Italian American wife started hanging around the store. Good-looking and in her early thirties, she chatted him up and eventually invited him to meet her in a Grammercy Park hotel room. One way or the other, before his midteens, he had learned all that he needed to know about sex. The showgirls were one thing, she was another. "Not only was she exciting," he recalled with great fondness and not a little gratitude, "she was kind and generous." She even took him along on a short vacation to Canada, passing him off as her brother so as to share a suite. This affair lasted an amazing six or seven years, with encounters as often as every week or more, sometimes in the back of the drugstore. Neither partner found any reason to end this real, if somewhat curious, love saga until Abe's life changed dramatically. He had turned twenty and she almost forty, when he explained that he had become serious about another woman, whom he someday would marry. His longtime lover, never one to demand or expect fidelity, amiably accepted that fact. She was more than willing to maintain a more complex relationship, but the young man could not bring himself to do so, effecting a certain sadness in both of them. "She understood," he reflected. "She knew I wasn't in love with her, just attracted to her. She had gained something, and she always knew that I had to break it off someday."

Actually, Sylvia Marrow had already spent several years preparing Abe for a monogamous future. A friend of his sister's, when she was fourteen and he seventeen, she announced to him her plans for their future marriage. "Have you asked my mother?" he recalled joshing the girl. "Have you asked *your* mother? Come back when you get authority!" Her father, an immigrant Jewish clothes store merchant, was making most of his money in the booming stock market. Her mother bought season tickets for the opera. Sylvia was a serious ballerina until a gland operation incidentally damaged an inner ear and impaired the necessary sense of balance. By the time she entered Hunter College as an anthropology major and he was nearing graduation, she had made Polonsky her real career in a partnership that would last until her death in 1995. This was more good luck, balancing a lot of the bad luck ahead.

Meanwhile, life at the famous DeWitt Clinton High School proved good for Polonsky. He made friends, excelled at English and physics, and became a published writer through his prize-winning paragraphs in a *New York Times* juvenile contest for best observations on the important news stories of the day.[18] Thanks to a friendly teacher's advice, he also started reading John Ruskin's essays.

That outlook, the interpretation of civilization from the more collective Middle Ages to the present energetic anarchy and increasing urban-industrial ugliness, influenced young Polonsky greatly. As a biographer of Ruskin would write, "the democratization of imaginative perception" demanded "active seeing" accompanied by the kinds of symbolic language learned by the keen observer, anticipating the ways in which a better civilization would encourage all of its participants to comprehend the meaning of what they see.[19] (Later, he would learn to his delight that another favorite author, Marcel Proust, had translated Ruskin's *The Stones of Venice* into French.) The piles of novels that his father would bring home from the line of used bookshops on Fourth Avenue and selectively pass along as he finished them also influenced Abe profoundly.

The teenager was making mental notes, too, on the workings of politics, more or less as his world-wise father explained them. Idealists might write literature and newspaper columns about reform, but Tammany ruled. From the drugstore Polonsky watched the softer side of corruption, not so much the protection rackets and prostitution as the vote buying, the sports betting, the charity occasions, and the myriad ways in which the political machine provided thousands of menial jobs for the relatives of clients and supporters. Both sides of corruption were America.

2

City College in the 1930s is one of the big stories of American intellectual life, now told most often through the intellectual origins of youthful left-wingers like Irving Kristol, destined to move to the neoconservative Right, or Irving Howe, clinging to the near-left of center. At the time, and for many graduates to the end of their lives, however, the school was seen quite differently. Notwithstanding an undistinguished faculty (with some sparkling exceptions) and a worse than undistinguished administration, City had its stars. Basketball coach Nat Holman was the People's Choice, the ultimate strategist of cooperation (Holman himself occasionally contributed, later in the 1930s, to the Young Communist League's

Champion Youth Monthly). Teamwork, ball handling, and even the
famous stall, not physical gigantism, put CCNY on the scoreboard and
held the opposition at bay. The students, vaguely socialist in their sympathies if fiercely dedicated to their own professional advancement,
hoped through the New Deal to approximate that success within
American society at large.

Polonsky's choice of City was natural. Like the host of other future
prominent Jewish intellectuals, artists, and businessmen, he could pay a
mere $2.75 bursar's fee, have his books provided free, and live at home.
Heightened by a combination of family aspirations, individual ambi-
tions, and dire economic realities before and after classes, the students'
collective motivation for an advanced education was arguably greater at
City than at any other contemporary American college. Nearly all of
City's students had immigrant parents and had passed through the New
York City public school system; almost as many were Jewish. The more
prestigious and expensive private colleges remained as good as closed to
Jews, and getting into City was so difficult that no one could seriously
doubt its students' intellectual caliber. (Prestige, of course, was altogether
another matter.) The Depression had shocked the families of youngsters
who expected to gain a secure foothold on life as they acclimated to the
New World, only to see their hopes struck down by the economic collapse that so many left-wing relatives had stubbornly predicted. Most
students continued to be haunted by financial insecurities that only
added to the frustrations of working for a degree that guaranteed no job
in depressed America. Naturally, competition was fierce. Added to that,
the all-male student body set a tone for intense homosocial relations,
along with an undercurrent of homosexuality.

Radicalism was never absent. Polonsky's college friend Meyer Liben
reflected decades later in a celebrated essay for *Commentary,* "what happened at Berkeley [in 1965] . . . might happen, or looked as if it might
happen at City every Thursday between 12 and 2 in the afternoon" when
the student activity clubs met and outside speakers came onto campus.
This was an exaggeration, if a pardonable one. Sentiment against the
Reserve Officers Training Corps (ROTC) could hardly have been
stronger during that era of national disillusionment with the First World
War and generalized Jewish resistance to warfare. But the mildly socialistic Social Problems Club—temporarily banned from campus in 1931—
offered the closest thing to an organized left-wing movement on the campus of the early thirties. Unlike the radical students of later decades, City
boys had even less sense of generational rebellion than they had leisure

and still less inclination toward cultural revolution beyond literary pursuits and mostly imagined bohemian-sexual adventures.[20] But they did have an enemy. President Frederick Robinson's reactionary administration prided itself upon efficient control and countered unregulated "free speech" with city cops on special assignment, Irishmen prepared and perhaps eager to bash Jewish heads. The antiwar sentiments that wise college administrators of the 1930s adeptly directed toward "peace assemblies" and other benign manifestations Robinson turned into near-riots through such provocations as inviting officials of Mussolini's fascist government on campus as honored guests.

The cerebral politics on campus, more constant than the active kind, took place in the famous Alcoves, the basement beneath the cafeteria. An alcove bench was designated for each course, and some students sat down in the cool (or warm, according to the season) for a break between classes. Notoriously, most of them chattered, trying to best each other through force of logic and citation of experts. But in drama, poetry, and fiction, at least, taste took precedence over politics: the favorite authors of Polonsky's class of 1932 were the nearly apolitical modernists Eugene O'Neill, Edward Arlington Robinson, and James Branch Cabell.

At first, Polonsky found himself bored and restless at school, for reasons that he never could pin down. Perhaps the instructors were not to his taste, or perhaps he had not yet learned how to ace his courses without attending classes (as he soon would), meanwhile devising his own education. Devoting himself to the track team until a kindly coach admitted that the slim lad was most useful for pacing the truly promising runners, he began failing his courses and feeling deeply guilty for disappointing his family: "I'd been a shmuck!" He escaped middle-class life for a few months by following Melville's Ishmael with "October in his soul," shipping out to sea on a Morgan Lines freighter for Galveston at twelve dollars a month plus board. Getting the job was not difficult, and he liked his shipmates. Ordinary Irish and Italian working-class fellows, including a former schoolteacher or two, they taught him how to play cribbage and steer a big boat. (Did they know that he was a Jew? "They must have thought I was some kind of Protestant. They never discussed religion, just card playing.") The officers aboard quickly learned that his specialty was lettering and set him about painting door signs for most of the trip. Four months later, as the ship docked in Texas, a black Episcopalian minister was waiting with a message from Polonsky's father to come back. He returned as a beloved prodigal son, vowing this time to do better.

The second time around, Polonsky worked harder at his courses. He reveled in the philosophy lectures of Moses Raphael Cohen (Polonsky said: "If a student complained, 'I disagree with that fact,' Cohen responded, 'I'm glad you know it's a fact!'") and in the five volumes of *The Life of Reason* by George Santayana, Cohen's personal friend. Reading the great philosophers was enthralling, and Polonsky used to sneak into Richard McKeon's philosophy lectures at Columbia with his new friend Paul Goodman, the future pacifist, educational theorist, and early New Left philosopher.

Polonsky, whose close friendships to this point were almost exclusively with women, now experienced real male bonding. Leonard Boudin joined the pair of Goodman and Polonsky, and Polonsky found a left family of real prominence. Leonard's uncle Louis B. Boudin, an 1890s immigrant from Russia, could be reckoned as an intellectual force in the Lower East Side even before Eugene Debs first ran for president in 1900. This Boudin soon became America's premier Marxist economic thinker, his classic *The Theoretical System of Karl Marx* (1907) answering contemporary challenges to Marx's predictions. His influence peaked just before 1920 and crashed when he could not reconcile himself to the multiple orthodoxies of the new communist movement. Still, he taught informal economics courses to young radicals, practiced his trade representing political dissidents in court, and in 1932 delivered *Government by Judiciary,* a two-volume Marxist history of American law. Leonard followed in his uncle's legal footsteps and would one day represent several of the Hollywood Ten (and Polonsky as well) against the House Committee on Un-American Activities. Though he was no joiner, Leonard would be sympathetic to the Left all his life, and he remained closer to Polonsky than to any other City College chum.

Meanwhile, Bernard Herrmann—a musician who would compose the scores for *Citizen Kane, Jane Eyre, North by Northwest,* and *Psycho*—proposed one day that he read something "by the French guy, Proust." Polonsky claimed the two had met and immediately had become pals when the thirteen-year-old Herrmann roller-skated up to him on Fifteenth Street and introduced himself. (Thirty years later, a terrified Herrmann denied that he had ever known Polonsky.) Polonsky picked up *Swann's Way* in a literary bookstore at Radio City Music Hall and found himself instantly entranced. Proust was the author whom Polonsky, without knowing it, had been waiting to read for a long time.

Until his death in 1999, Polonsky himself remained intrigued by this choice at a moment when other future radical classmates were selecting Marx, Lenin, and even Stalin. Proust, a severely asthmatic little boy born of a Jewish mother and stockbroker father during the uprising of the Paris Commune, grew up overprotected and intensely precocious to join the Left Bank literary circles then embracing the avant-garde. He became the intimate of such talented writers as future cinematic innovator Jean Cocteau and future surrealist poet Philippe Soupault, and even made the acquaintance of a visiting Oscar Wilde. He was bisexual but more devoted to *observing* than to acting upon the world in any way. A handful of critics greeted *Du Côté de chez Swann* (1913), the first volume of *Remembrance of Things Past,* with wild enthusiasm as a literary masterpiece, but only a small audience found it. The second volume, published in 1919, won the author instant and lasting fame.

In *Swann's Way,* Proust recounts a village life remembered from vacations outside Paris. Describing love and more general social relations in close proximity, his treatment of interiority and unconscious motivations exceeds any writer's except, perhaps, James Joyce's. Unlike Joyce, Proust offers these insights through the narrator's analytical observations, constituting a continuous reflection in typical French philosophical fashion, elevated to a high literary plane. Contemporary readers prepared by Henri Bergson's philosophy of daily life and subsequent generations tutored by Freud found in Proust something lacking in even the great favorites of realism. Reading all the way through to the last translated volume of Proust's series, Polonsky realized he would have to learn French language skills to go further. The head of the French department at City College advised him to take a beginner's course and get a dictionary. Thus his French reading commenced. A long lifetime after discovering Proust, Polonsky still quoted Proustian aphorisms (half-jestingly, of course) to explain his own happy and unhappy experiences, and still taught Proust among other literary moderns in an aesthetics course for University of Southern California film students.

In the later 1930s, and obviously under Proust's influence, Polonsky would devise a novelette about a miserable file clerk who cannot face his empty life and ponders suicide: "Had he dreamed, he could have dreamed his life through that night for there was time enough." But he did not dream, and so "when he slept, he slept, and when he ate, he ate, all in due course without any ambiguities like sleeping with a friend . . . or eating between opinions and fine phrases. . . ."[21] We need not doubt that the young man with "lank light brown hair, and of course, rimless octagon glasses upon a fine straight nose, thin nostrilled and elegant" was in some sense Polonsky and that he had projected upon fictional characters an interiority of near-universal human experience.[22]

One of his two surviving pieces of unpublished early fiction seeks to translate the mood of emotional (and sexual) uneasiness to a realistic setting and to impose it on an issue that would be central to nearly all of Polonsky's work: women's consciousness and their relations with men. "Last Clear Chance," written in 1931, is a young man's first-person tale of romantic consequences: pregnancy and the prospect of abortion. The couple meet on a hot summer Manhattan morning. Though she reminds him physically of a beautiful bird, she is a fully developed human with needs that correspond only roughly to his own. As he tells the story, she first was ardently in love with him and he reciprocated indifferently, hurting her unintentionally at a time when "even a glance can make nights sleepless." Soon, the relationship reversed, so that when he declared his affection she turned coy, making him frantic. Their relationship filled with tension and quarrels. After months apart, a reunion proved easy, despite her tears, because in mutual romantic suffering "there is a process of stripping personality of its uniqueness" and humility becomes "the quality of all clear passion." The reunion leads to extended moments of passion ("that weighted night") in which the protagonist offers as graphic a description of sex as Polonsky would ever write:

> Somehow your emotions detach themselves from the sensations that generate them, and get caught in a rhythm, formal almost as in art, the tenderness becomes pity, pity profound as that moving the soul looking on human goodness and everything that is human dying and breaking either through wickedness or by fate; and the passion catches you and immolates you, so that you feel a kind of terror in the presence of an impulse transmitted through a million generations of life; and suddenly you have descended once more into the flux of things and risen above it at the same time. Afterwards comes that calmness for spirit and weakness of the body that the Greeks called *leusis,* created by having felt and known. That is why the release is like death, because there is nothing left over. The soul is used up. It is finished, like a fine sentence. I said, I'm not hurting you. No, she said, and her voice came very small to my ears, as if we were so far away from the world that sounds sounding there for us to hear had to go to the world and return before we could hear them. Suddenly she clung to me, murmuring, more. And then the warm darkness of that evening closed in upon us. It was warm and secretive like a womb, and life and art are born in those half-darknesses.

She obviously lost her virginity in gaining him, and remembering all this, he cannot and will not arrange the abortion; he offers marriage instead. They part for the moment (because he has things to do, people to see, probably classes to attend), but they stop to watch the pigeons at South Ferry. Moving away, she appears once more to him like a "giant white bird" as she steps out in the street—and into the path of a giant truck. The vehicle somehow manages to stop, averting tragedy, and the lovers begin to run toward each other, "frantic with fear of a loss that had to come" in some other way, some other time, the loneliness that even the deeply loved feel around them.[23]

Polonsky read these and other literary experiments to the roundtable of friends in Clionia, a campus literary club. Founded in late 1930 by half a dozen bright boys, it included Polonsky's future brother-in-law, Milton Millhauser (future father of a Pulitzer Prize-winning novelist, Polonsky's nephew Steve Millhauser, in the 1990s); future *Partisan Review* editorial board member William Barrett; and some irregular members, including Leonard Boudin and Sylvia Marrow, who was just starting at Hunter in 1931. Practically everyone in Clionia was a student of the creative writing teacher Theodore Goodman, no intellectual giant, but an engaging and encouraging figure who methodically taught students the newer canon of Twain, Turgenev, Thoreau, Joyce, Lawrence, Conrad, Sherwood Anderson, and such avant-gardists as George Sand and Havelock Ellis. The Clionians mostly read their work aloud to each other, poetry or prose, as they aspired to becoming men of letters. The only requirements for membership were verbal capacity and literary interest. Compared to the rival and more politically minded club Phrenocosmia (whose regulars included Louis Feuer, one of those contemporary radicals destined for neoconservatism, and Joseph Lash, future near-communist, Eleanor Roosevelt intimate, and anticommunist liberal of note), Clionians were the true aesthetes.

Meanwhile, Polonsky also wrote poetry, admired the Latin poets, and even studied Greek long enough to read it with difficulty. He found an American voice in Whitman, a poet radical and homosexual, unreservedly democratic, and influential upon the world's artists as few Americans were likely to be. Fellow Clionians had other reasons to admire Whitman. Little groups of politicized literary intellectuals Polonsky's age on various campuses contained quite a few homosexuals, a carryover from the 1920s, when the Left had been so small that it included everyone outside the norm, giving it a detached, aesthete's edge that staunchly orthodox communists abhorred. Far from exceptional, Clionia's regulars comprised at least a third gay men, perhaps more. First educated in life by women, Polonsky was now educated again, in artistic self-consciousness at least, by gay intellectuals.[24]

With "Teddy" Goodman's encouragement, Clionia regulars revived *Lavender,* a campus literary publication of the twenties that had tem-

porarily passed into evanescence. Organized for an annual issue in spring
1931 (postponed from the fall because Joe Lash had failed to organize a
fiction section), it featured Millhauser as editor-in-chief, Polonsky as literary editor, and Theodore Goodman as faculty advisor. By the next
spring's issue, actually published only weeks before graduation, Polonsky
had become the editor-in-chief as well as the most prolific contributor
along with Paul Goodman (who had that honor in the previous issue).

Polonsky the published little-magazine writer was a thoroughgoing
modernist. His best piece, "The Lovestory of Peter Snark," reentered the
stream of consciousness, this time of a particularly foolish fellow. Snark,
at forty and badly overweight, rather absurdly fantasizes a romance with
an eighteen-year-old working-class girl ("How small her waist, really
aristocratic and patrician") with whom he has merely walked through
the park. Two years in college had made Snark an aesthete—more than
a bit like some of the Clionia circle, perhaps; a fellow fictional character,
more like the real-life Clionians in his success, sends Snark a note revealing that he has published a humor piece in the *New Republic* and hopes
to discuss Walter Pater again. But Snark flatters himself by disdaining to
spend what little cash he has to please a girl out only for a good time.
When he insists that they take a bus ride instead of seeing a show and
reaches to hold her while they ride atop it in the pelting rain, she calls
him a "fat old fool" and dumps him. That's all, at least on the surface,
nothing more than mockery of the would-be intellectual and his imagined lover. Blubbery Snark will make another appearance as the antihero
of Polonsky's unpublished modernist novel "The Discoverers," this time
with the bankroll to back his sexual demands, but just as ludicrous and
socially useless.[25]

Polonsky's other literary engagement of the early thirties reached the
whole college crowd around him rather than the few hundred readers of
Lavender. The tabloid *Campus,* perhaps best known for its sports coverage, had the usual student news, some literary coverage—and a humor
column, "Gargoyles," inspired by the silent sentinels of campus buildings. One and one-half student generations earlier, during the 1914–15
school year, future song writers Yip Harburg and Ira Gershwin had
invented the column as "Gargoyles' Gargles."[26] Polonsky took over that
venerable institution in January 1931, and kept at it erratically until May
1932, shortly before graduation, sometimes writing several times per
week, sometimes only once every few weeks. Under his hand,
"Gargoyles" boasted a variety of literary satires and jests at the leading
ideas (that is to say, ideologies) of the era. He was smart-alecky enough

to write one column entirely in Latin, full of in-jokes for the campus cognoscenti. He was also, in another way, learning to speed-write, as the movies later would require. The usual college-age sex humor stands out in one of his typical literary satires, "The Way of Most Flesh." It begins,

I have a little pervert;
   I beat him when he sneezes
He ought to learn to hide dirt,
   And not do what he pleases

Chorus: Inhibitions, prohibitions, that's the way to cure the young
No physicians or opticians, Freud Freud Jung Jung Jung!

He mocked and simultaneously borrowed from Virgil, Wordsworth, Joyce, and assorted others, leaning heavily upon Lewis Carroll, but also returning inevitably to sex ("Too young, by far to bear the yoke / Of marriage, love and passion / She'd rather hear a smutty joke / and pet— but in her fashion"). When he jokingly listed "my hates," Polonsky did not spare his own milieu: "Prudes, Virgins and the Bible as Literature"; "People who like Catholicism because of its beauty"; "Aesthetes and the Social Problems club"; "Literary manifestos and manifest litterateurs."[27]

Funniest of all, along with satires of graduation ("The Social Problems Club shall be disbanded and formed into ham sandwiches to be sold at the Officers Club at reduced rates") and of the football team ("For what other colleges have you worked? What salary do you expect?")[28] were Polonsky's lampoons of the growing Depression literature by and about communists, such as the imaginary tabloid headline describing the Hunger March in Washington, "NUDE WOMAN FIGHTS POLICE IN RED ORGY," and the follow-up, "Cops Belabor Reds in Throes of Insanity. Five Babies Shot and Beaten! Naked Women Scratch Out Eyes of Police (police deprived of good show)." Polonsky closes his send-up of the "DAILY WOIKER" with the exhortation: "Comrades! Now is the time to rise, Comrades! Are we to endure this brutal Capitalistic Imperialism that exploits our Hunger Marches, Comrades! . . . This proves that the Woiker must rise in his strength and demand no war, no exploitation, no imperialism."[29] In another column, he stole New York Mayor Jimmy Walker's line, "The only thing they've got against me is my wise-cracks."[30] Speed-writing and wisecracking, he was in training, though he did not know it, for radio and *The Goldbergs.*

Behind the humor, Polonsky badly wanted to complete a classical edu-cation and, like several in his crowd, he succeeded. His friend Paul Goodman, drawn mainly to philosophy, went on shortly to teach math and the Greeks to ninth-graders and to write "cubist" novels. Polonsky simply took in the knowledge and unknowingly prepared himself for a life of Hollywood story conferences, where the quick comeback was the only defense against studio tyrants and cultural poseurs, but where he would almost invariably be the most cultured figure in the room.

The Polonsky of the early 1930s did not take politics very seriously. When Phrenocosmia's devotees gibed their rivals about their apolitical sensibilities, the Clionians did not dispute the charge. While a small and insular Young Communist League unit around campus was merely "noisy," Polonsky recalled, he would cast his first ballot not for the Communist Party's William Z. Foster or even for socialist Norman Thomas, an extremely popular choice on the more upper-crust campuses of Columbia and Vassar. Polonsky voted for Franklin Delano Roosevelt: a very Jewish choice.

If anywhere, Polonsky found his politics these days in his fiction. By the time he was twenty-one, he had composed his first crypto-political work, the unpublished "For Dancers Only." This somber, sardonic piece is slightly less than a thousand words, but it carries the weight of a savage critique not only of an oppressive state apparatus but of the observers who contribute their visual consumerism to the theater of cruelty. We learn finally that the unnamed "dancers" are actually being hanged as an eager crowd gathers. (That same year, Yiddish feuilletonist Moshe Nadir half-jokingly asked readers of the left-wing daily *Morgn Freiheit* whether he or the red flag would first hang at Union Square.) We never learn anything about the victims except their "dance," a movement of limbs and torsos through which they "relinquished . . . the deepest instinct that contracts the life of man, his life and his pity . . . his sense of life." The crowd, obviously fascinated, allows itself a ribald joke about two of the dancers' rigor mortis erections. The artful quality of the story is not in the surprise ending but in the economy of expression, and above all the treatment of the anonymous rebels:

> The fame of those who were to perform had become a popular story, and after their deaths would be a legend among the legends in that bright and frightful land. But now these three were alive, and in their quiet approach nothing of their personal lives was to be seen. They walked like usual human beings, without grace, without courage, and without dignity. Still, there must have been in these three something so pure in its humanity as to reveal to any watcher what was still intact in himself or else, why the furor, why the silent passion of the crowd, why the public statements of eminent leaders. . . .
> Although everyone had been waiting for hours in the sun, no one said, "here they come." When the three appeared, it was enough. They were there.

The "bright and frightful land" is not some distant place, of course, but America. And the rebels? It is hard to say and it does not really matter. Rebels of any kind, violators of custom in a philistine kingdom where, as Nadir wrote, the man who can spit the furthest wins the great contest, a land where there is no room for promenading.[31]

Where did that leave Polonsky among the budding cultural Left, whose several wings began to take flight in the early 1930s? That question had a clearer answer for a number of his classmates who were soon to join either the Popular Front or Trotskyist/*Partisan Review* milieux. Alan Wald's comment on poetry in the 1930s applies more generally to the educated strivings of contemporary intellectuals to become artists: "neither means nor ends alone, but the dialectical relationship between means and ends" distinguished the artistic from the merely political. The task at hand was to "rework experience" (emphatically the artists' own experience) not didactically but imaginatively, so as to "communicate a new form of consciousness to the reader."[32]

The radical artist who is both an aesthetic avant-gardist and a political left-winger usually has—and in the 1930s emphatically had—a considerable problem, and not only because of the cultural commissars' wish to dictate form as well as content. The Communist regulars, the intellectuals of the small Leninist splinter groups, and the older generation of socialists or wobblies *all* assumed that artistic form was essentially invested in content, a view that Polonsky would in later decades renounce as the bane of the radical film. These otherwise feuding left-wingers therefore considered naturalism the great breakthrough in late nineteenth- and early twentieth-century American literature, à la Theodore Dreiser. At the grassroots level of literary production, poets and feuilletonists in a dozen languages of the ethnic-left literature thus continued, in the same familiar manner of realism and uplift.[33]

The fashionable, mostly apolitical or antipolitical literary scene of the 1920s both at home and in spiritual exile had highlighted entirely contrary impulses, of course. Ernest Hemingway, Gertrude Stein, T. S. Eliot, Ezra Pound, and other core modernists had exulted in form; their experimental media obviously constituted their messages. But during the 1920s only expressionism, mostly in graphic forms or the theater (or both, in set designs), affected the Left's more experimental English-language or Yiddish art, following the fashion of the contemporary Soviet artists. The consolidation of Stalin's rule soon flung the hard-won radical aesthetic backward toward "proletarian culture" and "proletarian literature," including the search for worker-authors among the Left's potential constituency. This move understandably depressed many self-avowed intellectuals but was closely in keeping with older left-wing traditions of heroic working-class autodidacts.

A similar naturalism, along with political fidelity to the Communist Party, inevitably proved the driving force of the John Reed Clubs that sprang up around the country after 1932. Publishing their own magazines, the clubs encouraged young writers like Richard Wright, Nelson Algren, Meridel Le Seuer, and thousands more who would never be famous or even published. The sheer creative energy made this intellectual leftward shift one of the exciting literary moments of the century, despite the restraints clamped upon the Reed Clubs by party functionaries. But the same movement saw the kinds of distinctions and intellectual categories detailed by the likes of Eliot or Pound as mere moral evasions and artistic heresies, even as they offered a secret pleasure (or guide) for self-consciously left-wing experimentalists of the early 1930s like Waldo Frank or Louis Zukofsky. The notion that artistic form had its own logic, a special way of seeing that transmutes doctrine into sensation, seemingly had no place in a breadline-filled America.[34]

Left-wing fiction writers were nevertheless encouraged, and poets (albeit less in artistic form than social content) as well, at the prospect of having a real place in literature and in life. Some of the most talented understandably disguised their personal aesthetics, quietly honing their talents and bringing them to full expression only as the political strictures regarding form began to ease. Given that Russian attitudes would continue to dictate Communist literary politics, these writers really had no other choice—except to abandon the major movements of the Left or to work in commercial media.

In criticism proper, prevailing Marxist notions tended notoriously, if not invariably, toward reductionism and vulgarity. The polemicists' shafts at bourgeois literature were not entirely misdirected, nor was the "great tradition" of American realism that Granville Hicks praised in his then-famous treatise of the same name either imaginary or used up. Writers, like other artists, needed more elbowroom than Communist aesthetics allowed. But the temptation to turn a predilection into a political-ideological lever proved well-nigh irresistible. Thus, as Raymond Williams later observed, "What looked like fundamental theoretical revaluation, in the attempted assimilation to 'ideology,' was a disastrous failure and fundamentally compromised, in this area, the status of Marxism itself."[35] The sort of distinctions made by Eliot quickly became a polemical weapon with which the editors of the modernist *Partisan*

Review famously counterattacked the philistine impulses of Communist intellectual regulars during the later 1930s. In the others' vagaries, political *engagés* and aesthetes saw their own justification—or so it seemed to each side in the politically charged literary wars of the day.

Why would Polonsky the young aesthete *not* choose over politics? As customarily posed in terms of the New York Intellectuals, that question mainly considers criticism, poetry, and fiction. The sizable scholarship in this area also emphasizes Trotskyist and/or aesthete literary-political and aesthetic views formulated in the later 1930s, by which time Polonsky had already determined his personal course. But in theater, in painting (including murals), in music, in dance, and above all in film, the political aesthetic was never so clear. Communist theater critics certainly had their favorites, like Clifford Odets or Lillian Hellman, but these playwrights either attained great popular attention because they touched an ethnic (that is, Jewish) nerve or appealed to the "serious" Broadway audience. Within the small but far from insignificant world of Yiddish theater, the Yiddish art theater ARTEF was at once demonstrably proletarian, intermittently expressionist, and militantly pro-Soviet. (Likewise, the best of theater criticism for the Yiddish world usually appeared in the ARTEF's indispensable booster, *Morgn Freiheit*.)[36] In the still smaller world of outright political drama, Theater of Action experiments such as street-agitation overrode the usual aesthetic issues. By 1937 when the TOA's successor, the Workers Laboratory Theater, with members like Elia Kazan and Sandy Meisner, merged into the WPA One-Act Experimental Theater with Nicholas Ray as stage manager, the tide had definitely turned from the avant-garde toward the realist (including "Method") current of the contemporary left-of-center mainstream.[37]

The mid-thirties' political shift from revolution to reform thoroughly redefined the categories in any case. Painters, dancers, composers, theater actors, and playwrights, among others, went from underemployment to government payrolls on projects with New Deal–flavored political aesthetics. Deployment of the grand themes of American democratic traditions sometimes turned the vulgar Marxism of the early 1930s on its head by celebrating the transformation of former Indian territories into Euro-American farmland or by commemorating the sacrifices of a wholly unnecessary First World War. But they also encouraged the most vital public theater the nation has ever seen, and on a smaller scale allowed young composer Aaron Copland, for example, to move from "Into the Streets, May First!" (his first performance piece) to "Outdoor Overture" (publicly performed in 1938 by students at New York's High

School of Music and Art), on to ballet scores for *Billy the Kid* and, still later, the celebratory *Appalachian Spring*.[38]

By comparison to these large public experiments, the literary quarrels within the Left were small-scale and insular, not gaining their chief importance until decades later, when the cultural and the political Left had been crushed and the former dissidents had become triumphant figures of cold-war liberalism. For an artistic intellectual like Polonsky, the choices were not merely between modernism or agitprop or between aesthetic autonomy and art as political weapon but weighted by personal experiences as well as artistic or political issues.

3

Polonsky had already begun mulling over the implications of his coming graduation in June 1932 when his father gave him a short lecture from the anecdotal history of European literature on how literary men must find some practical means to support themselves. Some members of his family still dreamed that the young man might enter medical school, realizing a father's unfulfilled aspiration. But he enrolled instead in Columbia Law School, paying his way by teaching night classes in English literature and in creative writing at his alma mater.

Part-time teaching made economic sense, but it was also a means of sustaining a campus life that pleased him greatly. Doing so required only a bit of deception: the college presumed that within a reasonable time following his appointment he would complete his graduate course work, write a thesis, and take a Ph.D. in English. He never really intended to complete the doctorate, however, because he had set his cap on somehow becoming a professional writer. Happily, the unprecedented unionization of teachers at City made it possible for him and others like him to continue teaching. He would not have to make a final academic-career decision in the near future. Meanwhile, he could live a normal adult life, even to the point that his 1937 marriage to Sylvia Marrow following her graduation was part of a happy drift ("we had been seeing each other for so many years that in a sense we were married already") toward an uncertain future.[39]

Teaching afforded ongoing contact not only with students but also with fellow faculty, who needed to organize in order to deal with an always hostile administration. This life of formal and informal day-to-day contacts and obligations gradually transformed Polonsky's modernist artistic sympathies into political ones. He felt the economic issues more keenly with his marriage. (He recalled getting married in City Hall during a lunch break and returning to try a case before a state supreme court judge.) He may have felt the political issues more keenly as well, because for most of their fifty-some years together Sylvia would remain the determinedly active political member of the family.

Even more important to growing political tendencies was the world-wide transformation of the Left. Until the mid-thirties, the American Communist Party had all but prided itself on its status as a pariah organization. Early in that decade, some twenty thousand party members and a periphery of perhaps a hundred thousand more (mostly older immigrant workers who preferred other tongues to English) had sought to establish a network of outright left-wing unions and had urged workers and farmers to resist Depression conditions—violently if necessary. Here and there—especially where they already had a following in Jewish neighborhoods—they had achieved considerable success or at least had widened their following considerably. They could rely upon their women's cadre (Jewish housewives in sections of the Bronx and Brooklyn) to lead rent strikes as left-wing workers and youth moved furniture back into apartments after the attempted evictions of working-class tenants. They could rely, likewise, upon ethnic supporters from Finns and Hungarians to Yiddish-speaking Jews to take their propaganda among the workers who had gained least during the good times and often stood at the center of semi-skilled industrial labor in the giant factories suffering severely with the slump. Meanwhile, contributions to major defense and civil liberties causes like the Scottsboro case in Alabama and the Harlan County, Kentucky, coal miners' struggle (which brought CCNY campus leader Joe Lash to Harlan and closer to the party) gained widespread publicity and admiration for the Communists' work on behalf of capitalism's victims.

On occasion, the Communists' practical achievements were nothing short of spectacular. The San Francisco General Strike of 1934, more than any other single event, presaged the rise of the industrial union movement. But not even such red mobilization encouraged the kind of following enjoyed by sister parties across most of Europe, large parts of Asia, and Latin America. And very often the American Communists squandered their advantage, isolating themselves and their allies through overwrought propaganda and sectarian sniping. Thereby, they gave competing left-wing groups a chance at leadership roles in local activities like organizing the unemployed. Among the intellectuals they often made worse blunders, demanding loyalty to rigid views and practically driving dozens of fellow CCNYers no less culturally minded than Polonsky into the arms of left-wing and liberal anti-Communists.[40]

But younger Communist activists in particular, less cerebral than intent on agitation, had begun to learn crucial lessons as well. Sometimes racing ahead of party positions by building cooperation with demonstrably nonsocialist leaders like Harlem minister "Father" Divine or by joining mainstream unions as individuals without revealing their political identities, they struggled to break out of their normal political isolation west of the Hudson. Meanwhile, Hitler's rise and the German Communist underground's obliteration after mistaken hopes of early widespread resistance prompted serious rethinking in the Kremlin.

The Seventh Congress of the Comintern, held in Moscow during 1935, crystallized the new position. An American delegation readily agreed that vigorous antifascism, including mustering non-Communist allies, would be needed to replace the prognosis of (and planning for) impending world revolution. Such an antifascist program would necessarily demand a series of structural reforms within bourgeois society, but must also allow ample room for maneuvering. Against the pointed disagreement of some hardline American Communist delegates, Popular Front theorist Georgi Dimitrov forcefully argued that the New Deal did not tend toward fascism. Rather—and this was a dramatic departure with far-reaching implications—the reactionary forces of monopoly capital now ranged against Roosevelt in business and the press represented the main danger of the day.

This also marked a stunning shift of immediate political course. By unstated implication, the Communist Party could actually (if not quite openly) support Roosevelt. The American Left had *never* made such an accommodation toward a major mainstream politician, and certainly no Communist had ever even imagined it. Other adaptations quickly followed. In just a few years the historic secularist disdain for Jewish holidays (religious in background and at least spiritual in symbolism) that had prompted the most rabid anticlerical satires gave way to fervent communal merrymaking and the Exodus story's reclamation for the Jewish Left.

With amazing speed and dexterity, Communists repositioned themselves to advance in the ranks of New Deal reform agencies and of the new mainstream unions then organizing industrial workers. Indeed, Communists and their allies swiftly imparted their verve to the most creative agencies and unions. The new Communist leader, Earl Browder, personally led the transformation from the counterpart mentality within party circles, even down to the detail of his own wife's returning from unstylish flats (the proper choice of the communist proletarian woman) to heels. Proposed and briefly adopted as the party's new mass slogan, "Communism is the Americanism of the Twentieth Century" effectively captured the changed mood.

However much the startling turnabout may have outraged traditional-minded leftists (including many Communist old-timers), it was eminently sensible to Abraham Polonsky and thousands of other young Jewish radicals. Hitler loomed large in their world, a murderous threat to their people, ever more menacing as the decade wore on. Roosevelt could hardly be a protofascist when the Second New Deal of 1935 pushed his administration's agenda leftward, installing Social Security and as much as putting unemployed leftish artists, theater people, and street scholars on the Works Progress Administration payroll. By 1936, Roosevelt depended upon the labor movement, especially his supporters who launched Labor's Non-Partisan League, to bring in the votes. During that year's love fest between liberals and the large majority of the Left, Polonsky joined the Communist Party.

The same Polonsky who voted for Roosevelt in 1932 increasingly viewed the New Deal as a way forward for the Left as well as the nation. The antifascist urgency of the Popular Front, but even more the struggle of untenured City College instructors, prompted Polonsky to formalize his day-to-day activities with Communist Party membership. For him, at least as he looked backward, that moment would always be the party's best. At once a collection of free individuals (especially at the local base) and a distant bureaucracy, it presented a paradox not to be conquered or denied. To be a Communist but to take as few orders as possible either as artist or activist was unendingly problematic. But, then, so was the idea of being a radical or revolutionary in the bourgeois United States— even during the Depression. Polonsky always seemed to mix fatalism and idealism, as his films and novels would reveal abundantly.

The presence of the Teachers Union (TU) at CCNY made him a solid unionist. Launched as an American Federation of Labor union by Manhattan schoolteachers in 1916, the TU had been radical from the beginning and had suffered for it. During the first Red scare in 1919, hundreds of its members were threatened or arrested, and more baited by yellow journalists charging "reds in the classroom." At the same time, unionizing teachers faced formidable difficulties convincing the public (and many teachers as well) that educated professionals such as them-selves—however badly paid—had the right to join trade unions. Boards of education, especially during the conservative 1920s, thwarted the TU's growth and sought to eliminate it entirely. Membership nevertheless increased again during the 1930s, with locals taking root among primary and secondary schoolteachers and especially among the heavily exploited substitute teachers. The Teachers Union also experienced a burst of energy in a handful of college locals, nowhere stronger than at the city colleges, Columbia, and Columbia Teachers College.

Radicals found the TU exciting, and it accomplished real goals through hard work on campus and in the political arena. Before the TU, the college president in the city system had the unquestioned prerogative to approve or end the appointments of everyone on campus, from the deanery to the janitorial staff. Through TU members' legislative efforts, by 1938 any teacher who had been reappointed for a fourth year and had met other requirements automatically earned tenure at his or her existing level, from tutor to instructor to full professor. Other sweeping legislation on departmental structure democratized procedures from faculty appointments to promotions, an achievement that the *Nation* magazine saluted in a special award to the president of the board of higher education. Characteristically, a lone (and secret) Communist working in the City College registrar's office had actually drafted the crucial legislation.[41]

The red college teacher obviously did not fit the profile of what Communist Party leaders liked to call the "iron battalion of the proletariat," heavy industrial workers regarded as the backbone of the forthcoming revolution but rarely recruited with success in the numbers desired. After 1935, as the party rolls swelled, nearly half of its members could be found within New York State, disproportionately among the displaced petit bourgeoisie of teachers and dentists (largely Jews barred from medical school) from working-class districts, along with workers in light industry, small businessmen with family-owned shops, and lower-middle-class housewives. By 1938, when the CPUSA reached its prewar peak of fifty-five thousand members (with perhaps a million or so more in associated movements including Communist-led unions), its radicalized milieu had seriously undermined the muscled gentile image of the Communist "American worker." Even as the Communists maximized their influence on the labor movement by leading a half-dozen of the largest and most dynamic new CIO unions, they fitted more comfortably into the politics of the Popular Front at the New Deal's leftward fringe. They were, more than anything, an intelligentsia in the making.

For this new constituency of the Left, the weekly literary magazine the

New Masses, often previously shrill and pseudo-proletarian, now became almost charmingly sophisticated, at least when it was not primitively lambasting Russia's critics.[42] Like the greatly improved *Daily Worker,* it was one of the party's new faces, along with a bright cadre of accommodating near-liberals. Always hindered by rumors of terrible events in the Soviet Union and the heavy-handed orders of functionaries at home, on occasion caught entirely off guard by Stalin's antics, Communists now seemed despite it all a bright, mostly youthful, demonstrably idealistic, and determined bunch. As their rivals on the Left engaged in interminable internal struggles, Communists alone had the organizational capacity to get things done. They were certainly the only group that had the contacts and strategy to maneuver within the New Deal apparatus. Ideologues among the intellectual (and sometimes cultural) ranks felt compelled to press for political uniformity, especially on issues where dissent was plainly rife. Nonideologues like Polonsky simply fell silent, declined to attach their names to any of the documents then circulating among liberals to legitimate or denounce Moscow's policies, and hoped that time would replace Stalin's tyranny with something better.

The Popular Front milieu also included many young men and women who were exceptionally talented in the popular arts. The aforementioned Yip Harburg and several other future blacklistees, along with his lifelong friend (the distinctly "progressive"—that is, close to the Popular Front) Ira Gershwin and Ira's brother George, had helped invent the Broadway musical during the 1920s and '30s. Other Communists and near-Communists would "discover" black folk music and write anthems like "Ballad for Americans" to celebrate American liberalism; they would refurbish Abraham Lincoln's memory, adorn post offices and assorted public buildings with many of the era's memorable murals, and sometimes write the popular jokes against anti-Roosevelt Republicans. Even more than in the finer arts, an "invisible international" (as scholars later characterized the connections of left-wingers after the dissolution of the Comintern in 1941) existed among like-minded, mostly Jewish intellectuals who found semi-creative commercial work for each other or who converted their new colleagues to Popular Front liberalism.[43]

Unlike the committed strike journalists or literary insiders, few of the commercially connected artists who actually joined the party contributed in their own names to Communist-connected publications. Polonsky would later say that his aesthetic sense was so far removed from the contents of the *New Masses* or *Daily Worker* that to attempt a contribution could only have resulted in disappointment and isolation. Communist aesthetics never drew him into the party or kept him there. As a wonderful case in point his next career move involved commercial artistry far from either the formal artistic logic or political mobilizations of the Left. Law degree in hand, he began working in a New York law firm of modest progressive intent and show-business connections. One of the firm's clients was Gertrude Berg, who combined in herself the producer, writer, and star of the enormously popular radio show *The Goldbergs*. When Berg herself appeared on the company doorstep one day seeking help in writing a courtroom scene, the task was passed on to the junior Polonsky, who—although a complete stranger to the show—drew on his writing background to dash off several pages of dialogue. He succeeded so well, he says proudly, that she could hardly tell whose script was whose.

Berg was so taken with his skill in scripting that she asked him to continue, a way of taking the weekly burden off herself. For $200–$300 per week (a great sum in those Depression times), he was glad to do it. No record indicates any particular episode to which Polonsky contributed, but the show's scripts reveal clearly the pattern in which he worked. The announcer opens the program by setting up the situation, as often about husband Jake's current financial plight as about romantic mix-ups. The siblings jab at each other in characteristic adolescent fashion. Molly exerts herself to "make nice" for family unity's sake, meanwhile ruminating on solutions. (For instance, would it be ethical to offer false impressions to a possible business connection?)[44] In the only film ever made from the series, *Molly* (1951), Berg herself expressed its inner philosophy. To Jake's complaint that he will "never conquer the world," Molly answers properly, "We only want to live in it."[45] A more humane, Jewish, left-of-center observation could hardly be imagined. The radio episodes that Polonsky helped devise certainly offered nothing original. They had the comic-Odets quality of foolish-or-wise-but-always-lovable Jewish petit bourgeois family life, so unlike Father Coughlin's vulgar anti-Semitic stereotypes heard over the radio in those days or the ethnic self-denigration of the "cheap" Jack Benny.

Years later, Polonsky learned that Berg had always had help on scripts; he was both successor and predecessor in a long line of talented youngsters who helped get the work done and never challenged her creative control. Hardly political herself, she nevertheless felt close to the social circles of lefties. (Actor David Loeb, a cast member for decades and her costar "Jakie" in the film, would commit suicide during the McCarthy era after she unsuccessfully tried to protect him from blacklisting.) Polonsky appreciated the opportunity not only to break into radio but also to spend social time with Berg's real-life family, a kindly group of husband, father, and several children, all dependent upon her fortunes.

"In life," Polonsky's fictional Aunt Zenia says, "one thing leads to another. There's no other way. That's why it's always too late to turn back but never too late to change." Berg invited Polonsky to join her in 1937 on a trip to Hollywood, where she had been offered a screenwriting assignment for a picture with the juvenile songster Bobby Breen. (By coincidence, Polonsky's future Hollywood comrade, director Bernard Vorhaus, was about to direct three B pictures with Breen.) There, Polonsky discovered an unexpected taste for the movies. "As soon as I saw this magnificent nonsense going on, I said, 'This is the work for me.' I not only became an inmate, I wanted to run the asylum."[46] He stayed six months, suggesting some dialogue to Berg for the odd but forgettable 1937 musical *Make a Wish*. Therein, a Hollywood back lot magically becomes a summer camp in Maine, and singing prodigy Breen guides struggling composer Basil Rathbone (best remembered as the favorite Sherlock Holmes) in a budding romance with the boy's widowed mother, played by Marion Claire. Plenty of misunderstanding, a dash of romance, and a gallon of music gave Polonsky little actual work to do and plenty of time to do it. He also encountered some of Hollywood's left intellectuals, including future comrades like Paul Jarrico, as well as the visiting André Malraux and Ernest Hemingway on tour to raise funds for the Spanish Loyalists. Most important to himself, he used his leisure developing the plot, setting, and characters of his first novel.

After returning to New York with Berg, Polonsky, like dozens of other writers who finally ended up in films, also began working in radio drama. The later New Deal years saw the rise of quality drama, including audio versions of many serious contemporary films and a striking amount of original material. Polonsky's old friend Bennie Herrmann, already a working musician at CBS, helped him get small jobs mending dramatic scripts, a talent Polonsky relied upon two decades later while blacklisted. Gaining the confidence to quit the law firm, he adopted a work routine that he would follow for decades thereafter. He would write in the morning, meet friends for lunch, and do his other work in the afternoons. During the late 1930s, this meant balancing a living between CCNY teaching assignments, struggling with writing a serious novel, and contributing occasional radio dialogue for *The Goldbergs* or, on a higher level, *The Columbia Workshop Theater* and Orson Welles's famous series, *The Mercury Theater of the Air*, where his friend Bennie conducted the orchestra.

These were not only learning years for the future writer of dramatic films but also a time of extending himself among like-minded political types in show biz. Welles and his *Mercury Theater* offered a home for talented left-wingers like future screenwriter Howard Koch, William Alland (a fellow Communist and future friendly witness who later practically defined the "creature feature" as producer of *Creature from the Black Lagoon* and a series of spinoffs), and Koch's secretary, future fellow blacklisted screenwriter Anne Froelick, to mention only a few. Polonsky had his own projects and knew such people only vaguely if at all. But in his small way, he had entered a fertile zone for political involvement in the popular arts as a working member of the invisible international.[47]

Decades later Polonsky recalled that during his Hollywood sojourn with Berg he ran into a former Manhattan newspaperman. This past acquaintance insisted that the only reason to write movies was to make enough money to get back to New York. (Unfortunately, the fellow always drank up his would-be bankroll.) Although Polonsky felt differently, Hollywood hardly seemed a realistic prospect for an intellectual who had abandoned an attorney's career. He assured Sylvia that between teaching and writing assignments, he would always manage to make enough money for them to live on.

4

What Polonsky might have missed by not moving to Hollywood in the late 1930s is purely a matter for speculation but nevertheless involves large and interesting questions. The McCarthy era set-piece attacks on left-wingers who became screenwriters started as early as 1936, when cynical newspapermen, watching the Left's leading playwright sinking into Hollywood melodrama, asked rhetorically, "Odets, Where Is Thy Sting?" Odets's Hollywood debut, *The General Died at Dawn* (1936), an Orientalist drama involving American commercial imperialism, actually had about fifteen good minutes, par for the products of dedicated left-wing writers trying to make a living in Hollywood. To say the least, it was not *Waiting for Lefty*. But film work, with all its weaknesses, was an opportunity to achieve something that the Left of the theatrical world, the ethnic neighborhoods, or even the industrial unions could never do: reach millions of entertainment-hungry Americans from all social classes.

Especially at its upper levels, the Communist Party that Polonsky joined did not appreciate this kind of success, other than the prospect of hefty financial contributions by movie people to the continually underfunded cause. Party leaders had neither the artistic-cultural background nor the show business know-how to pose, let alone answer, the questions of how the Left might best respond to the remarkable appearance of social themes in films and theater. In literature, at least, they had *commandante* types like novelist Mike Gold who sought to define a proper "proletarian" style—until overruled by the quest for prestigious liberal writers more suited for Popular Front political initiatives. In Hollywood, they were truly at a loss.

This presented the Left with an unprecedented opportunity, as well as a daunting problem. Besides going to films routinely at least once a week, nearly every urban or even small-town American with fifteen cents and free time (massive unemployment allowed for lots of the latter) would dodge a rainstorm or temporarily escape a heat wave by ducking into a theater. A large minority of the population above the absolute poverty level and many well below it considered movies their grandest form of entertainment and—to the special dismay of would-be uplifters—of social instruction. Stars had been more recognizable than presidents since at least the early 1920s, and movie magazines practically pushed aside crime pulps on the newsstands, especially for younger female readers. That hundreds of young and underemployed, mostly lower-middle-class, left-inclined men (and a few women) of some artistic bent or literary interest should want to try their luck in Hollywood was hardly surprising. But they earned the literati's special scorn, an extension of the sentiment that popular visual culture was dragging down the mass mind and corrupting it with false images. Polonsky and his college friends more or less shared this attitude: a movie might be sociologically significant as well as entertaining, but it could not be fine art in the defining sense of commitment to meaning and expression.[48]

Earlier deployed against literary "yellowbacks" (pulp best-sellers) and later transferred to television, the uplift complaint assumed that if the masses were not wasting their time on these entertainments they would be reading "good" books, just as if they were not wasting their time on jazz and assorted popular tunes they would be listening to "good" music. To this generalized attack on "escapism" Communists—indeed all left-wingers—added the charge that films offered particularly bourgeois fantasies of personal solutions for social problems, censoring everything real and dangerous. It was a good point by the early 1930s. Even silent film had more political freedom and working-class content (not to mention heroes, above all the avowedly left-wing Charlie Chaplin) than the films that would follow for a considerable time.[49] The new Production Code, introduced in 1930 and tightened in 1934, censored not only sex but a huge variety of potential heresies, from unpunished crimes to bathroom humor. More than ever, filmmaking became a factory-style operation with set plots and predictable endings. To be a successful member of the Hollywood scene was therefore a special sin, for the literary classes (not excepting the Right) and the Left alike.

Across the country, then, Communists sneered at Hollywood writers as sellouts. Even Hollywood's left-wingers often wondered among themselves why they were not out organizing the working class or at least producing documentaries, as a small and demonstrably unsuccessful group of left-wing artists attempted to do from New York. Decades later Polonsky observed that the radicals' role in Hollywood was simply beyond the understanding of contemporary Marxists and in good measure remained so. He added,

> You can't possibly explain [it] by saying, "They came to Hollywood for the money," although indeed they did. You can't possibly say that they came for the glamour, although some did in fact. [But] if they had come only for money and glamour [they would all] have become stool pigeons, to hold their jobs, to continue making money and doing pictures. . . . According to Marxist theory, no decent pictures could be made in Hollywood.

Polonsky nimbly responded to the familiar charges of sellout by denying the premises:

> This dilemma was not solved and it couldn't be solved because it was artificial and didn't exist. Film making in the major studios is the prime way that the film art exists. That doesn't mean that film, as an art form, does not exist apart from the studios. But when you want to get into making movies . . . then there's only one thing to do: you try to make feature films for studios. It may not be the best solution to an artistic problem. It may end in the total defeat of every impulse that the writer has, the director has and the actor has. But the fact of the matter is, that's the only choice, and that is why so many people who became Communists in Hollywood didn't rush to go elsewhere.[50]

All the same, the status of left-wing writers in Hollywood could not have particularly encouraged the observant Polonsky. Like most other employees of every kind in "open shop" Los Angeles, they worked within an autocratic system. The moguls not only threatened firings at the first talk of unions but successfully demanded employee contributions to defeat the Democrats' 1934 candidate for governor, famed socialistic novelist Upton Sinclair. The rise of fascism in Europe and the civil war in Spain gave the Hollywood Left strong causes and their first opportunities for full-scale mobilization. But an organized Communist

Party still barely existed in Hollywood, remaining so thoroughly under-ground that famous and politically committed writers often feared to be seen in public with known party members.

Nor did their films offer much self-satisfaction. Indeed, scholar Michael Denning's equivocal description of 1930s filmwriters' influence on the films they scripted—"hard to judge"—is too sanguine for most of the early efforts.[51] Promising beginnings like John Bright's scripting for several outstanding Cagney films and Mae West's *She Done Him Wrong* led to career crises when writers showed enough spunk to take on the boss. Bright himself tried to throw producer Darryl Zanuck out a sec-ond-story window. A few recognized talents, notably quiet about their left-wing leanings, got the best assignments, but only a handful of their films could be considered artistic successes, let alone political statements. To consider for a moment the most successful left-wingers, Sidney Buchman was already highly paid for the garish, biblical *Sign of the Cross* (1932) and destined to become more so for *The Awful Truth* (1937), *Mr. Smith Goes to Washington* (1939), and a raft of later fine films. So was Donald Ogden Stewart (a rare Harvard grad in Holly-wood, known even before his film days as "America's funniest writer") for the Bing Crosby vehicle *Going Hollywood* (1932), *The Barrets of Wimpole Street* (1934), and such later films as *Love Affair* (1939) and *The Philadelphia Story* (1940). Dorothy Parker, who quipped to a later interviewer that the studios had no contract clause compelling writers to see their own films, could claim the shmaltzy *Suzy* (1935) and *A Star Is Born* (1937).[52] The rest of the studio-union pioneers looked back with-out nostalgia upon their Depression-era assignments, mainly low-budget titles like *The Sins of the Children* (1930) and *The Right to Romance* (1933). Most of those who reached their career apex during the war or shortly after and then went on to the blacklist were only getting started in the late 1930s. Some of the most talented, including Jules Dassin and Elia Kazan, were just then coming out of left-wing theatrical experiences or documentary filmmaking.

Yet the merely cynical look back, even to the time of Polonsky's early Hollywood visit in 1937, could be misleading in several important ways. First, in spite of the paucity of work in which a writer could take politi-cal pride, a large handful of films had made valuable points along the way. Depression realist shockers like *Hell's Highway* (1932), *Mayor of Hell* (1933), *Road Gang* (1937), or *They Won't Forget* (1937) treated most sympathetically the conditions of the homeless and incarcerated. *Our Blushing Brides* (1933) and *Success at Any Price* (1934) captured

the emptiness of bourgeois social life (and the relative absence of bourgeois morals) during the Depression. Powerful films against war, *The
Man Who Reclaimed His Head* (1935) and *They Gave Him a Gun*
(1937), carried the popular mood of revulsion with the whole experience
of the First World War. Quietly protofeminist films to which left-wing
writers made script contributions—Katharine Hepburn vehicles *Alice
Adams* (1935) and *The Little Minister* (1934), as well as Lillian
Hellman's *These Three* (1936, a lightened version of her stage hit, *The
Children's Hour*) or the delightfully iconoclastic film adaptation *Becky
Sharp* (1935)—foreshadowed an efflorescence of keenly gendered
women's films as *Holiday* (1937) and *The Philadelphia Story* looming
ahead. Escape-to-jungle films like *Sinners in Paradise* (1938) and *Five
Came Back* (1939) showed the true colors of plane- (or ship-)wrecked
Americans, and their capacity to work cooperatively for survival. Even a
low-grade science fiction film like *The Devil-Doll* (1935) opened on
Devil's Island and closed in Paris with revenge of the wrongly accused
against the rich and powerful. A miniboom of populist cowboy films and
sophisticated sex comedies, an occasional high-profile political shocker
like *Mr. Smith Goes to Washington* (1939), even left-written family films
like *The Adventures of Huckleberry Finn* (1939), signaled that a new era
of Hollywood radicals' prestige and creative influence was on the way. In
truth, after Polonsky's Hollywood visit in 1937, the opportunities grew
steadily greater, if always shaded by exploitation of themes, sharp limits
upon artistic experimentation, overt censorship, and on-the-set dumbing-
down rewrites that often ruined the scriptwriter's most creative work.

Perhaps the forgotten social-theme film *The President's Mystery*
(1936) best displays the fascinatingly paradoxical status of the screenwriting Left. Lester Cole—ironically best known, decades later, as the
last of the unwavering Communist Party members among the former
Hollywood set—had responded to a story in *Liberty* magazine by
Franklin Roosevelt (more likely, one of his writers) musing on the fate of
a rich man who chose to disappear from view. In the film, a corporate
lawyer played by Henry Wilcoxen abandons his practice and his faithless
wife in order to discover himself. He quickly finds a bankrupted factory
town whose canning plant is ready to reopen but is prevented from doing
so by scheming corporate bosses bent on monopolizing certain markets.
Keeping his identity secret, Wilcoxen develops a plan for cooperative
enterprise, winning the trust of the public and the love of the factory
owner's well-meaning daughter, played by Betty Furness. After a near-
riotous clash with authorities, the workers win the day, but sections of

the upper classes also evince virtue. The message is just slightly to the left, in short, of the New Deal.

Hollywood would absolutely not allow the making of any pro-union film, let alone a revolutionary one. But by emphasizing certain popular themes, left-wing writers (also directors and, by the 1940s, actors and producers as well) could elevate those themes into an improved and, at times, almost transcendent liberalism. Especially at the highest level—a play adaptation like Lillian Hellman's script for *Dead End* (1937) that carried too much prestige to be easily ruined by studio heads. Meanwhile, at the lowest levels of children's films, action comedies, detective stories, and romances that studios hardly noticed in production, a certain freedom prevailed.

Still, for financial and technological reasons, artistic experimentation had barely appeared in Hollywood. The expressionism so vividly present in corners of American theater could hardly be found in movies outside of animated features and horror films. Until the second half of the thirties, Hollywood left-wingers themselves hardly considered cinema as more than filmed theater. Even within their own circles, the conversation had only begun.[53]

By the close of the furiously productive years just before Pearl Harbor, future victims of the blacklist had nevertheless scripted well over two hundred films, including critically acclaimed features, box-office smashes, strong-minded "women's films," riveting detective dramas, bold (for the time) treatments of class, ethnicity, race, and even homosexuality. In those same exciting years, screenwriters' and actors' unions had begun to dig in their heels and press for both dignity on the job and participation in artistic decision making. That this all happened in nouveau riche Hollywood is the more remarkable. Marxist hard-liners, if there had been any in Hollywood (gravel-voiced actor and nonparty member Lionel Stander occasionally claimed to be the only one), might well have looked suspiciously upon the ease of transition from revolution to reform manifest in the Communists' own swift turn toward the liberals. The deep political hopes now suddenly invested in the Democratic Party, as much in California as in New York State, the practical abandonment of the anticolonialism that had been the international version of antiracism, not even to speak of the warm reviews in the *New Masses* of certain Nelson Eddy/Jeanette McDonald features, all demonstrated that Communists were eager to go with the flow. The New Deal certainly suited the Hollywood Communists' mood, their self-envisioned place in the world, and their career hopes.

To all this, the announcement of the Hitler-Stalin Pact on August 19, 1939, was a stunning blow. Steadfast party members could justify it among themselves as necessary and even inevitable, given the unwillingness of France, Britain, and the United States to stand up to Hitler. But they could not justify it to the large public that the Communists had built around antifascist unity over the previous few years. Blacklist victim Carl Foreman much later observed shrewdly if inaccurately that the Communist Party in Hollywood died at that moment and carried on afterward as a ghost.[54] In reality, the party's membership grew during the war to several times its pre-1939 size, and its respectability multiplied many times. In 1939, party members and close supporters were still to write their most popular and, in most cases, their best films. But their moral position as a group had been seriously damaged, and a reviving economy had thrown the inevitable decline of capitalism into doubt. The Hollywood that Polonsky entered in the 1940s would be starkly different, but the '30s remained a memory of a politically more hopeful time, now almost certainly lost forever.

A continent away from all this, for Polonsky the decade closed as curiously as it had begun at City College with Paul Goodman and the bohemian crowd. While the critics argued and the Hollywood Left of semi-educated brain-workers craved creative control of their dialogue, Polonsky worked at the novel that he never saw successfully into publication. The leftist Modern Age Books advertised *The Discoverers* but then dropped it during a shuffle of editors. Had the manuscript been published, readers would have found Polonsky holding firm to his Proustian beginnings, utilizing a modernist perspective but with a large difference. Now that he was a Marxist with political experience and a union veteran, he saw the characters dragged down by their social isolation and their self-involvement.[55]

This is, however, too simple an analysis by far of the work's imaginative qualities, which demonstrate how distant Polonsky remained artistically from both the Communist literary/aesthetic world of the earlier hyper-proletarian *New Masses* and from the liberal, didactic literature of American democratic tradition that was becoming ever more fashionable as war neared. "The Discoverers" offers a complex narrative with asides (as in Polonsky's other novels) aplenty, both descriptive and philosophical. His handsome, wealthy, twenty-nine-year-old protagonist—the same age as the handsome if unwealthy Polonsky—Charles Veer is hardly more than a shadow on the setting of Physalia, an imaginary seaside California beach settlement named for the rather grotesque, notoriously stinging Portuguese man-of-war. This "small and regular universe, revolving in its orbit of social life and pleasure," holds little more than sun and surf, morning games, shopping trips, music, and entertaining at night. It is a place of "pleasant, civilized voices," the usual rounds of love affairs (some heterosexual, some homosexual), and rather more earnest conversation than one would expect among the leisure class—except, of course, in an era of economic crisis.

Most of the story figures around an unlikable young man, Windy, doubly heir to money and to a girl, Louise, who cannot decide whether to ridicule him for his buffoonery or accept him as a good match freeing her financially to live the life of individual freedom and excess that she imagines. Add to the cast a famous novelist and a naive boy almost old enough to leave for college, a frankly gay African-American in his thirties, and a ghost (a young woman whose memory remains a key to Windy's character). The novel largely shifts from one conversation to another, while behind it all the initial sprawl of beach development (lone white houses looking like "tombstones" and an absurdly overdone grand hotel), with its promise for further exploitation, provides the key to American-style consumption.

Like any number of characters in later Polonsky novels, Veer is a former rebel. He revisits his radical past, thanks to a bookseller's bringing back to mind a college pamphlet that briefly won him notoriety. ("He recalled now how carefully he had written the work, how he had forced himself to . . . write plainly, simply, keeping his determination clear. For a whole week he had known himself utterly, and he had never known himself again.")[56] But Veer has lost the spark in accepting the empty existence of the comfortable rentier. Imagining himself to be the only one with a sense of humanity in these surroundings, he does justice to most of the rest of the crowd but flatters himself.[57] A nearby blue-collar city of "cheap joints, saloons, dance-halls, ten-cent movies, pool harbors and whorehouses" fascinates and delights him with the contrast to Physalia, but he is no different from the bohemian gentility whose "depraved tastes" bring them there to go slumming.[58]

Resolution is in fact impossible, which may be a major weakness of the novel. The characters wander. After the novel's climax, a ritual humiliation of Windy at a party with all the major figures on hand, Louise and Veer go off on an automobile adventure with the gay mulatto Fenman as their driver. Speed and motion together block out any concrete thoughts: the three of them have resolved to settle for experience alone. Within the immensity of the night, everything else dissolves "back into the heap of the universe, blank, even and finished," the "blank fluidity of energy everywhere the same."[59] Nothing else matters, which is to say, nothing ever mattered beyond the subject's self-perception.

All in all, "The Discoverers" is a remarkable performance—perhaps a farewell to existentialist themes—from a writer moving in very different directions. Polonsky freely admitted that its plotting is insufficient, with any narrative energy displaced to character studies through description and dialogue. He added that he populated its pages with "most of the people I knew under different names, having conversations of the sort I was used to."[60] In that sense, he was working through the frustrations of the contemporary intellectuals. But these psychological character studies would become building blocks for studies of social tensions of different kinds.

5

Polonsky's bridges were meanwhile burning behind him. In March 1940, in the wake of the Hitler-Stalin Pact, the New York state legislature passed a joint resolution forming a committee to investigate the state's financing of New York City's public schools. Submitted by two Republicans (upstater Herbert A. Rapp, and the body's only Republican from Manhattan, Frederic R. Coudert, Jr.), the legislation prescribed only "investigation," as would later be the case with so many other committees. Of thirteen issues to be studied, the eleventh was "the extent to which, if any, subversive activities may have been permitted to be carried on in the schools and colleges of such educational systems." Under the leadership of committee vice-chair Coudert, the hearings focused entirely on that issue, even if the final committee report offered no evidence of such activities. (The only "subversive" actually discovered, unnamed by the committee but eventually arrested by the FBI, was a paid Japanese agent teaching at City College!)

The Hearst press nonetheless struck a political bonanza with the committee hearings, running banner headlines like "100 OF COLLEGE FACULTY HERE BRANDED AS RED." The conservative Taxpayers Union demanded the closure of City College until all "un-American professors and students" were eliminated. (The Taxpayers Union's president insisted, with unconscious hilarity, that a *majority* of the students there were "confirmed Communists.") Dozens of teachers fell under scrutiny, amid the continually blaring publicity of the yellow press. As later in Hollywood, the committee left the actual firing to others. Thirty-six teachers with alleged Communist affiliations, having been "named" by informers—themselves mostly embittered or frightened ex-Communists—were thus placed on trial by the board of higher education. The board made it clear that anyone admitting to being a Communist would be fired. Unable to settle on a legal strategy, a small handful of teachers made the mistake of denying their party membership. They soon found themselves serving jail sentences for perjury, while confessed Communists were free to enjoy their new unemployment.[61]

Polonsky eluded any potential pursuers, mostly because the committee wanted to nail the party leaders on campus, but also thanks to the intervention of remote events. The Rapp-Coudert inquiry halted shortly after Germany invaded Russia, as it became clear that Communists would once again be the most ardent of liberalism's antifascist activists. Had the investigations continued, Polonsky insisted, he would have willingly admitted to being a Communist and faced firing. As it was, he suspected his always-uncertain future as a teacher was inevitably reaching its end. He had also had a taste of the witch hunt. Some of the friendly witnesses for Rapp-Coudert would resurface when the public school investigations resumed in the early 1950s under new legislation. By then, Polonsky was long gone from New York. But the whole political experience, especially Polonsky's intensive examination of the friendly witness character type, proved a valuable preparation for things to come.

THE GOOD WAR—
AND AFTER

FROM THE CLOSE OF THE 1930s to Pearl Harbor was a strange time for Polonsky and the other left-wingers and, indeed, for the rest of America. The film community and the many antifascist committees that united liberals with the Left added to the growing drumbeat of support in the press and among the elite for the United States to go to war. At last the public realized the dangers of fascism and the inevitability of armed involvement. Yet questions remained. The popular audience, as contemporary movie critics noted quizzically, could feel simultaneously and with no apparent sense of contradiction the urgency of an antiwar film and of newscasts that all but demanded an armed response to Hitler. Of course, moviegoers would not make the decision. Seeking a third term in 1940, Franklin Roosevelt promised voters not to "send your boys to any foreign wars." Both he and sophisticated observers knew better. The Hitler-Stalin Pact of 1939 destroyed the Russian Communists' credibility while compelling American Communists at least temporarily to turn against their liberal allies, thus opening the gates to the first major Red scare since 1920.

The American Communists' defense of the Russian turnaround so discredited the Popular Front that the political complications of the moment were lost. Any left-wing support for the New Deal now would logically have shifted gears on domestic issues as well. Congressional losses in 1938 and an economy surging with a rush of war orders seriously undermined the New Deal's prospects for reform. Hollywood

Communists had swallowed hard when Roosevelt forsook the Spanish Loyalists to hold Catholic (that is, pro-Franco) voters. They also grimaced when he allied himself with racist Dixiecrats to hold the Solid South. But by 1940, when Congress's shift away from government programs had become clear, especially in matters of arts and culture, the high New Deal years looked more and more like the Golden Age. The idea of government in the public interest during peacetime had always been more a matter of rhetoric than of principle but nonetheless enjoyed a certain ideological importance during the Depression. Now it would be reduced to little more than Social Security and eventually to the GI Bill, highway subsidies, and other schemes intended mainly to benefit the upwardly and outwardly mobile.

Nor did Roosevelt's administration, after the announcement of the Hitler-Stalin Pact, discourage the prosecution of Communists via congressional and state legislation that foreshadowed the Truman administration's "security" measures and McCarthy-style political showmanship. Within the presumably left-leaning world of labor, Roosevelt now seemed to turn from his solidly progressive CIO supporters of 1936 to the conservative American Federation of Labor, whose rising leaders (like future AFL-CIO president George Meany) were best known for their rigid Catholicism, their visceral hatred of left-wing ideas of all kinds, and their quiet tolerance of labor's organized crime legion.

Militant unionists grew restive. CIO champion and mineworkers' leader John L. Lewis, who became the Communists' patron and ally during the second half of the 1930s, threatened to form a national labor party in 1940. Only at the last moment did he backpedal to support Roosevelt's liberal Republican opponent, Wendell Wilkie. Much as they had during the First World War, factory conflicts intensified with war orders and the rising demand for labor, but an increasingly Jewish and lower-middle-class Communist Party was ill equipped to exploit them.

Left-wingers knew as well or better than anyone else that war was finally coming. Arguably, the threatening catastrophe impelled Polonsky beyond his 1930s modernism and academic career toward an entirely different existence, scarcely less literary but immensely more practical. For Polonsky, though, the change was a more or less spontaneous decision to abandon his past as a part-time teacher and would-be novelist to become a full-time writer-organizer. He would travel far in every sense— geographically, politically, and artistically. Only a few years after he had repositioned himself, first as labor educator and then as intelligence field operative, postwar Hollywood found him in the startling role of a left savant, the most sophisticated and self-confident figure in his extraordinary crowd. But every shift was Polonskyan, more imaginative than even he could have expected.

1

Polonsky still had to deal with one more major piece of political-intellectual business. To meet the crisis posed by the Rapp-Coudert hearings, he would write a three-act play, "Out of This World." The highly ruminative drama was not at all a modernist piece like "The Discoverers" or a popular performance like his upcoming genre work in magazines and film. The "friendly testimony" of a brother-in-law spurred the play, which also more dimly reflects the Soviet Union's Show Trials (which Polonsky like many Communists privately considered catastrophic but did not publicly protest), with their defendants' coerced "confessions." It captures a crisis of conscience due to become ever larger in his own milieu.

The play is set in a drawing room, or more properly the living space of an upwardly bound Jewish family, "one of those new, modernistic apartment buildings located in a not too fashionable section of the city," equipped with radio-phonograph and modern kitchen, set with excellent taste.[1] These are Polonsky's first stage directions. Though his screenwriting would become notorious for such detailed directions, he clearly knows what he wants to see, and for good reason: his characters have the taste of cultivated people, but no answers for problems they could not have anticipated in their younger lives during the rapidly receding Depression. They are not elderly by any means, ranging in age from around twenty-seven to thirty-one years (just the age of his former classmates at CCNY). But the atmosphere and their own success make them feel old. Ben Fisher is a lawyer working for the City of New York. Ben's wife, Ruth, a socialist at heart, is now an inactive rank-and-file follower of the Left, evidently never joining any organization but happiest at a demonstration or public event. Her former boyfriend (and their mutual dear friend), Dave Temple, made his mark as a highly successful commercial photographer but for social reasons turned to documentary work. Ben's father, Max, who lives with the couple in the apartment, is a frequently failed immigrant businessman and egotistic antisocialist. One more character, Ralph Ryder, sets the plot into motion. A man "too busy changing the world to have time to live," he has been energetically defending civil service workers who are about to be fired as Communists.

Since his college days Ben has insisted that "radical democrat" is "the only phrase that makes sense in American politics" and is immune to the charge of being a Communist. Precisely for that reason, he is free to choose whether or not to extend himself for his friends' sake. When he is served with a subpoena to appear before a hearing very much like the real-life Rapp-Coudert hearings, his room for indecision narrows.

The assorted characters take sides. Max, who has already borrowed money from Ben and intends to borrow more to launch a restaurant, repeatedly urges his son to repudiate his friends and get on with realizing the materialistic American Dream. Dave, appalled that Ben might capitulate to cling ignobly to his career, also has a hidden motive: he is still in love with Ruth, who wants a baby (and allows herself "accidentally" to become pregnant) for the usual reasons but also to fill the emptiness left by the social movements' evanescence. She is the most conflicted, and she sees clearly that despite their relative prosperity, their circle has not "begun to live." She also knows that her husband is not ready for parenthood and that through some moral compromise he may destroy her faith in him.

Very much like the friendly witnesses of Rapp-Coudert or the later Hollywood witch trials, Ben knows that he will be asked directly about his friendships and observations in the thirties, above all concerning Ralph. He can refuse to answer, which will seriously damage his career, or lie, which will open him to perjury. Or he can destroy lives by giving the committee the answers it already knows but wants to hear from a distinguished witness. While Max blames all the difficulties on "troublemakers" who refuse the security that America offers and Ruth implores him to lie if necessary (echoing the decisions of the Rapp-Coudert defendants), Ben wavers. Then he falls, testifying willingly, as he explains to her later, after realizing on the stand "who I was, what I was, what I wanted to have from this world. And I terrified myself with the utter horror of being destroyed, of being driven out of the common ordinary place I had found to live in." Pleading for her to stay with him, he concludes that when forced to choose self-protection, "all your theories and attitudes crumble," leaving "your filthy, dirty, vicious humanity that clings to endurance . . . [so that] you are ashamed and you try to live on." An eloquent plea for careerism.

At that moment—with apparently too much coincidence but very much as in the real-life Rapp-Coudert hearings—the news of Pearl Harbor interrupts. Ben is still thinking above all about saving his own skin. Very much like another character in a Polonsky novel a dozen years later, he attempts to destroy a past that has become uncomfortable and alien by burning books, in this case his own radical library. The Communists' sudden heroism reflected from the glimmerings of Russian resistance to the Germans makes no difference to the committee pursuing Ralph. With a series of further self-evasions and rationalizations brilliantly foretelling the McCarthy era, Ben insists that he has upbraided the committee by explaining proudly "the rock that our past friendship was founded on" (including "how sincere and innocent you were"). By clinging to his formal libertarian position while testifying that Ralph has read Marx and Proust and may be a Communist—but also insisting that it is no business of a friend (or a committee) to know about such things—Ben has cleverly found a roundabout means of betrayal. At one level, he knows what he has done makes him "despicable," a "nothing" (words that actor and friendly witness Lee J. Cobb would use to describe himself a decade later); at another level, he has conspired to hold onto his pride while actually holding on to his career.

At the play's anticlimax, Ruth tells Ben she is leaving him to create her own identity and her child's in the best way that she can. She cannot live with the lies necessary to continue their marriage, and notwithstanding her self-recognized limitations and weaknesses, she has chosen to live.

Polonsky had no doubt of his artistic talent, even if he would leap into a wider public arena at the earliest opportunity and then leave to fight the fascists firsthand. The play was never performed either as the political fund-raiser he had originally planned or in any other venue. But Polonsky had cleared his mental desk for other work.

2

"The Discoverers"'s rejection even after a modest advertising campaign may have triggered what Polonsky later described in private correspondence as a dramatic shift not only in literary genres but also in literary intent. What might have been a modernist career as a man of letters imagined by his circle at City College instead became an engagement with pulp literature and the slicks: a suitable irony that would make more sense as time passed. Undertaking what he described as a private joke or dare between two close friends and aided by the publishing connections of a one-time literary partner, Polonsky channeled his talents into *The Goose Is Cooked*, a genre mystery collaboration with Mitchell Wilson. Polonsky would never again collaborate on fiction and usually bemoaned collaborating on film scripts. But by no mistake, genre was his meal ticket.

The Goose Is Cooked is a very funny novel, an "entertainment," as Graham Greene described his own commercial sideline creations. Published in the Inner Sanctum Mystery series that capitalized on the title of the famed creaking-door radio show, it carried the byline of "Emmett Hogarth," and was dedicated to Mitch and Abe (the authors themselves) and to Sylvia and Helen (their wives). Coauthor Wilson, a physicist working for Fermi at Columbia and a left-winger, would be denied government clearance for the Manhattan Project but vindicated as a successful popular writer on scientific subjects. The authors, both mystery readers in their leisure hours, took turns producing chapters. One would write a chapter, the other would respond, and so forth. Polonsky then rewrote the entirety, which is obvious in his own favorite character, the police detective, who by some slight coincidence is also a City College graduate, an ardent Proust reader, and witty Marxist who quips, "Marxism is a great thing. It changed *cherchez la femme* to *cherchez la economic motive.*"[2]

The plot revolves around the murder of Seward Salem, an aging radio electronics entrepreneur from the 1920s who had cheated his partner but fallen on relatively hard times before being found electrocuted in his laboratory, thus "cooked" with "juice." Twenty-seven-year-old protagonist Peter Whitman (bearing the name of Polonsky's favorite American poet) is a hard-working but poor technical assistant, in love with Salem's adopted daughter, Joyce. Peter resists the attention—it may or may not be seductive—of Salem's wife, Meg, a "dark and sleek," stylish woman just his own age.[3] Joyce shows some interest in Peter, but she also seems linked somehow to Stephen Jay, a young technical and entrepreneurial whiz who had been on the verge of securing a substantial loan from Salem to launch a technologically groundbreaking electronics line. Nearly everyone in the book had a motive to kill Salem, including a number of secondary characters. Cathy, a working-class girl dragged into the plot by virtue of being picked up by Jay, claims nearly "every woman in Greater New York under seventy has had to fight off Seward Salem at one time or another. The chorus girl's union wants to have him declared unconstitutional."[4] But who had both the motive and the opportunity?

The narrative cruises along with detective Marty Cohen, who shepherds Peter around New York and Westchester County by car and on foot, questioning potential witnesses and the presumed killer. There's little deviation from formula here and some real pleasure in it. Clues steadily appear, then complicate the situation instead of clarifying it.

Stephen Jay turns up dead, apparently murdered by the same electronic means as Salem. Peter gets his opportunity to press his feelings of love upon Joyce in her moment of vulnerability, discovering her "strong, unbelievably strong, as she held him to her."[5] But his beloved Joyce, an apparently respectable girl who frequently avers her love for her stepfather, turns out to have assisted Stephen Jay in murdering Salem when the old entrepreneur discovered that the supposed technological breakthrough was a fraud. She then went on to kill her co-conspirator.

By contrast, Meg—having married a rich older man in order to live an easy life and then realizing the consequences of being under the thumb of an "absolute louse"—is irreducibly complex and definitely in charge of her own sexuality. She confesses that she loves Whitman at a point in the novel when she might be lying and even be the murderer, yet we cannot help admiring her. Looking gorgeous in pajamas but "entirely self-contained . . . she asked nothing of him. . . . [because] at the moment she had no need for him." Thus she taunts Whitman, "Could it possibly be . . . that you're in love with me and you don't know it? That the very idea of loving me has shocked you so that you can't admit it to yourself? You consider it impossible to be in love with your boss' wife but it's traditional to fall in love with his daughter. Traditional? It's the great American dream."[6] She brings Peter ever closer to escaping from a typically immature American mixture of keen engineering skills with a complete lack of social understanding.

Meg and Peter's relationship is much more interesting, in fact, than the main plot. That crypto-feminist message, buried within the genre's conventions, would have to wait to be developed more fully. Meanwhile, within the year, a magazine offer expanded Polonsky's opportunities in genre fiction.

His serialized novel *The Enemy Sea*, published first in *America* magazine during 1942 and put into hardback by Little, Brown the next year, could be described as his major literary contribution to the war effort. Indeed, he dedicated it to the determinedly left-wing and interracial National Maritime Union, whose members were not only manning the waters but working actively with resistance groups in Greece and elsewhere to prepare the overthrow of Fascism.[7] The novel also scored a financial and personal literary hit. *America* paid him $15,000 for what he calculated to be three weeks' work, and he was able to mix genre and antifascist political material very much as the Hollywood Left had reached its widest audience with real or implied war-action features like *Pride of the Marines* or *Casablanca*—the former virtually the adopted favorite of the Marine Corps and the latter an all-time cult film—before their writers went on the blacklist.

The Enemy Sea was Polonsky's first book to earn real reviews. It also was just as much a genre job as *The Goose Is Cooked,* intimately close not to the detective novel but to popular screen war-action dramas. A *New York Times* reviewer reflected, "A bald telling of the tale would make a superb movie scenario; all the sure-fire ingredients are there— action, brawls, intrigue and suspense."[8] But Polonsky also wanted to make a philosophical statement, and as some film critics would later complain about *Force of Evil,* he sometimes impeded the action to do so. But his weaknesses were surely his strengths, as well as vice versa. The novel got him a serious look from Hollywood.

Protagonist Danny M'Cloud is like the Jimmy Stewart character of *The Philadelphia Story* removed to rougher times. Polonsky mostly chose gentiles to typify wider America, and Danny is no exception, a midwestern litterateur who has become a big-city ace reporter. He has never been comfortable with urban sophisticates or able to put across to them his artistic work. But at least he has been happier. During the 1930s, when "young people had come alive" with political and economic interests, he successfully wrote for magazines and even had a popular if less than bestselling reportage book.[9] By now, liking the big city more than he had expected or wanted to, he has more philosophical depth than his fellow former proletarians, but pays for that depth with a stubborn inability or unwillingness to stay on track with the rat race. The passage describing him closely is one of the best in the book, and deserves quotation at length, with M'Cloud ruminating on

> the paradox of his flesh, the big workingman's body which had lived leanly back in those hard days on his grandfather's farm. There the flat acres and flatter sky, the terrible winters and more terrible summers, had kept the flesh docile; and in the strength with which he met the long hours of work he had been free. It was easy to enjoy his transparent senses, the day rising or passing, the long lift of muscle when he stocked the barns. You could pause a moment and take it all in measure: the fragrant dust that stirred in the dark, the animal recesses of the barn. You could wipe your face and turn back to the fork, and everything fitted, action to thought, thought to action. He had been a young man and he lived.
>
> But there was a bubble of creation in his mind, and one winter it had floated loose. Then Chicago saw him and finally New York. The blunt-faced, blunt-fingered giant of a boy had come to the cities. And they had taken him. It had become possible to express what he understood so that they would listen. His bare words, his small sentences, his plain insights couldn't touch the verbal barriers of the literary world. They didn't want him, and they were the

readers, or so they said. He made a silly figure at the parties he went to, and as his big body went soft, that hard core of poetry in his nature flattened too, until finally he gave in.

And so he had become a journalist, because he was shrewd enough and slick enough and dogged enough when he wanted to be. If they wanted it, they could have it. And he gave it to them. At night he tried to write of the secret things he knew, the muddy brook behind the church, and Sunday night with his old Aunt Ellen. He knew those things: the old bum in town who had civil rights granted to no other tramp; the agonies of frustration; the deep, the passionate tenderness of the village druggist. But you couldn't say those things when your mind was filled with the slick days. And so finally he had stopped trying, and it seemed that one night he had died, and he was through.[10]

Through, that is, except in his love for Carrie Tennant, a top war photographer ("one jump ahead of the fascists and two jumps ahead of the censor") in whom he saw condensed all of the lure and unrealized possibilities of cosmopolitan life. [11] So far, she has kept him at arm's length, and out of misplaced pride, he has not pressed her for more. It would be easy enough to say thus far that Abraham Polonsky had precious few ideas about midwestern farm life that he had not acquired from books and found himself operating along the lines of Sherwood Anderson's *Winesburg, Ohio*. But as the *Times* reviewer commented, Polonsky was preparing the reader for a political message that became clearer as the plot developed.

Carrie has got herself and Danny into a risky assignment covering the oil tanker *Aruba*'s trek from Galveston to New York (reversing, of course, Polonsky's own earlier adventure). The job would be merely dull and dirty in peacetime, offering a novelty story at most. But this was wartime. With the merchant marine losing more men than the navy to enemy fire and normal sea hazards, an oil tanker was nothing more than a floating bomb. Even before the ship leaves port, Danny realizes that Carrie has carefully planned the assignment to give her one more chance with the aristocratic former magazine writer Larry Denhim, who dumped her after a romance a few years earlier. Now (and this is already a bit suspicious) Denhim is a common ship's officer in charge of the gun crew, presumably doing his patriotic duty. Carrie's sudden announcement that she and Denhim are about to be married by the captain is part of a ruse (of which she is innocent), but the truth soon comes out.

Danny is alert to the signs of a conspiracy whose leading figure turns out to be none other than Denhim. Contemptuous of Danny ("You belong to that Hoosier school of feeling in American life, but that went out with the Mississippi pilots. The town-meeting mind and the Sunday-school heart aren't tough enough for this world and this war") in the same way that he is contemptuous of American "softness," he has chosen the Nazi way.[12] Sophisticated devotee of T. S. Eliot, John Crowe Ransom, James Burnham's *The Managerial Revolution,* and E. E. Cummings (all non-left modernists, including some of Polonsky's own favorites), he has plotted a rendezvous with Nazi subs off the Florida Keys in the Gulf Coast. After the subs refill with oil, they will sink the *Aruba* with most of its crew and spirit Denhim and a few others away to Germany to survive with a tall tale of natural disaster.

Here the story shifts, though never entirely, to adventure. Danny and Carrie are thrown into a cabin together as the crew works below under loaded guns preparing for the subs to reconnoiter. Two events are key to Polonsky's narrative. First, the couple discover a potential savior in the African-American cook, Stark, whom the Nazis hardly consider capable of thought. Stark plans an escape with the quiet help of the captain, a philosophical democrat coerced by the Nazis' hold over his family back in Germany. Stark—we never learn his first name—soon begins relating his own life, bit by bit, revealing an intelligent workingman and potential hero. Second, inspired in no small degree by Stark's example, Danny comes alive in a way new to himself. Through realizing that he can readily sacrifice his life to defeat Fascism, however small his contribution to that effort may be, he gains unexpected strength and resolve. His "peacetime muscles, those bar and restaurant muscles, those living-room muscles, those golf and tennis muscles" were not the "work muscles" that would allow him to do the really heroic tasks—like swimming to the mainland ten miles at a time, from one island to the next, as they had planned for Stark to do.[13] But he can throw himself fiercely on a Nazi beast, learn to operate a machine gun, and dodge bullets as needed. He also gains virility in Carrie's eyes, without deceiving himself that what she admires in him amounts to much more than she had mistakenly revered in Denhim.[14]

But the point is the action. Like a movie serial, the excitement moves in episodes, with our hero and heroine left hanging at the close of scenes, just as in the magazine installments. Danny's growing appreciation of Stark, however, sets an unusual background for the adventure. Momentarily doubting that Stark has given in to the Nazis, Danny ruminates, "For Stark he had profound tenderness, because this was just the white man's world. It needed no further tags, no labels or new political beliefs. This was the same old world. And yet, Danny had imagined for a while on that first day out . . . that Stark was an undefeated soul, one of the great resisters, who had measured mere living against the living he wanted and made his choice."[15] If for this moment Danny downgrades Stark to "nothing but the tragedy of the man who had nothing to lose and no courage to fight," the truth soon hits him: "And then Danny felt the drench of shame. It flooded him with humiliation. It drowned the self which had generously conceded nothing to Stark, Stark who was bearing the whole burden of revolt just because he was a Negro and ostensibly servile. . . . Stark was taking all the immediate risk, and any casual blow."[16] This was a real literary issue at a moment when African-Americans had barely won the right to enter the army as more than cooks and scullery workers. Danny and Stark escape to an island. He has only begun to appreciate fully Stark's intelligence and resolve under fire when the Nazis search them out. Stark is shot dead, but Danny hides the body. Returning to the ship for a life preserver that might enable him to reach the mainland, he is caught but temporarily convinces the Nazis that Stark has escaped and that they will have to abandon the entire project. Denhim tells the reunited lovers they will probably live happily together—then reveals that Stark's corpse has been found and that their deaths will be almost immediate.

They are saved because the sympathetic captain has shrewdly planted the ship near a sand bar and opened the sea valves to let her settle there, rather than sinking her in open sea. Some of the crew's brave proletarians are lost, but others survive with the pair, "lost in their freedom."[17] The survivors are further saved from thirst and exposure because the captain earlier had radioed a report of a torpedoed ship.

To this adventurous conclusion Polonsky offers a charged anticlimax. The news of the rescue has been carefully kept out of the papers. The lovers, together but not fully reconciled as Carrie continues to obsess about Denhim's betrayal, are invited along with the crew's leader to listen secretly at the official inquiry into the downed ship, with its captain and Denhim, now on trial, testifying to their presumed tragedy. Danny realizes, as they listen, that Carrie "would be hating Denhim and at the same time she would be remembering the pleasure of loving him, the gestures of love. . . ."[18] Suddenly realizing that his deception has been exposed, Denhim blushes, and Danny realizes in typical antifascist pop psychology of the moment that fascists "lived in a child's world of ambition. . . . It was infantile . . . not to think ever of defeat, or even imagine it possible. An adult could find a measure of victory even in defeat, saving honor, or habit, or hope. But an infant was defeated completely. And then he was ashamed. He was caught."[19]

As his life and work went on, Polonsky repeatedly would make the point that there were worse things than defeat, the betrayal of ideals being at the top of the list. But here he has two more revelations for the reader. Given the chance to save himself by admitting that he purposely placed the ship next to the sandbar, the captain prefers to spare his family in Germany. He has compromised himself like the mass of German civilians who are neither Nazis nor potential resistance members. Finally, in a "typical bar," Carrie asks how she can be forgiven now that she has no choices remaining. After the "magnificence of Stark" (the novel's penultimate paragraph reiterates the African-American contribution) and the humility of the captain, "There was no room left for any of the old civilian pride. He paid for the drinks and took her out into the street, into the incredible poetry of daily existence."[20]

Amid the interesting prose, stirring action, and the expected attack on Nazi amorality, Polonsky hit some themes less familiar to contemporary readers (or moviegoers). Left-wing screenwriters and directors had pressed, almost completely without success, to add nonwhite characters to war films; with limited exceptions, none nearly as strong as Stark emerged until at least 1946, when a certain realism and psychological depth began to transcend the all-out-for-victory mood.

More to the point of the writer's oeuvre, Carrie is nearly the typical Polonsky woman: possibly more chaste than his usual heroine, but dynamic, full of failings and contradictions, yet capable of self-reflection during a crisis. Like Meg, she is not easy to accept. From early on Polonsky portrays her as someone who has sold herself, her very considerable talents, to achieve her success, even if she means to do good with it. Despite her courage and despite her being on the side of the angels, she has, like so many Americans of all types, lived largely on the surface. She is also capable of growth, however, given the space for political and personal reflection. Danny finally concludes that for them to have a life together, "She would have to have changed as he had changed, or else that was an end."[21] Actually they needed to grow together, a metaphor for the nation.[22]

The names by which the antagonists are always identified, Denhim and Danny, are so close that one quickly suspects they are unwilling partners in a dyad, two halves of the male American psyche.[23] Of course, few Americans even from the aristocratic upper classes actually chose the German side, but the upper-class WASP racists (and America was full of them, not only in the South) considered themselves naturally superior beings, while the farm boys and city lads were mostly slow to commit themselves against the fascist threat. Life in America, as Polonsky says repeatedly, was too easy in its individual comforts for that kind of resolution; only the war could call it forth again from the personal decency that had earlier aimed at other goals.

Life, of course, proved still more complicated. When Hitler and Stalin's notorious nonaggression pact divided Eastern Europe in 1939, the wider effects on the Hollywood Left were incalculable. Prestige organizations like the Congress of American Artists and the Hollywood Anti-Nazi League virtually collapsed. Erstwhile liberal allies such as screenwriter Philip Dunne understandably felt betrayed.[24] What had been important leftward movements among American artists and intellectuals, once lost, could not be reconstructed.

Their faith in undiluted capitalism restored by the rising prosperity of war orders, conservatives glimpsed an opportunity to regain lost ground. As the New Deal wound down and the anti-Roosevelt contingent in Congress grew bolder, legislators abolished the Works Progress Administration's Federal Theater amid much red-baiting. The left-wing artists who had secured employment and reached a maximum audience through the theater found themselves out in the cold. The gears of outright repression began to grind into action, and congressional hearings on Hollywood commenced for the curious purpose of investigating the movies' purported pro-war bias. Yesterday's grassroots suspicions of the weapons dealers labeled "Merchants of Death," entirely well founded and elaborately documented by congressional investigations, could be shrewdly turned into suspicions of Jewish influences on popular culture. Thoroughly dependent upon the protection of New Deal personalities and causes, the Popular Front Left was now seriously endangered.

The trade union apparatus, more highly valued by the Communist Party than any other "mass" leadership, was threatened as well. Ever since the 1936–37 sit-down strikes had brought various elements of the Left together into a vital if short-lived alliance, the volatile United Auto Workers had seen a factional donnybrook. Polonsky's near-future opponents, Walter and Victor Reuther, earlier sympathizers with (and visitors to) the Soviet Union, had quickly moved on to build a power bloc of anti-Communist socialists and others. The cold war had in effect begun.[25]

In the internecine struggle, the Reutherites solidified their camp among conservative Catholic unionists and socialists alike, backed by the press and local police "Red squads." Communists had, however, dug in skillfully at major unorganized shops like Ford Motors as well as those unionized plants that profited wildly from war orders but also sought to eliminate union interference. With the assistance of the Left-led National Negro Congress and ethnic fraternal organizations, they effected a common cause among the divided communities of black and foreign-born workers. If employers and the press railed at the Reds, many ordinary workers responded warmly to the newly confrontational Communist cadre, which was temporarily unburdened of their political attachment to Roosevelt and its costs.[26]

The fractious United Auto Workers mirrored, in complex ways, the far more bureaucratic Congress of Industrial Organizations at large. The Communists had not only supplied crucial organizers to markedly undemocratic unions like the United Steelworkers, where they never had any significant influence beyond the regional level; they had also supplied the national leadership and rank-and-file enthusiasm for some of the largest unions and for most of the handful that aggressively organized women and non-whites. The United Electrical Workers (for a time the largest CIO affiliate with some half-million members, but later badly reduced by raiding from anti-Communist unions); the International Longshoremen's and Warehousemen's Union; the National Maritime Union; Mine, Mill and Smelter Workers; the Fur and Leather Workers; the Food, Tobacco and Allied Workers; and the United Office and Professional Workers Union, to name only a few, provided the CIO's cutting edge, especially on the crucial issues of inclusion.[27] Elated to end their isolation, Communists, too, had generally accepted willy-nilly the emerging labor elite's bureaucratic rules, foreshadowing the upper ranks' consolidation against them—including not a few former Communists.

Under these circumstances and with the added strains of the Hitler-Stalin Pact, Polonsky most unexpectedly found New York Communist and sympathetic CIO leaders tapping him for an educational leadership role. He had no union experience outside the TU, of course, but suitable candidates were hard to find. Decades before their emergence as Manhattan's favorite upper-class suburban retreats, Westchester County and the lower Hudson Valley were still largely industrial or rural, with small and medium-sized factory towns either generally weak in labor organization or dominated by the older craft unions of the American Federation of Labor. An affable teacher who foresaw the end of his CCNY career and had already considered moving out of Manhattan to concentrate on his writing, Polonsky was ready for the job. As educational director of a CIO district and editor of *Home Front*, the district's new monthly tabloid based in Tarrytown (home to a GM auto plant), he could encourage the local CIO initiative and simultaneously carry on the political work of the day.

Tarrytown and its environs were no Youngstown or Detroit, "burned over districts" of major left-wing activity or rivalry, or for that matter, no center of labor militancy, however nonpolitical. The more the region acquired wartime production facilities, the more it became known throughout the Left mainly as a district to be colonized economically from nearby New York. In short, it was not a promising site for political recruitment. Even had he wanted to, Polonsky could not have waged a militantly antiwar propaganda campaign—and like many Jewish Communists, he had no heart to do so. Pearl Harbor and the United States' entry into the war changed almost everything, but not enough for Polonsky to become an open Communist north of the Bronx. He held instead to the familiar and accurate unions-are-good-for-workers line, quietly teaching Marxism (or "economics") to the most alert and open-minded of the union members. In his humorous way, he relished the unionists' public meetings with the Westchester Republican ladies' clubs because "his" blue-collar workers were so amazingly eloquent and well informed.

In another way more apt to Polonsky's daily energies, the move suited his shift from a teacher and writer closely involved on the Manhattan scene to a writer who gave himself the freedom to write almost single-mindedly while saving time for a satisfying political involvement. Shortly before Sylvia gave birth to their first child, Susan, in 1941 (Abraham, Jr., was born in 1942), Abe rented a house in picturesque Briarcliff Manor, just outside Peekskill and home to an exclusive girl's school. (His major social problem, as he remembered, was having an amiable dog who wandered into classrooms and had to be retrieved. His greatest social triumph was sharing duties with townfolk organized to search the skies for German planes at night.) From there he could take the train to New York for classes—although he progressively lightened his teaching load before finally resigning—and on other days drive to Tarrytown to work on *Home Front*, which he largely wrote himself, or to teach labor and economics classes. Sylvia missed the city terribly; Abe thrived on the countryside life. The efficacy of this change was evident in his hefty magazine payments for *The Enemy Sea*, quite enough to live on in those times.

Decades later, Polonsky remembered mainly the difficult conditions for CIO mobilization. The AFL guarded its territory carefully, often with paid sluggers, and its thugs repeatedly threw would-be industrial union organizers "into the cold Hudson River" to warn them off the district. His life was not as heroic as it might have been in some cauldron of class conflict, but it proved decidedly interesting. He chose a little Hudson Valley town for the bank robbery in *Odds Against Tomorrow;* similar industrial towns of the region in his novel *The World Above* seemed not so much picturesque as run-down and dreary, with working-class flats as bad as Greater New York's slums but more lonely. Beyond the industrial villages lay the estates and modern-day castles and institutions of the wealthy—institutions like *The World Above*'s fictional private mental hospital outside Nyack or like Briarcliff itself. In short Polonsky beheld a world of contrasts, different from those in the city and rich new ground for his imagination.

Polonsky remembered the high point of his labor activities as a regional United Auto Workers convention where his circle neatly out-maneuvered the Reuther faction's effort to purge the Left. They did so not only by arguing their positions but also by outbidding the opposition with promises of union jobs. In their fervor for wartime unity and the democratic tradition, Communist Party officials liked to pretend they had won on principle alone, Polonsky recalled wryly; this was their idea of the new order, with all the cards on the table. To him it was still politics, a realm where Tammany rules remained the law and indifference toward them was the poorest Marxism imaginable.

Such small victories, however sweet, could not hold up long. The Communists' insistence upon honoring Roosevelt's appeal for a no-strike pledge amid vastly accumulating profits gave the Reutherites the perfect opportunity to prepare a devastating defeat for their opponents. With the once-rebellious conservative faction now returning to the bosom of the union under Reuther's calculated patronage, the outcome was never seriously in doubt. Still, the battle dragged on, local by local, into the early 1950s. Communist loyalties at the local level—especially among black workers—died exceptionally hard. As Polonsky might have anticipated, Walter Reuther talked a good line, supporting labor democracy and civil rights. But the UAW bureaucracy operated day to day like any other union. African-American auto workers ended up on the bottom or out in the cold as automation and the administrative apparatus combined to pacify labor (with good benefits for white retirees) and as manufacturers gradually prepared to shift production out of union facilities and out of America entirely. Polonsky's labor work had been in vain. Even knowing the conclusion in advance, it was not one he could have accepted.[28]

Polonsky's career in labor had never been more than part-time, in any case, and from his first days in Tarrytown he had another agenda. So cataclysmic were the events from August to December 1941 that he could

not have remained on the home front without exhausting every opportunity to join the armed struggle. He recalled hearing radio broadcasts
with the news of Germany's invading Russia. The Germans had compelled the Communists to straighten out and return to antifascism, not
only in Europe but in the United States as well. As Sylvia guessed before
Abe could say a word, he was going to Europe, one way or another, very
likely fool enough to get himself killed.

Enlisting proved no easy task for a man over thirty with thick glasses.
Responding at once to the declaration of war, he learned over the course
of 1942 that nobody wanted him. His brother, whom the Air Force had
assigned to the Office of Strategic Services (OSS), suggested that he join
the latter as a civilian. That way he could do valuable work for the war
while retaining his civilian status and the freedom to depart if and when
the assignments became unpalatable. Thus Polonsky shows up in the
memoirs of leading OSS British administrator Sefton Delmer. Recalling
events of 1944, Delmer writes of an effort to reach German soldiers and
civilians, hastening their collapse in the battlefield and at home. The
famed American sociology professor Howard Becker, working with "a
writer of film scripts named Polonski [sic]," asked to borrow the radio
apparatus "for a one-shot broadcast which he and Polonski had worked
out." They put onto a German frequency moments after it closed down
for the evening one night in 1944, and in "what must have been one of
the most fantastic broadcasts of the war," German General Ludwig Beck,
widely (and correctly) believed to have committed suicide when his
attempted overthrow of Hitler failed, announced that he was in a secret
hiding place and appealed to the German people to cast off their heavy
burden of guilt by removing the Fuehrer.[29]

A second broadcast, from Radio Luxembourg, offered a sort of *Our
Town* serialized for combat, purportedly reporting a Rheinish village's
revolt against Hitler. Now the burgomaster was appealing for help from
Allied soldiers. For two weeks installments continued, "with dialogue,
sound effects and messengers dramatically interrupting with bits of late
news." Of course, the mythical city's liberation, met with the burgomaster's fervent greetings, was a fiction. But Polonsky and his new friends
had reworked Orson Welles's *War of the Worlds* hoax to replicate the
dramatic wartime news broadcasts. They had, in effect, put technology
to work with the imagination.[30]

The story behind the story is less dramatic, if in some ways much fun-
nier. After Polonsky refused to accept a home-front desk job in the OSS,
he was called to a State Department office in Manhattan, within which

the agency had hidden its offices. Officials there warned him of the danger and then sent him on to Washington, where he was given "intelligence and operational" examinations such as being locked in a room with a half hour to escape. (He hit the solution in moments, breaking the second-floor window and leaping out.) OSS instructors taught him how to use various weapons, including the new plastic explosives, and told him that he was being sent secretly to the London office in April 1944. "Secretly," he soon learned, meant on a huge troop ship with thousands of soldiers on board and a brass band sending them off from the Brooklyn Navy Yard. All just a cover, he quipped, for his mission, and the best applause he ever received.

Given the real cover of an embassy job, in London, he was first asked to help translate German (which he had never learned!), reassigned to interview famed Nazi defector Rudolph Hess (he claimed that they chatted about the future of computers), and then sent to the Lake Country to question captured German generals (who wanted to talk mostly about their pensions and postwar retirement). Every now and then he would visit London as the blitz continued. Finally, after months of delay, he was ordered to join the D-Day invasion force as an army major, his newest and final cover.

Amid the tragedy and drama of D-Day landings, Polonsky, along with a continually inebriated naval commodore, several army colonels, and a jeep, landed somewhere on the coast of France. The colonels promptly drove away in the jeep, leaving him and the drunken officer to get to Paris by themselves. ("My wife is right." he remembered thinking. "They're going to get me killed!") Notwithstanding the snipers, French families were returning for the liberation, and the famed decision of the German commander in Paris to abandon the city rather than fight to the end made the trip almost safe. In Paris, Polonsky was quickly accommodated at the Hotel Ritz, where the commodore had never given up his social contacts, even during the Occupation. There, Polonsky and OSS officials made plans to capture Radio Paris outside the city and begin propaganda broadcasts. The aged German technicians still on duty at Radio Paris were happy enough to surrender to a handful of young Partisans (which is to say, Communists and near-Communists), leaving the station in perfect running order. The broadcasts began, mostly aimed at persuading German civilians to prepare for quick and peaceful surrender.

Polonsky had always suspected that the military order of command empowered stuffed shirts and braggarts, and every experience confirmed his expectations. But he found the civilian leadership even more contemptible than the military disorder. Crossing into Germany with the troops, he learned that he could actually break into *Reichswehr* military channels and create confusion or call for outright surrender. By tacit agreement, however, military channels remained sacrosanct even between armies slaughtering each other; radio interference would make strategy impossible. Yet, as supreme commander, Eisenhower simply wanted the war to end, and his office went so far as to recall Polonsky to the States to address the Joint Chiefs about jamming German radio frequencies. Even in the last days of the European war, they refused; they were less interested in casualties than in establishing the ground rules for future wars. The OSS did, however, offer Polonsky an assignment to help block Mao in China by propping up the vastly corrupt and fumbling Jiang government. That was his cue to resign, and he had a good excuse, if he needed one: he was on his way to Hollywood.[31]

First, however, Polonsky had one more quasi-military assignment after he returned from Europe in February 1945. *Reunion USA*, a series actually broadcast during 1945 over ABC but originating in Los Angeles and composed by members of the Left-led Hollywood Writers Mobilization, constituted a serious effort to explore the postwar situation. Claiming ten million listeners (the third most popular short-run show of the network that year), *Reunion USA* pointed to the complications of adjustment for family and GI. The GI's sharp turn from his war experience, and no less his mate's transition from her assorted wartime roles, demanded a serious rethinking. As Sam Moore (Communist president of the Radio Writers Union, and scripter for *The Great Gildersleeve*) complained, most fiction writers and not a few social commentators simplistically suggested that a pretty girl was all the GI needed to bring him back to "normal." "Perhaps," Moore speculated, "the radio audience is not a horde of twelve-year-old mentalities breathlessly awaiting the wolf jokes, the childish love stories of adapted movies, the slow-motion 'problem' dramas presented by soap manufacturers," but something more meaty.[32] This would be Polonsky's last and most serious radio drama, "The Case of David Smith," costarring Howard Duff. Firmly rooted in the realism of wartime observation and a public minipanic over reports of the "neurotic soldier" who often could not fight at all and was destined to return to civilian life "unbalanced" and, perhaps, dangerous, the script at least constituted a serious effort to aid the massive readjustment.

As narrated by a Captain Myers, the half-hour drama commences with Captain Smith's psychiatric investigation by a colonel, a trained psychologist, and a psychological popularist. At first glance, Captain

Smith looks like a familiar case of debilitating melancholia following three years in a Japanese prison camp. Smith's wife, Myers says, is a "pretty, placid, pained . . . middle class matron at twenty-two" who felt "let down" by her husband. She relates somewhat petulantly that he could not let go of the war, put it all behind him, and return to "normal." He is changed in many small ways, too. Even his first postwar ice-cream soda tasted "bitter."

Mrs. Smith reveals under questioning that her husband joined an anti-war organization in college and had wanted to become an anthropologist but then idealistically enlisted. Later, we learn from an officer, Smith volunteered to go behind Japanese lines to organize the resistance on an island somewhere in the Pacific. He promised the natives freedom in return for fighting, but when the island was recaptured the essence of the old colonial order "was reestablished with due order and a little shooting." Such was the real-life experience of colonized peoples from Africa to Vietnam. Nominal independence might come, but the Americans did not intend to liberate the slaves from global economic domination, then or ever. Smith's and, hence, Polonsky's postwar message is unmistakable: "I believed in the promise I made them, the promise of freedom. Who is going to keep it, and when?"[33]

A commentary by Franklin Fearing, a non-Communist psychology professor at UCLA and consultant to the series, immediately followed the narrative. Fearing, who would shortly direct the film journal *Hollywood Quarterly,* explicates the message and clearly states his admiration for Polonsky's skill:

> This is not a story of a soldier who became psychoneurotic because of experiences in the war. Let us be clear on this point. It is a story of what happens when a soldier returns and looks at civilian life and tries, as he must, to find some meaning in the world that he now confronts. . . . He now seeks some evidence that the world of civilians, in which he finds himself, understands, if only faintly, the reasons for which the war was fought and the price which must be paid for peace. If, instead, he finds a complacent willingness to return to the past or glib talk about our enemies in the next war, he will retreat in horror and revulsion.[34]

This was serious radio drama.[35]

Polonsky's intermittent radio career was almost ended. His last work in radio would be a failed but ardent effort toward an executive role. Optimistic about their prospects in the assorted media, a group of radio writers around their beloved union president Sam Moore (destined for blacklisting) proposed to buy out an existing station in Los Angeles and to broadcast serious drama along with the usual entertaining fare. The Hollywood Community Radio Group, as they called themselves, got as far as applying to the Federal Communications Commission for licensing, with Polonsky testifying. The project, which might have succeeded during the era of wartime good feelings, collapsed when commissioners baited the usually agile Polonsky into admitting that Communists would be allowed to espouse their political views under certain unspecified circumstances. Nineteen forty-six was already too late, although the attempt prefigured the Bay Area's progressive radio station KPFA and the pacifist-leftist listener-sponsored station network, Pacifica.[36]

Polonsky's literary career was about to go on hold, but he quickly sold three last pieces with revealing features. The first, "A Little Fire," in *Collier's*, August 3, 1946, was a sort of exotica or science fiction adventure with strong continuities from "The Case of David Smith," taking two zoologists to a Pacific isle shortly after the war. The military establishment has chosen to test atomic weapons on Brany Island, "a telescope into the past, into evolution, life." On the island live the Menapi, an ape species closely allied with man but also rat-faced and smelly. ("Like man it eats anything and everything, including its own kind.") For their own protection, some of the Menapi are removed once and for all to a zoo, with their own man-made island.

There, watching the Menapi collectively scramble to catch and kill a helpless and terrified squirrel, the zoologist hired to observe them is sickened by the nearness of their behavior to humans'. Worse, the creatures learn to make fire, and thus "to release the enormous potential of natural energy which made the difference between the beasts of the field and the life of civilization." Then the zoologist suddenly realizes that most of all the Menapi want meat—*him*. Furiously beating them back, he makes his way from the zoo island in a boat while his "mind rode down the ages and saw the huddle of men through the dim centuries fighting the world outside and the anarchy within." Soon he is safely back in civilization, with the "nylon-covered legs of girls, the coated men, the elaborate baby carriages of our own young."

The zoologist soon learns that fire has destroyed the Menapi just at the moment when the original island was disappearing into the ocean after an atomic blast. "Taken from the dark past into a world teeming with controlled furies," they had been doomed. But their doom and its small lessons seemed minuscule compared to "the big experiment that the whole world had conducted at Brany Island."[37] Were humans about to make monkeys of themselves and their own aspirations?

Published November 1946 in the more prestigious *American Mercury*, the second piece of fiction explores a theme that would be considered difficult in any period and represents a high point in Polonsky's published short prose. In "The Marvelous Boy," a young woman with the curious name of Urna Langsam, a teacher who specializes (very unhappily, but with resignation) in caring for mentally handicapped children of the wealthy, is given charge of a banker's thirteen-year-old son. Until now, her sexual life seems to have consisted of her own hands meeting each other (although we can easily imagine what else "her hands and their unusual life" might represent). But perhaps because the boy knows only how to shake hands, she can feel "the flow of her blood in the boy's body, in his hands, and projected in her mind, like hope, was joy, a softness rising and prolonged." Soon his hands are living within hers, so to speak, and she devotes herself wholly to him, training him to feed animals so that they come to him eagerly.

The boy manages to mold clay into the shape of a bird in flight (hence the title of the piece), reminding her improbably of Rodin, her favorite artist. After a traumatic park-bench encounter with a stranger that she takes as a near rape, she distances herself from the boy, perhaps afraid that she is unconsciously luring male spirits. Later, as she strokes a coat that the grateful banker has given her, she concludes that she must have somehow invited the park-bench assault. Now she as much as invites the boy to fondle her. Thwarted by his indifference, she pulls back again. Soon, his woebegone father (with whom she can almost imagine her own future) leaves the boy alone with her once more. This time she is animated fanatically with "a single desire: to show herself, to have herself seen." When the boy runs away from her nakedness, she is left lying ashamed on the bed, wishing the boy dead; when she suddenly realizes that he has just thrown himself (or, perhaps, simply fallen) through an open window, she feels free. Of course, she is not free at all and, emotionally at least, she never will be again.[38] Urna Langsam is a Polonsky woman who is anything but in charge of her sexuality, unable at the cost of her sanity to sort out her wants and her needs. Looking back, Polonsky was surprised to have had something so sharp, complicated, and avant-garde accepted by Mencken's old magazine, which at the time was shifting from mixed fare to political ax-grinding for the extreme Right.

The last, and definitely the most commercial of the three pieces was "No Neutral Ground," published as "The Month's American Mystery

Novel" in the June 1946 *America* magazine. It had several melodramatic illustrations, including one of a woman with her nightgown opened revealingly, for those days, to a low-cut slip, looking at a shadowy man entering a barely illuminated room. Anthropologist Paul Ryder is returning to America after eight years in the jungles of New Guinea and long months in a Japanese prison camp. His face, shattered by a gun butt, has been rebuilt through plastic surgery. Now he has military orders for a mysterious mission. On the plane home, Ryder meets a perky and surprisingly intelligent and independent-minded Lucy Hyatt, the half-sister of the distinguished Dr. Varian who sent him on his original odyssey. Typically for Polonsky, Lucy will provide the key to the story ahead.

Ryder's intelligence officer, an important general, explains that his task is to ascertain the correct route through the island where he had been imprisoned, in order for Allied forces to retake it in the Pacific counteroffensive. Waiting for him and the general at Varian's mansion outside San Diego, Ryder finds a mixed military and civilian group, including his former girlfriend, Irene, now married to Varian.

As Ryder comes to realize that the proposed trail has been wrongly described, every member of the group becomes suspected of working for the enemy. Surrounded by armed guards and studying a large physical map of the island, the group puts him on the spot. Irene accuses him of not being Ryder at all, but an islander who served as commercial assistant to the Japanese. What possible motive could have prompted her to enter a plot against him, even setting a death trap? Polonsky's answer is psychological: as Ryder realizes, "having no energy or talent of her own, she was ready to exploit life through the man who was her husband." The "blind, uncontrollable desire to be safe in her expectations of life" drove her into treason, a treason against humanity shared by fascism's supporters everywhere but observed here with special intensity by Ryder because he once loved this collaborationist.[39]

Surviving a near deadly attack and exposing the traitors Irene and Varian, Ryder resolves to lead the Partisan mission. In true war-romance fashion, he knows that Lucy will be waiting for him when he returns. She is no gaudy bauble of helpless female dependence but a real woman who has her own aspirations and desires and is not afraid to express them. Women's strength and growing self-confidence is the hope of the world, their weakness a catch-basin for reaction. With all its built-in limitations, this ostensibly personal message approaches the best that wartime films and fiction had to offer on gender themes.

3

By this time Polonsky was more than ready for Hollywood, and if it ever would be, Hollywood was ready for him. The very week he was leaving for London on his OSS assignment, Paramount had offered him a five-year contract at $750 per week. Formally, the studio was sending him to London to cover the air war and make a documentary on it. He postponed leaving just long enough to fly to Hollywood (his first flight, ever). When Paramount executive William Dozier kept him waiting, Polonsky lobbed four-letter New York style insults at him from the outer office where future friendly witness Meta Reis held sway. He had as much as ordered his own future exile from Paramount.

Looking beyond the war, Polonsky had good reasons for confidence. From left-wing screenwriters' point of view, the forties were the golden years, nearly up to the time of the blacklist. A considerable majority of film credits by later victims of the blacklist (and friendly witnesses as well) date to that decade and, for the obscure or the lucky, to the first year or two of the 1950s. Plenty of work existed, and for the best-known and most productive writers it sometimes paid extremely well. Most of those who lasted beyond two or three film credits usually found as many projects as they could handle in one genre or another, from detective to westerns to women's films or comedies and musicals. Of course, these were rarely the projects that writers and directors would have chosen; even the most successful writers would repeatedly declare that their best scripts remained either unproduced or butchered.[40]

Yet despite the shallowness of the Roy Rogers epics (the first one pairing Roy with Dale Evans was written by comrade Gordon Kahn, while Michael Wilson scripted several suspiciously antiracist Hopalong Cassidy films) and notwithstanding the plethora of witless "let's put on a show" musicals, vapid slapstick comedies, and formula detective films, the movies were growing up. Little as most future blacklistees were likely to see their real hopes fulfilled, the Hollywood branch of the Communist Party played a considerable role, directly and indirectly, in this maturation. Polonsky's artistic admirer and close political ally during those years, John Weber, offers the strongest evidence.

Born the same year as Polonsky but more proletarian in his immigrant New York, Jewish background, Weber showed intellectual promise as coeditor of his high school press, working simultaneously as a copy boy at the *Morning World,* Heywood Broun's paper. But he dropped out of the same City College campus that also first overwhelmed Polonsky.

Weber threw himself headlong into Communist politics, rigorously training and doing assorted work in the unemployed movement and union
organizing drives. In 1938, New York leaders dispatched him to
Hollywood. There, he found the bare rudiments of a communist movement and established an informal and secret party school, along with fellow Communist Arthur Birnkrant, a future playwright and aide to
Sidney Buchman. Some three hundred writers, actors, directors, producers, and technicians thus received the most formal, serious theatrical and
political education that most of them would ever have the opportunity to
acquire. Along with Marxism, they also imbibed United States history,
sociology, and practical lessons in screenwriting from talented studio
veterans.[41]

The school closed in 1940, with the sudden collapse of the Popular
Front, the growing emphasis on legal defense, and the sharp reduction of
the (barely) salaried party apparatus. Within a year or two, a more public version of the school would grow up within the Los Angeles branch
of the League of American Writers. It performed many of its precursor's
tasks until the war's end, when the LAW itself folded and still another
version, the People's Educational Center, took shape. Attending these
informal schools were not only Communists and sympathizers but a
wide spectrum of liberal students (not to mention plentiful FBI agents)
who could take eminently practical courses in film and theater along
with the inevitable political classes. Instructors remembered mainly
young women and mainly West Siders, which is to say a high proportion
of Jewish progressives similar to those among the broader, mostly middle and lower middle classes of the Popular Front.

The Hollywood party itself flourished in wartime, so far from being a
pariah that the patriotic activities of its favorite organizations gained
wide praise and the eager participation of determined careerists like B-
film star Ronald Reagan. Elsewhere in the party's national centers of
influence, the men in large numbers went off to war (often among the
first to volunteer, after Pearl Harbor) and women swelled party rolls,
which reached an all-time peak of 85,000, more than 50 percent female.
Many of the left-wing writers, actors, and technicians also managed to
don uniforms and see armed action, but most continued to work in film,
making the documentaries and docudramas of orchestrated, antifascist
patriotism. The Hal Roach Studios in Culver City, taken over for the
duration by the army (and known popularly as "Fort Roach"), turned
out such footage by the mile. Still others worked directly on armed
forces–sponsored home-front-booster films like *The Negro Soldier*

(1944), which Polonsky's friend, African-American documentarian Carlton Moss, wrote for Frank Capra.[42]

Meanwhile, the commercial business boomed. At least in some quarters, party membership actually served as entrée to film careers: the ultimate test in Hollywood. Veteran Hollywood radicals would later describe the new members as left-wing "Hollywoodniks," metaphorical successors to the self-seeking "allrightniks" of New York's Jewish quarter during the 1910s but perhaps also predecessors to San Francisco's more successful literary "beatniks" of the 1950s. Unlike the handful of party members during the Depression, these numbers were large enough to add up to a movement, with all of its instabilities: most, but not all, of the friendly witnesses drifted into the party and out again during the 1940s. Fund-raising events in the luxurious homes of figures like director Frank Tuttle, star Lucille Ball, or even Charlie Chaplin, with prestigious German exiles like Berthold Brecht and Thomas Mann on hand for wit and observations, offer some of the happiest pictures anywhere of the Left in popular culture.

If communism would never really become "Twentieth Century Americanism," its adherents nevertheless offered ideas of Americanism for an age of renewed abundance and imagined peace. Surrounded by glamour, they actually lived out those ideas, at least to an extent. The dissolution of the Communist Party into the Communist Political Association in 1943 seemed to complete the picture. Now normalized, with the stain of subversion removed—or so they hoped—the organization recruited some of the prestigious intellectuals and artists who previously had held back from making this special and ultimately hazardous commitment. Among them were later persecuted figures like Dalton Trumbo, the highest-paid writer in Hollywood during the war. Left-wing Hollywoodites saw party popularity as a totem to the advanced liberalism they envisioned for the future.

Leading New York Communists had often hinted since the middle thirties that the Californians were going too far—the contrast between the People's World and Worker offered daily proof in style, if not political line—and the wartime mood seemed to prove it. Even into the early postwar period, Polonsky told Nancy Lynn Schwartz, "the Hollywood Party was like Sunset Strip. Thousands of people used to go there [and] hang around a little while" altogether casually, as if they considered it more social club than political organization. In other parts of the country, the Left offered plenty of opportunity for sacrifice; in Hollywood, it was for some years both fascinating (as in other parts of Hollywood life, celebrities might turn up at any moment) and joyful. Other branches of the party around Los Angeles, mainly older immigrants and trade unionists, shared this world only peripherally. One of the great ironies of the friendly witnesses' later breast-beating, Polonsky observed, was how eagerly the penitents denounced "a way of life that they had enjoyed tremendously . . . excitement and dedication and the fun of working together."[43]

Work they did, along with the fundraising and merry making. Those trained in classes and in private hours with comrade-chums aimed their own careers at the industry's newer possibilities. Thanks in no small degree to the Left and its quietly cooperative friends, from John Ford to Orson Welles and Rita Hayworth, far more significant films could be made once the depressed and sometimes desperate thirties had disappeared into memories. Almost always, as happened with the modern southern gothic *Among the Living* (1941), the sharpest political dialogue would be muted or dropped and scenes would be altered to suit the whims of a producer or the Breen Office. But no one could doubt the seriousness of *Escape* (1940), *The Little Foxes* (1942), *Casablanca* (1942), *Woman of the Year* (1942), *Hangmen Also Die* (1943), *Dragon Seed* (1944), or a dozen more that earned strong notices from the *New York Times*'s Bosley Crowther, among other critics.

Perhaps most apparent, even in the war films that would remain predictably gung-ho until the final American victory in the Pacific, the added psychological elements transformed a previously contrived innocence or literalness of intent (among the good and bad alike) into shadowy images of moral ambiguity. This psychological impetus, which itself quickly degenerated into a vulgarized cliché, has often been viewed as a negation of and successor to the Marxist materialism of the thirties—all the more understandably because the party apparatus patently feared and frequently denounced psychoanalysis. But as consummate left-wing intellectuals, Hollywood left-wingers were more sensitive than anyone in popular culture to the possibilities of its revelations. Screenwriters Leonardo Bercovici and Daniel James tried to establish a formal dialogue among fellow writers and prominent Hollywood psychoanalysts in 1946. The effort failed, reportedly due to both sides' dogmatism. But the logic of probing the uneasy postwar American psyche, torn between the urge for materialist security and the loss of collective purpose, grew steadily more inevitable and more artistic. The troubled souls of Cary Grant's wanderer in *None but the Lonely Heart* (1944), who perceives his inability to connect with fellow beings, and of Kirk Douglas's character in *Champion* (1949), who realizes that he has been made into a fighting monster, carry the weight of the times brilliantly for screenwriters Clifford Odets and Carl Foreman.

Along with such psychological treatments, leftist filmmakers reached their bedrock, a special talent for critiquing the bitter consequences of materialism and the dangers of American-style authoritarianism. During the war, the all-out emphasis on victory and renewed collective confidence on the home front fostered a rigid dichotomy of idealist patriotism and escapist entertainment. Nobody delivered better than left-wing screenwriters faced with projects from the action-packed *Thirty Seconds Over Tokyo* (1944) or *Back to Bataan* (1945), among several dozen others, to the sweet *Sunday Supper for a Soldier* (1944) and a score of lookalikes, to the slapstick Abbott and Costello feature *Hit the Ice* (1943) and musicals like the 1944 *Meet the People* (an adapted Hollywood Theatrical Alliance hit whose singing proletarians turn their shipyard into a stage) or the 1944 *Knickerbocker Holiday* (based on the Kurt Weill and Maxwell Anderson Broadway musical that explores the birth of the free press in old New Amsterdam). But influential early noirs *This Gun for Hire* (1942) and *Murder, My Sweet* (1944), likewise *Talk of the Town* (1942), *Our Vines Have Tender Grapes* (1945), *Out of the Fog* (1941), even comedies like *Make Your Own Bed* (1944), and the few features with African-American stars or black actors (the 1942 *Tales of Manhattan* and the 1943 musical *Stormy Weather*), to mention only a few written or directed by left-wingers, returned strongly to class themes. A large handful like *The Very Thought of You* (1944) and *Tender Comrade* (1943) mixed home-front patriotism with class issues, developing character in female protagonists prepared for the rigors of collective struggle and postwar rebuilding.[44]

As America emerged triumphant, such commentary quickly became more thoroughgoing and uncompromised, not so paradoxically at the same time that political odds turned sharply against creative-minded left-wingers. Easily one of the most remarkable and underrated films of the time, *A Medal for Benny* (1945), directed by party member (and Christian socialist) Irving Pichel, finds a small California community prepared to honor a local hero fallen in the Pacific. To the horror of the city fathers, it turns out that he was a Mexican-American former juvenile delinquent from a barrio that they were planning to efface. Pichel (and conservative-minded screenwriter Frank Butler, father of Communist writer Hugo Butler) offered a picaresque but in-your-face challenge to middle-class white Americans who wanted to return to living as if the war against fascism's only effect was their own material improvement.

Abe in New York with his dog,
Bessie, around 1917.

As a student at
City College.

A portrait of the
aspiring artist as
a young college
graduate.

During his first stay in California, around 1937.

Polonsky, at left, with an unidentified
friend in France during the war.

An official portrait of Polonsky in
London during the war.

The film noir neorealism of *Body and Soul*
(1947). John Garfield, as boxer Charley Davis,
has his arm raised in victory.

Lilli Palmer (right) with Anne Revere in
Body and Soul. Like Polonsky, Revere
soon would be blacklisted.

With John Garfield
and Beatrice Pearson,
while shooting *Force
of Evil* in 1948.

Realistically, such films could not survive long in Truman's America. But for a few years more, the output was staggering. In the admired noir *Act of Violence* (1949), directed by Fred Zinnemann and written by Robert L. Richards, the Van Johnson lead, who betrayed his buddies to the commander of a German prison camp, is pursued by fellow ex-GI Robert Ryan into a California boom community. They converge on a state builders' association convention of drunk and frivolous partyers cashing in on the good times. Dozens of other features from 1945 to 1951 admired by film buffs radiated the artistic-political values of Popular Front screenwriters facing terrible times: *A Walk in the Sun* (1946), *Cass Timberlane* (1947), *Till the End of Time* (1946), *Brute Force* (1947), *Deadline at Dawn* (1944), *From This Day Forward* (1946), *The Asphalt Jungle* (1950), *Crossfire* (1947), *Kiss the Blood off My Hands* (1949), *The Big Clock* (1948), *Raw Deal* (1948), *Naked City* (1948), *Thieves Highway* (1948), *Another Part of the Forest* (1948), *The Five Fingers* (1948), *The Strange Love of Martha Ivers* (1947), *All the King's Men* (1949), *Life with Father* (1947), *Gun Crazy* (1949), *The Boy with Green Hair* (1949), *The Bishop's Wife* (1947), *Give Us This Day* (1950), *Underworld Story* (1950), *Whirlpool* (1949), *Cyrano de Bergerac* (1950), *The Search* (1949), *The Men* (1950), *Try and Get Me* (1950), *Pinky* (1949), *Not Wanted* (1949), *Gentleman's Agreement* (1947), *Intruder in the Dust* (1949), *Home of the Brave* (1949), and the original version of *Cry, the Beloved Country* (1951). With their more obscure counterparts that might claim twenty good minutes—the social-minded (pro-Indian and antiviolence) westerns like *Broken Arrow* (1950) and *Man from Colorado* (1948) and the small independent features on the legacy of war and fascism—they outpaced politically and, arguably, artistically any other half-dozen years in Hollywood production history.[45] Polonsky's contemporary film work, as we shall see in the next chapter, stands at the center of this remarkable tableau.

The Left's often rosy optimism, of course, had been dead wrong and its sometimes sober pessimism dead right. The Hitler-Stalin Pact had long since given the Right the wedge that they would try out briefly before the war, revive in wartime, and finally use most effectively after the war to crush the Hollywood Left. At the pact's signing, California's Democratic governor Culbert Levy Olson, elected with radical support in return for promising the release of "class-war prisoner" Tom Mooney, turned quietly against the Left. Although Olson did not actively join the conservative campaign to uncover Communists' and other left-wingers' alleged infiltration of the poverty-oriented California State Relief

Investigating Committee, he did nothing to hinder it. Popularly referred to as the Little Dies Committee (after Martin Dies's congressional committee), the Relief Investigating Committee reorganized in 1941 and changed direction entirely. Run by a former ally of the Left, state assemblyman Sam Yorty, and chaired by another former Popular Front figure, state senator Jack B. Tenney, the committee become a joint fact-finding committee, in effect a state Un-American Activities Committee.

As recently as at an August 1939 Hollywood Anti-Nazi League rally, Tenney himself had demanded the Dies Committee's dissolution. Then, after being defeated as president of an American Federation of Musicians local, he had avidly switched sides. Hardly a year later, he successfully sponsored a bill to ban the Communist Party from the California state ballot. (The bill was later declared unconstitutional.) In a dozen years, he would run for vice president on a ticket with Gerald L. K. Smith, a classic anti-Semite popular among white Southerners and their California-transplant kin.

Tenney's committee failed to send a single Communist to jail, but it foreshadowed events to come. Nineteen forty-four saw the founding of the Motion Picture Alliance for American Ideals and of the Free World Association. The Alliance's conservative members ranged from studio exec Walt Disney and director Sam Wood to celebrities Gary Cooper, Clark Gable, Irene Dunne, Ward Bond, Barbara Stanwyck, and Spencer Tracy (the last two ironically famous in part for their artistically formidable roles in left-written films). The progressive Association featured celebs like Rosalind Russell and James Cagney, Motion Picture Academy president Walter Wanger, and as the dinner speaker of choice, United States vice president Henry Wallace. Compared to the Association, the Alliance offered little substance, but the Red Hunt had just begun, and the Alliance, not the Association, could count on the Hearst papers and the gossip columnists for constant publicity and support.

In March 1944, the Alliance broke an old prohibition, venturing outside Hollywood to bring the heavy-hitting national Right's intervention in the movie business. Dramatically, MPA representatives traveled to Washington to offer a message for a conservative senator to plant in the *Congressional Record:* "totalitarian-minded groups" were busy disseminating un-American ideas and beliefs in the movies. As propaganda, the message excited mainly the anti-immigrant congressmen who actively opposed increased immigration of Jews and other specially persecuted European groups. But the tactic gave the Dies Committee an ideological opening to set up shop in Hollywood the following month.

At the Hollywood hearings, the likes of Captain Clark Gable of the United States Air Force denounced communism, with Stanwyck and Cooper loudly applauding in the audience. Dies charged (and not without reason, at least party member-for-member) that Hollywood was "the greatest source of revenue in this nation for the Communists and other subversive groups." The Alliance immediately offered Dies $50,000 to leave Congress and become their director. In retrospect, Dies's refusal inadvertently may have been a lost opportunity for the Left because of his avowed anti-Semitism and racism.

The inevitable jockeying in Hollywood went on amid national events. While the Right snarled, future blacklistee George Pepper—president of the musicians' union and a past personal foe of Tenney—and future television producer of *The Adventures of Robin Hood,* Hannah Dorner, jointly headed the Hollywood Democratic Committee for Roosevelt in his campaign for an unprecedented fourth term. An election-eve broadcast of the renamed Hollywood Independent Citizens Committee for the Arts, Sciences and Professions (HICCASP) united radio giant Norman Corwin with Cagney, Groucho Marx, Keenan Wynn, E. Y. Harburg, and assorted others in a show that reputedly delivered a million additional votes to reelect the president. So long as FDR lived and the New Deal coalition survived, the Left could not be wholly isolated by the red-baiters.

Within months, however, FDR died, and Harry Truman took office. The Left was arguably dead before the blacklisting began but did not yet know it. Even if they had known, Hollywood's dedicated radicals could not have changed events significantly, and most would not have turned tail and run in any case.

When Dalton Trumbo was quietly flown to San Francisco to write a United Nations speech for Walter Wanger, he delivered flourishes of wide-eyed optimism about imminent world peace. Other screenwriters on the scene in San Francisco were immediately skeptical and soon enough proven correct. The cold war was around the corner.

Meanwhile, all the gains that the Left had made with and for Hollywood labor were suddenly thrown into doubt. The AFL's International Alliance of Theatrical and Stage Employees (IATSE), operating in the studios as a mob-infiltrated company union, provoked a jurisdictional dispute with the progressive-led Conference of Studio Unions. Declining on patriotic grounds to support a CSU walkout during wartime, the Communists sheepishly threw their energies into picket-line duty after the Japanese surrender. But during a flare-up of conflict in early October 1945, the IATSE (aided simultaneously by the sheriff's office and mob sluggers) broke through picket lines and successfully painted their opponents as Reds. The CSU held on doggedly, but the IATSE's total triumph was around the corner. Polonsky shared the quietly offered view at the time that CSU leader Herb Sorrell had allowed himself to be outmaneuvered; Sorrell unrealistically envisioned a Hollywood on the verge of industrial unionism with himself a sort of Harry Bridges of the studios. Instead of ducking an unwinnable conflict, Sorrell marched the CSU into the breach. Frequently denying membership in the Communist Party (but relying utterly on Communist support), Sorrell went down with his union and later turned bitterly anti-Communist.

Not long after Polonsky moved his family to Hollywood in 1945, the Communists began to contribute in other ways to their own approaching disaster. In spring 1945, party leader Jacques Duclos's essay in the French Communist press bitterly criticized American leader Earl Browder, the very symbol of the Popular Front, as badly mistaken in his prediction of postwar amity. No one doubted that Duclos had taken his cue from Moscow. Within months, the American Communists had made their largest turn since 1941, this one irrevocable. Reestablishing the Communist Party, a symbol of the struggle against capitalism, they loudly insisted that some kind of New Deal–style global amity could lead to a socialist conclusion.[46]

But American communism's moment of glory had passed everywhere, not just in Hollywood. True, postwar strikes filled the landscape, and for a time class resentments ran deep, while demands by women and minorities for change foreshadowed the 1960s. Abroad, stirrings in liberated Europe and, even more, the dawning anti-colonial movements radiated grand hopes. But with the recovery of the American economy and with Truman running the United States' global politics, Communists were only fooling themselves. Not even Stalin's death could have changed the basic equation. All that remained was to resist the worst possibilities.

In Hollywood, meanwhile, Polonsky not only attended his first West Coast Communist event, a party branch meeting, but hosted it at his house. There, a virtually one-sided discussion obviously following the national leadership's direction savaged Earl Browder, yesterday's favorite. Polonsky, who had always been critical of the ousted leader's exaggerated positions, pointed out the foolishness of so sudden and complete a reversal. Such outspokenness at a branch meeting rather than privately between friends was heresy. Voices rose for the new screenwriter's expulsion, a move worse than comic. Like many who had gone into service, he was still "on leave" from the party and had not yet rejoined! Others might have quit the party at this point—some certainly did—rejecting Marxism in particular and radicalism in general for a career-safe liberalism. But Polonsky stayed, notwithstanding his contempt for the blindly pro-Russian, dunderheaded New York leadership and its faithful followers.

Personal stubbornness aside, Polonsky had another reason for rejoining the beset organization. He refused to leave the political mobilization to the movie colony's hard Right. Push was just coming to shove, and as Polonsky later reflected, alternative leftist groups might become wiser on Russia (in fact, so they were by a country mile), and for now the Communists alone had a network in place to organize neighborhood and factory resistance against the coming right-wing wave. Hollywood liberals, who rightly had been aggrieved by the Communists' abandonment of antifascism with the Hitler-Stalin Pact, could be counted upon to fold under pressure, as indeed they did.

The Tenney Committee recommenced its hearings in 1946, this time under conditions far more favorable to its operation. At the same time, Representative John Rankin (only a few years later convicted of bribery and sentenced to prison) had replaced Dies and was demanding a look at film scripts for features yet to be produced. Tenney's own 1946 hearings focused on the purported Communist influence at UCLA and the role of the People's Education Center, famous—or notorious—for drawing instructors or guest speakers and performers who included some of Hollywood's best-known actors, musicians, directors, and writers, from Dudley Nichols to Johnny Mercer. Leveling the familiar charge that taxpayers were funding supposed red activities, Tenney had special success attacking the UCLA students and faculty. He secured from the regents resolutions barring all such off-campus activity without advance permission, on threat of expulsion or (in the case of faculty) outright firing. Thus the loyalty oath system, the most sweeping form of McCarthy era academic repression, began in earnest.

Tenney took special aim at the *Hollywood Quarterly*, a highly cerebral venture set into motion by a win-the-war conference of the Hollywood Writers Mobilization and its well-placed allies on the UCLA campus in 1943. The names of Communists on the new journal's editorial board troubled Tenney more than its contents, which he hardly mentioned. Whatever its difficulties elsewhere, the Left threatened to come of age in Hollywood.[47] Tenney's harassment prompted John Howard

Lawson's resignation from the *HQ* board. Invited to replace him was the new fellow in town, none other than Polonsky.

The shift was significant. On the surface, it was a tactical move, because Lawson had been the figure most identified with party leadership in Hollywood since the early days of the Screen Writers Guild and the production of his most controversial film, the Spanish Civil War classic *Blockade* (1938), starring an almost unbearably sincere Henry Fonda. Lawson was the scion of a well-off Jewish family that had lost its capital. During his early career many observers considered him one of the first American-born playwrights likely to achieve international artistic stature. Lawson's *Roger Bloomer* was the earliest expressionist play produced in the United States, and his highly touted 1925 experimental feature, *Processional,* ran for ninety-six performances in New York. By the mid-1920s, Lawson had become the dominant figure of the experimental New Playwrights Theater. If not for personal ambition and political commitment, he might have made a brilliant career in the lively leftish theatrical scene of the next decade. His Hollywood experience was artistically disappointing, however, despite properly respectful notices for two outstanding 1943 war films, *Sahara* and *Action in the North Atlantic*. In fact, Lawson had long since transferred his main attentions to left politics and theoretical concerns.[48]

In 1946, the Maltz controversy exploded around party members, pushing Polonsky for the first time toward the center of the internecine fray. That February, the *New Masses* published an essay by screenwriter Albert Maltz, "What Shall We Ask of Our Writers?" outlining a position widely (if quietly) held by many intellectuals at the time: art should not be judged by the personal politics of the writer but by the quality of the art itself. If Marx could unabashedly enjoy the writings of royalists like Balzac who in spite of themselves revealed the true character of class relations, then why should the party refuse to acknowledge the work of someone like Trotskyist James T. Farrell, who had written the renowned Studs Lonigan trilogy about Irish-American working-class life? The question was valid and rife with potential for the kind of fruitful discussion joined informally by Hollywood writers and nonwriters of all kinds. But party leaders, already feeling threatened on all sides, had only one response: shoot the messenger.[49]

So many friendly witnesses later dated their disillusionment to 1946 and the polemical firestorm around Albert Maltz that the episode seems almost to have alienated the broader Hollywood scene. The relatively good left-liberal relations evaporated, and with them the plentiful well-paying work. At a special meeting of the Hollywood branch in actor Morris Carnovsky's basement, the large majority (not excluding some who would soon enough become friendly witnesses) sided with the party leadership.[50] Only four voted for artistic freedom: Polonsky, John Weber, screenwriter Arnold Manoff (later to become Polonsky's television-writing partner), and Maltz. Days later, a dejected Maltz submitted a dossier of his "errors" both "downtown" (that is, to the Los Angeles party leadership) and to the *New Masses*.[51]

The consequences continued to roil the party's intellectual waters. Outraged but unwilling to stand openly, assorted party intellectuals as much as demanded and were granted a bizarre public meeting where several thousand New Yorkers saluted and applauded Maltz in absentia not only for his willingness to bow to party discipline but also for his erroneous but provocative essay! Hard-line party chief William Z. Foster himself paid tribute to Maltz and insisted that the movement opposed "thesis literature" and the regimentation of artists, even if "Trotskyites" must still be opposed without reservation. Fellow film-writer Arnaud D'Usseau's declaration captured the middle position: "We can have ideas, we can be very brave, but these are futile unless we have technique."[52] In short, on supporting the Soviet Union, no compromise; on artistic matters, continued vagueness, a nonresolution that left open ground for both backtracking and further political bullying.

As one of the vocal dissenters, Polonsky later told Nancy Lynn Schwartz that the Maltz episode was at the time and afterward a classic case of overblown symbolism. Hollywoodites naturally resented any pressure on artists and particularly on writing. As Polonsky looked back, "party politics were a drag to people in Hollywood who were more radical in the human sense. Back East they carried on the radicalism, while in Hollywood we suffered the idealism." Disgraceful enough in its own right, to political veterans of the Left the party sentiment in 1946 was an "old outrage," an overreaction to changing political tides with a hardening line in Moscow and fear of losing the intellectuals and artists among whom the supposed vanguard of the proletariat was making its most noticeable progress.[53]

The studios and the Breen office had already so circumscribed freedom of expression in scripts that events in New York hardly could have affected it. Even during the war, when Communist postures were the most open, once-and-future party leader Foster had offered nothing more than an admonition for screenwriters to hold out against racist, elitist, and anti-Communist politics in their projects. Likewise, when cultural commissar V. J. Jerome occasionally came to Hollywood to demand stricter attention to party positions and norms—and he did so more often after 1945—the writers politely listened to his advice and then quietly forgot it. What writers might do positively, given all the limits on their creative expression, Communist leaders could not suggest and never would, not even during the extreme sectarian era to follow.

That communism might rule in far-off Russia but the studios ruled in Hollywood helped temporarily to preserve the milieu even as the world turned for the worse around it. So much had to be done simply to counter the revanchist anti-union mentality, often disguised as the studios' acceptance of "legitimate," safely conservative unionism unthreatening to corporate movie prerogatives and unquestioning of State Department motives. So much had to be done to fight the advancing cold war with its repressive intent. Likewise, so many things had to be done positively, especially in race relations but more broadly in creating a more critical cinema, that most of the Hollywood Left resolved to hold on and hope for better times and better leadership, from New York to Washington to Moscow.

For all that, the Hollywoodites did not have to be satisfied with a local party leader such as Lawson. Quick to condemn deviations, including those as unlikely as open support for Yugoslavia's independent-minded Marshal Tito against Stalin, Lawson continued to be respected—but less and less loved. Dictates based on 1930s ideas of proletarian rebellion no longer made sense; their repetition in party publications neither assured the screenwriters nor endeared Lawson to them. According to often unreliable FBI informers' accounts, Polonsky was quickly becoming Lawson's rival.

Organizationally, a rivalry between Lawson and Polonsky is not credible. Polonsky had neither the predilection nor the authority from New York to succeed Lawson. Sylvia Polonsky was the activist of the family and along with her sister, who was still more active, worked closely with the widely respected Dorothy Healy in the Los Angeles party branches. But the anecdote does contain an important kernel of truth. As John Howard Lawson's son reflected a half-century later, his father had been a troubled man, an emotionally distant "angry communist" long before the blacklist. He had earnestly wanted approval since his days at Williams College, when he burned with rage at the anti-Semitism in the world around him. His own disappointments in film reinforced his romantic notions of the Soviet Union from afar and of the Communist apparatus up close.[54] In film aesthetics, Lawson belonged to the 1930s of an unrealized American Eisenstein.

By contrast, Polonsky belonged to the new era, when the higher level of films logically raised intellectuals' (that is to say, Hollywood Communists') expectations for their own leadership. Polonsky liked to say that he did not make Marxist films, but that as a Marxist, he made films in the only way that seemed meaningful. Writers who found themselves stuck in slapstick films, melodrama, or in the lower ranges of musical comedy had little opportunity to experiment, no matter what their intellectual refinement or expectations. More sophisticated and successful writers like Donald Ogden Stewart had always worked on instinct, adding Marxism late in the process if at all. Carl Foreman, a former carnival barker, would prove the most innovative, arguably inventing the jump-cut during the late 1940s, to make narrative transitions without fadeouts and thereby challenging the audience. Foreman was still working on personal instinct rather than collective discussion even after all the discussion.[55]

Along with Polonsky and Lawson, only Michael Wilson and Ring Lardner, Jr., were respected as Marxist thinkers by their fellow Hollywood Reds, and neither was given to theoretical discussions. Nor did either of them choose to direct. At least until the later films of directors Jules Dassin and Joseph Losey (neither of them writers), Polonsky was sui generis, his spare critical writings likely to invite the collective sensation that he spoke for his fellow left-wing film intellectuals. Even those who continued to respect Lawson with all his faults could admire Polonsky as an intellectual and artist, an important model for future left-wing screenwriters (and directors)—if only reaction could be held at bay.[56]

4

Like most would-be Hollywood writers of all political hues, Polonsky got off to a rocky start with the studios. From the moment he entered William Dozier's Paramount office, he found his acid criticisms of existing movie standards unacceptable. According to Polonsky's account, Dozier charged out of the inner offices swearing Polonsky would never work in Hollywood. (A decade later, the same Dozier had Polonsky fired from television's *You Are There*.) Polonsky reminded Dozier that government policy guaranteed him the job he had left—albeit without really beginning—for the sake of war work. The standoff kept Polonsky in the studio, but he remained under a cloud. Like so many others, he mainly produced scripts destined never to be shot.

Two of those scripts are highly interesting and in some ways predict his later film work. "Paris Story" appears too complex and sophisticated to be filmed.[57] Set in Paris during the Liberation, it tells the three-cornered tale of an American major, Johnny; his former lover Oriane, a popular torch singer; and Oriane's confidant, the cynical *chansonnier* and comic Toc Toc. Underlying every attempt to sort out the past and present is Polonsky's observation that heroism in Occupied France was rare, at least until the Nazis were obviously losing the war, and collaboration (or at least unresisting consent) exceedingly common. Toc Toc's employer and patron throughout the war is one Lennery, a large-scale economic collaborator who retains his power and prestige despite the turn of events.

Before the war, Johnny had been in Paris representing an American firm that needed Lennery's signature on some legal documents. No one is innocent, and Toc Toc articulates it best: "Your rich client, M'sieur Lennery—this banker—financier—this lover of the arts—he lives off the stupid poor and we clever poor live off the stupid rich. It's a law of nature." Johnny, a typical American, is entirely indifferent to France's problems: he would prefer to have Europe simply disappear.

While Johnny is in Paris, Oriane rises from former cigarette girl to the city's leading theatrical performer. Unwittingly, unwillingly, and in spite of her warning him against corruption, Johnny falls in love with her. The scenes in a Mount Parnasse nightclub (with Toc Toc on the stage watching the couple) and on a bicycle ride to the country are among Polonsky's most evocative. Johnny entreats Oriane to marry him and come to America, where he would spend his life making her happy. "That would be too much for too little," she comments, adding that she cannot leave Paris or her career. But there is more, something characteristic of Polonsky on women's insight into the male idea of love:

> I know that when a man loves a woman, the front of his eye sees her, but the back of his eye sees someone else, a mother, a sister, an aunt, a childhood sweetheart, something of the past. You're not thinking of . . . me, but of you having me. But I'm thinking of me having you, and at the same time of myself, speechless in a foreign land. If I succeed here, then as we say my life becomes more than me. The poets and artists speak through me and thousands hear. I'm more than just Oriane who makes you feel like a traveler in a French Arabian nights.

When Johnny returns with the Liberation, he is warned that the girl he loved has disappeared in one sense or another. He quickly learns that Lennery's housekeeper was a German agent involved in deporting French women to Polish slave-labor factories. He interrogates Toc Toc in prison and learns from personal testimony how France caved in (expecting no help from America) and how the Resistance began. During the Occupation, Oriane asked Toc Toc, "I'm a woman of France. Could I learn before France did?" The two then worked secretly for the Underground. According to Toc Toc, Oriane was ordered to be murdered when caught, but Lennery's bribe saved her.

At last Johnny learns that La Bluette, a resistance leader in one of Paris's neighborhoods, is actually Oriane. In a dramatic speech to a street gathering, she insists that "the liberation of women from medieval prejudice" is a necessary part of the general liberation. She adds hopefully (if naively) that if America was, as Johnny had put it to her, a country that for a long time had not made up its mind about the future, now "America has taken sides with us for that future."

Back at Oriane's apartment, Lennery suddenly appears, and Johnny reveals that he represents the United Nations War Crimes Commission. Oriane insists that despite Lennery's reputation as a collaborator she will defend him because he protected her, knowing that she was working with the Resistance. After a series of hearings, Lennery is cleared of the worst charges and Toc Toc restored to the stage. The characters find themselves all together in a nightclub, where after some sparring, the lovers can be reunited. As they walk arm-in-arm up the stairs, Oriane tells Johnny, "I warn you. I've changed. I'm struggling to become more and more of something new—a new woman in a new world." He answers, "You can't frighten me with the future, Oriane, so long as it's mine."

Contrast Polonsky's unproduced script to *Reunion in France* (1942), a film directed by young Jules Dassin. French showgirl Joan Crawford, coerced into bravery by American agent John Wayne's sudden appearance at her window, helps him to cross the border, meanwhile believing that her patron, played by Philip Dorn, is a collaborator—as his manufacturing parts for the German war machine demonstrates. At the end of this chase film we learn that Dorn actually has been a patriot all along, supplying the Germans with nonworking parts (a ruse that in life would have been unlikely to slip past the ever-efficient German war machine). Crawford never reveals herself to be Dorn's lover, and the only moral ambiguity turns out to be a misunderstanding. By contrast, "Paris Story" demands a sophisticated view both of politics (or wartime life) and of love.

As Polonsky told an admiring *New York Times* interviewer in 1947, "Paris Story" simply "was shelved."[58] So was his adaptation of Dan Wickenden's novel *The Wayfarers,* in some ways an even more ambitious script. This project had a hopeful beginning when Paramount producer Harry Tugend asked him to work on a Depression theme and to get Edward G. Robinson for the lead if possible. "With the connections you have from the CP," Polonsky remembered Tugend saying, "you could see Jesus Christ" if the Savior happened to be in Hollywood at the time.[59] Polonsky talked seriously with the actor about art, Robinson's favorite subject, and sold him on the film. Its artistic point was to reconsider the unresolved contradictions of the 1930s, revealed through the life of the industrial town of Broadfield and its newspaper. We quickly learn that reporter Vinnie Rourke has been set upon the hot story of Andrew McBain, a local journalist-intellectual who has made good in the big city and abroad as a war correspondent and is now returning home. Rourke's boss, Norris Bryant (Edward G. Robinson's projected role), is a hard-drinking depressive. Ten years earlier, having previously borne him three children, Bryant's wife died in childbirth, along with a fourth child. Since then, he has had nothing to live for.[60]

The narrative is elaborated through reporter Vinnie's relationship with a glamorous local heiress, Carola, who says to him, "I wish you wouldn't pretend to have ideas," but is happy enough to use him sexually and call him "darling." She explains that the dead wife had been in love with McBain, followed him to New York, and then returned to Broadfield. If she had lived, things might have been very different.

The would-be film's real story becomes the editor's inability to deal with his failures, and his daughter Pat's rage at her family's defeat. Although she will not accept the reality, that defeat was brought on by the Depression rather than by her father's personal failings. At a family Christmas dinner, to which he has invited Vinnie, Bryant tries to straighten out his world. Both of the grown children other than Pat, however, represent facets of his dead wife, coarsened and narrowed.

The rendition is so talky that its theatrical character never evolves into film fare. Perhaps Polonsky was restrained by his desire to be true to the novel, which he described to a *Times* reporter as "a very fine book."[61] Still, the script has fine touches, like the memory of Bryant's dead wife, Laura, as a crusader for woman suffrage or the assorted women's speeches about their unequal relationships with men or Bryant's soliloquies ("I wonder how many millions have forgotten how to act . . . and then cry out at disaster like children lost on strange streets"). McBain, the town's hero, urges Vinnie to model his life after Bryant and base it on "human values." Eventually, McBain admits to Bryant that long ago Laura had refused to go to Europe with him and instead returned to live out her life with Bryant and the family. She is the missing character of the screenplay, but her determination to make things work provides the coda: "If you're still alive, spring comes every year. This time, use it." The studio didn't: they were finished with Depression themes.

After such disappointments, Polonsky achieved a success that he distinctly did not want and hardly regarded as his own. It was a co-credit, his first, for writing the earliest version of *Golden Earrings* for Marlene Dietrich and Ray Milland. He insisted that he meant this lighthearted romantic comedy to present a serious picture of the Holocaust as faced by the Gypsies, a fact little mentioned and quickly forgotten after the war. All that survives of that intent in the rewrite by veteran scripters Frank Butler and Helen Deutsch is a casual remark or two by Dietrich about the past ("they used to hunt us like wolves") and the future ("in this godforsaken land, they'll kill us all") after an encounter with a Nazi battalion. The rest of the film, under the direction of Mitchell Leisen, is played for camp, perhaps inevitably because—as the critics observed— Dietrich with mud on her legs and dark makeup on her face, throwing herself at the all-too-staid Milland, was still Dietrich and every member of the film audience knew it.

The Gypsies, in fact, come off as a merry band of antimoderns living the old rules of eye-gouging fights with the woman going to the winner. They reject baths as completely as they do fascism, while Dietrich ably assists the Underground (and Milland even learns to read palms). After his escape and the winning of the war, Milland comes back to one of the most improbable endings in a Hollywood famous for its improbable endings: Dietrich is still in the same location, and Milland leaps past her arms into the caravan wagon, where they hit the trail (past the Death Camps? through Communist Eastern Europe?) together. The press scoffed at "the Gypsy in Marlene" as "frippery," and complained that "general whimsicality" quickly became "weary" with overuse.[62] Polonsky went to a screening and walked out "after ten minutes." He could only laugh it off to experience. Although he could not envision them at the time, two vastly more important film projects lay ahead.

3

THE POLITICS AND MYTHOLOGY OF FILM ART: POLONSKY'S NOIR ERA

BY 1948, ABRAHAM POLONSKY cut quite a figure in Hollywood. How had it happened so quickly? The answers are varied and can be found in the talents he brought to films as well as in those he seemingly acquired overnight. They lay also in the whirl of local and world events that jeopardized Hollywood's progressives at the very moment when conditions had become ripe for a battle over the creative control of films.

Ian Hamilton's insightful *Writers in Hollywood* captures a certain spirit of the moment when it puts Polonsky at the center of noir, quoting his timely aphorism on the genre's power to reveal "where the moral authority is, in the undestroyed element left in human nature." What Hamilton describes as the cinematic symptoms of the age, "the early-hours back-street, the lone streetlamp, the drizzle, the flashing neon sign . . . the stairwells, the cramped elevators, the rain-flecked windshields," had many practitioners, but none who was more politically conscious of what he was doing.[1] That the same Polonsky of *Force of Evil* had only a year earlier written, in his own words, a "fable of the streets," with John Garfield as protagonist literally fighting his way *out* of the morass of contemporary corruption, pointed up another, less remembered quality of the interesting films of the age. Before the crushing blows of the loyalty oaths, the purge of the industrial union movement, and the repression of 1940s feminist and gay impulses—and before the grim finality of Stalinism settled across Russia and Eastern Europe—the future everywhere and in every field, in art as much as in politics or economics, seemed vastly more open.

The cheap moral victories of movie cops or spotless heroes enforcing contemporary laws and norms (even liberal ones, like abhorrence of anti-Semitism) revealed mainly Hollywood's self-indulgence and its exploitation of contemporary controversy. The deeper issues of moral erosion and individual alienation in the midst of postwar prosperity proved both far harder to express and less bankable. The film audience after the Second World War, numerically reduced in the face of television but also more self-motivated in its quest for serious film art, appeared ready for the maturity demanded. When Polonsky scored a hit with *Body and Soul,* he reached his moment of mass-culture truth.

Polonsky's artistic success, however brief, was possible because of a broader development in a key sector of the American cinema. The superior quality of the films by serious and political-minded artists (not all of them, by any means, on the Left) during the period just before the blacklist has often been attributed to the filmmakers' awareness that time was running out. Certainly, the moment of artistic freedom to which director William Wyler famously attributed the possibility of making *The Best Years of Our Lives* was brief.[2] Even before the subpoenas flew in 1947, the movie-making machine began slipping into the hands of East Coast financiers who would increasingly dictate the terms of studio survival. But this valuable insight overlooks the long quest of studio workers who wanted to shake free of the studios' control and produce their own films. Among them were not only writers, directors, and producers on the Left but stars like James Cagney and Hedy Lamarr. A crucial moment in the early postwar years had arrived and would soon pass. But before it ended, an intelligent cadre of Hollywoodites had begun to ponder aloud about the possibilities of film.

1

Until late 1945, the Hollywood Left's own published writings on film amounted to so little that the dismissive comments about "swimming pool Communists" and kitsch artists by cynics and hard-line anticommunists, liberal and conservative alike, might seem almost justified. If Hollywood's avowed Marxists and assorted Left followers had demonstrated more serious artistic intentions in their films, their critics jibed, why were these obviously fluent intellectuals silent on film aesthetics? In truth, the overwhelming majority lacked the theoretical background for criticism; they also rationalized that Hollywood unionism, along with involvement in assorted social causes from the Spanish Civil War and the

Second World War to combating the local racism against Hispanics and African-Americans, swallowed their available energies.

But their relative silence was due as well to the absence of proper outlets and to the risks of expressing themselves in public. Intelligent public discussion of cinema took place almost exclusively in the trade papers (especially *Variety*) or in the outlets of semi-liberal opinion—the *New York Times,* its local counterparts, and the opinion weeklies. The only magazine on the Left to examine films any more deeply than reviewing them had been launched during the 1930s as *New Theater* and renamed *New Theater and Film* only during its last gasp of publication in 1936–37. The invaluable dialogues among screenwriters, directors, actors, and technicians took place, then, in private, comrade-to-comrade and friend-to-friend, or were at most expressed in the classrooms of the Hollywood Left's informal academies. Other than *Clipper* and *Black and White,* the largely personal magazines that screenwriter Guy Endore had published in the few years before the war, the only outlets for outright Marxist film commentary were the official Communist daily press, the weekly *New Masses,* and the trade organ, the *Screen Writer.*

The *Daily Worker,* which earned a top readership of perhaps eighty thousand on weekends, was best known culturally for its alert sports page and for what wags called the "anti-movie" column that was almost as sure to pan anything that Hollywood produced as it was to praise whatever Russian filmmakers offered.[3] The *Daily People's World,* published in San Francisco with a Los Angeles edition, was somewhat better, but considering its location, offered surprisingly little in-depth treatment of films and film art. In any case, progressive screenwriters found the political logic-chopping less than useful for their own art and few of them would have dared put their own names on film commentary even if they had been asked. *The New Masses,* as the organ of the New Yorkish, pro-Communist cultural intelligentsia, could be more eclectic but cared no more for movies than for dance and far less than for theater. Astonishingly, none of these publications gave any indication in reviews, or even seemed to know, which films Hollywood Communists wrote.[4] The *Screen Writer,* even with left-wing editors like Gordon Kahn in charge, remained generally fixed upon the profession's immediate issues, from authors' rights to the sharpening political struggle within the union. At that, or perhaps precisely for that reason, the *Screen Writer* assumed as little as possible about its readers' loyalties and foregrounded mainstream liberals like James Cain who bore no red taint.

Criticism's gloomy state brightened somewhat with the October 1943

Writers Congress at UCLA. Here, greeted by a letter from President
Roosevelt and welcomed by UC president Robert Gordon Sproul, leading studio executives and liberal and radical writers from the United
States and abroad held plenary sessions and seminars about writers'
activities during the war and after. Darryl Zanuck, Norman Corwin,
Chet Huntley, Oscar Hammerstein II, Thomas Mann, and Walter White
(of the NAACP) were all present, along with numerous Hollywood left-
wingers on leave and in uniform. Anything approaching Marxist termi-
nology was, of course, underplayed in this atmosphere of unity. The tone
of progressive internationalism and militant antiracism, however, could
hardly be misconstrued. But after the University of California published
a six-hundred-page proceedings volume in 1944, any further open discussion ceased—until the *Hollywood Quarterly* appeared.[5]

As John Houseman would comment decades later, the *Hollywood
Quarterly* "created no major stir and exerted not the slightest influence
on the filmmaking of its time. Yet it remains the first serious cultural
publication in which members of the motion-picture industry were collectively involved."[6] The journal's fall 1945 premiere extended the
wartime alliance and the respectability it had brought to the Left.
Sponsored by UCLA and the Writers Mobilization Continuation
Committee, the *Hollywood Quarterly* secured a decisive measure of freedom from party control by virtue of its strictly academic and formally
nonpolitical status. Franklin Fearing, a respected sociology professor at
UCLA (and a nonparty member who had never taken much part in
Popular Front activities), served as its editor and chief intellectual sponsor; his student Sylvia Jarrico, screenwriter Paul Jarrico's wife and a
returning student at the university, was managing editor.[7]

If any overt left-wing political leaning could be found in the
Hollywood Quarterly's early issues, the names of its editors and some of
its contributors supplied the only clue. In fact, the publication took its
place quite simply as the first serious film journal in the United States,
with those most interested in the subject at the helm. Here, the distinguished psychologist Lawrence S. Kubie ruminated on "Psychiatry and
the Films"; Orson Welles's producer John Houseman wrote about violence in the cinema; former Office of War Information functionary
Dorothy Jones dilated about the Hollywood war film; assorted acade-
mics interpreted radio and film music; and famed animator Chuck Jones
took up his favorite subject.[8] A commentator could even ascribe
"genius" to conservative Walt Disney (for whom several of the future
blacklistees currently worked) and insist that his artistic failings were due

to the scale of films Hollywood demanded and not to Disney's personal limitations.[9]

Polonsky himself contributed his radio script, "The Case of David Smith," and two important critical essays. These latter largely set out his theoretical perspectives on the accomplishments, limitations, and possibilities of contemporary film, just as he embarked upon his brief and spectacular preblacklist career as a writer-director. During the journal's few years before the blacklist and the university system's loyalty oath, they were unique in being at once practical and theoretical.

The first essay was a close examination of the widely lauded *The Best Years of Our Lives,* long considered by many as the finest film of their time, albeit with the Hollywood system's built-in limitations.[10] The writer and director (award-winning Robert Sherwood and William Wyler, respectively) captured middle America "with truth, with warmth, with communication," even if the town's banker could be better understood as a model of the film industry itself. No political test is necessary, for within the film

> the area of human character which *The Best Years* makes available to its audience is a landmark in the fog of escapism, meretricious violence and the gimmick plot attitude of the usual movie. It becomes very clear that an artist who happens to bring even a tag [tad] of daily experience into the studio is making an immense contribution to the screen. *The Best Years* indicates for every director and writer that the struggle for content, for social reality, no matter how limited the point of view, is a necessary atmosphere for growth in the American film.[11]

Not that Polonsky was uncritical. The film follows the postwar adjustment of a banker, a blue-collar worker, and a lower-middle-class fellow with hooks for hands, weaving their three distinct experiences into typical Hollywood formulas, like the old stock plot of the worthy proletarian marrying the businessman's daughter. But writer and director had moved Mackinley Kantor's original novel from hokum toward realism, and their "immense patience for detail and emotional texture" had paid off handsomely. The very "passion for insight smashes the stereotypes, around the edges." Polonsky drew the obvious conclusion for directors and writers that "writing for the movies is writing under censorship," a censorship that "forces stereotypes of motive and environment on the creators." The answer, if possible, was "to press enough concrete experience into the mold to make imagination live."[12]

This was censorship different from the Breen Office's usual application of the term to sex and bathroom references, politically unacceptable interpretations, and certain types of unpunished crime or violence. The implied issues went to the heart of Polonsky's artistic concerns. The real story of postwar adjustment (as he wrote so strongly in "The Case of David Smith") was the false promise of peace and prosperity in return for sacrifices, and if *The Best Years of Our Lives* partially exposed this reality, it nevertheless supplied merely personal solutions. Although the Hollywood fog over the truth cleared from time to time in the film, "where the economics of life make naked the terror of a return to the bad old world," the "southern California mist" of Hollywood formula soon gathers again. The banker and his wife, blind to the society around them, thus turn aside their daughter's serious questions about their resettling into a middle-class life. Likewise, a spectacular scene of the working-class guy momentarily back in his bomber (now sitting ignobly in a junkyard) is ruined when the junkman interrupts the airman's idylls and offers him a job. Instead of epitomizing everything, the experiences epitomize nothing.

All this comes down to Hollywood's inability to deal with class, especially the working class. The "submerged majority of the public," their screen images rendered inarticulate, had thereby been cheated and so had film art. Doubtless, the film had done wonderfully in focusing on the people and their conversations rather than jumping around aimlessly as many such topical efforts would do, but *The Best Years of Our Lives* lacked something basic and thus remained incomplete. Polonsky closes, "Within its imposed limits and compromises the film is an enormous success, something like the war itself, which has invigorated many a European country and stirred vast colonial peoples, while here at home we have returned to cynicism from our betters, sharpened social conflicts, and a mood of vulgar despair among the artists."[13] Polonsky would not be moved again to make so definite and thorough a critical judgment of film art until he composed his "Manifesto for the Screen" in the early 1960s. His essay on two more films, the British suspense drama *Odd Man Out* and Chaplin's curious *Monsieur Verdoux*, has an even stronger emphasis on the meanings of realism.[14] Polonsky begins by pointing to the sense of crisis after atomic warfare, and the "great moral danger" that people everywhere will lose hope and stop trying. Then he asks the pregnant artistic question, "How . . . can the artist function in this crisis to feed consciousness with iron and fragrance?" In other words, how could "reality, reconstructed in art, issue into experience as a further mastery of the daily world?" The answers were "rooted in the ambiguities of the recent war and its qualified victory," not to be reduced or resolved through "metaphysical" formulations. The artist, as it stood, could neither satisfy nor even give pleasure to his audience "except with some fragment of reality," and there was the rub.[15]

Polonsky praised the masterfully directed *Odd Man Out*, which treats a daring robbery by an Irish nationalist leader and his pursuit by British authorities in some unnamed Irish city at some unnamed time in the recent past. The noir-style hunt through the endless night is beautifully done, and viewers find themselves finally "delivered into some darker kind of living reality." But the underlying purpose grows less rather than more clear as the film goes on.[16] Anticipating critiques of the psychological approach offered in friendly witness Elia Kazan's *Viva, Zapata!* (1952), Polonsky observes that society's artistic and political problems have come to be defined as those of the human condition itself, the soul in conflict with "abstract authority," rather than as a question of social forces (and the individual within them) facing a leviathan of capital or the state. A turn toward moralizing obviates the shreds of realism and leaves *Odd Man Out* finally unrealized.

Monsieur Verdoux suffers from a different problem because it had been conceived as a sort of fairy tale, the saga of a bigamist, adulterer, and murderer who does all these wrongs for the good of his middle-class family. Neither the stiffness of portrayal nor clumsy editing can obviate Chaplin's "marvelous flow of gesture." Polonsky, Chaplin's admirer, cannot quite bring himself to say that the film's incoherence makes it difficult to follow or, for many viewers, just to sit through. For Polonsky, the film's rigorous exposure of bourgeois hypocrisy "moves toward reality" while the presumably realist *Odd Man Out* moved away from reality.

Polonsky grants that the study of psychology in recent years— prompted by civilization's horrible trials during fascism, war, and the unpeaceful aftermath—has opened "vast internal structures of subconscious consciousness" with important insights. But even when creating "some works of sensitive discrimination," the so-called realists have more often than not abandoned the audience to moral chaos by fleeing any prospect of solution. Thus the "search for internal truth suddenly externalizes itself" into a "radical verbalism which accepts the status quo."[17] Polonsky thus acutely anticipates the inner emptiness of the great majority of Hollywood's moody "rebellion" films in the second half of the century.

Historian William Appleman Williams would, during the early 1960s, describe such blindness as American intellectuals' "great evasion" of the possibility that Marxism, or any other critique of America's endless economic expansionism, might have something serious to add to the heated discussion on pervasive social anxiety.[18] Polonsky, also seeking an American use for Marxism, follows the master himself to lay out the simple rule that consciousness stems from social relations, not vice versa, and must be understood concretely by detailing the relations. The strength of Polonsky's critique, however, is its faultfinding, which he states with such great irony and close intent that a long passage is worth quoting:

> You cannot pretend to examine life without opening a floodgate of truths. . . . But when these truths conflict with presuppositions rooted in interest, then you must obey the truth or refuse to look. In *Odd Man Out* the storytellers refused to look. To the senseless world they say: there will always be authority, needed, aided, loved; and there will always be rebels, both weak and heroic; and people are torn with fears of self and not-self; and man is a storm-tossed creature adrift on the dark seas of eternal conflict and misery; but if we have some inner dignity and charity toward others and ourselves, while we cannot change life, we can learn to endure it. If we cannot change human nature and the conditions of its existence, let us at least be kind to each other. Let us *indeed* be kind! We can get used to not being used to life, as many a suffering neurotic can vouch for.
>
> This is, of course, plain antirealistic perversity with which the psychiatrist is more familiar than I, and no decor of objectivity, not real street lights, street signs, tenements, mills, not any real object or place, makes this position aesthetically realistic. These works are not created from the point of view of mastering reality. You cannot master reality unless you recognize its content and this, despite its bravura clownishness, *Monsieur Verdoux* does. *Realism is based on content.* . . . The accidents of a literary verbal heritage or stylistic modes are not central to the method of realism.[19]

Polonsky had said what he wanted to say about film and perhaps wider aesthetics as well. These statements closed his theoretical discourse for a decade.

2

Abraham Polonsky's 1940s films *Body and Soul* (1947) and *Force of Evil* (1948) quite simply embody the highest achievement of the American Left in cinema before the onset of repression. They were also among the first to reveal the promise of independent films in the United States, and by that measure, they summarize the best work of the generation that created the critical American cinema.

Film production in the United States remained, with some exceptions, firmly under the studios' political and aesthetic control, even as European and Japanese filmmakers were creating a new vocabulary for world cinema after the Second World War. When a handful of the black-listees returned to their craft decades later, American films were still bound by the conventions of genre and the narrative syntax hammered out by decades of studio production. *Body and Soul, Force of Evil,* and comparable films of the early postwar period—*Asphalt Jungle, Brute Force, The Strange Love of Martha Ivers, Try and Get Me, A Place in the Sun, Naked City, Night in the City,* and *They Live by Night* come read-ily to mind—are therefore the culmination of the Depression genera-tion's struggle to emancipate American dramatic art from the film corporations' control.[20] From the perspective of the generation that sur-veyed the wreckage of the McCarthy era well into the 1960s, they would be among the last examples of the classic American filmmaking that could compare, on its own terms and within its own traditions, to the best of the new international cinema.[21]

Polonsky's cinematic story really begins with Enterprise Studios, which provided the framework for his greatest preblacklist accomplish-ments. A few new major bids had been made to produce films indepen-dently by 1947. Notable among them was Liberty Films, formed by Frank Capra, William Wyler, and others, but despite its name it achieved little liberty, due to the early box-office disappointment of the classic *It's a Wonderful Life* (1946, scripted in part by Michael Wilson, although never credited to him). David L. Loew launched Enterprise Studios in 1947. He and his twin brother, Arthur, produced such fascinating, artis-tic, and oddball films as *So Ends Our Night* (1941) and the *Private Affairs of Bel Ami* (1947). (David Loew also joined the Hakim brothers on Jean Renoir's heavily stylized 1945 feature, *The Southerner,* written by William Faulkner and future blacklistee Hugo Butler.) Advertising/ marketing executive Charles Einfeld had helped gather $10 million in revolving credit and with high hopes lured Ginger Rogers, Barbara Stanwyck, and Ingrid Bergman to the studio at competitive rates. Meanwhile John Garfield, whose contract with Warners had expired, had just set up a production company with his former business manager, Robert Roberts. The two simply joined their efforts to Enterprise, plan-ning to split the profits down the middle. Alas for creative dreams, Enterprise's one and only success in four years of production came to them as a great surprise: *Body and Soul.*

As Polonsky tells the story, his friend and fellow screenwriter Arnold Manoff had been working on unsuccessful scripts for several years in Hollywood. He was ready to give up entirely after six months of a failed attempt at a biopic about boxer Barney Ross—a Jewish war veteran who in real life had been arrested for drug possession shortly before. Manoff happened to be in Polonsky's office at Paramount and invited him to visit Garfield at Enterprise, two blocks away. On the walk over, Polonsky came up with the basic outline of the film, and he pitched it to a delighted Garfield and Roberts. Several hours later, he offered it to the heads of production at Enterprise, without fee. Polonsky had just returned to the gates of the Paramount studio when the guard stopped him and handed him a phone: Einfeld called him back to Enterprise. He had the job, although he was "on loan." By Hollywood rules Paramount got fully half of his thousand dollar weekly salary.

According to another version, the studio actually had canceled Manoff's original Barney Ross project, but would-be director Robert Rossen insisted that they could produce a different boxing picture and threatened to sue if such a film did not proceed under his direction.[22] The two stories are not necessarily inconsistent, but they do point to two overpowering personalities in potential conflict: Polonsky and Rossen. The two agreed on many things, including hiring the talented noir technician James Wong Howe as cameraman and a crew of helpers familiar with combat photography's handheld cameras. Rossen, unrestrained by the studio or Roberts, gave Howe the creative space that he wanted, and soon a small camera crew was racing around the boxing ring on rollerskates, something never tried before. Rossen also seemed to agree entirely with Polonsky's script, but as Polonsky quipped a half-century later, "you wouldn't want to be on a desert island with Rossen, because if the two of you didn't have any food, he might want to have you for lunch tomorrow." He promised not to change a line of the screenplay and then passed out new pages on the set until he was confronted.[23]

Rossen came with considerable personal as well as artistic baggage. The grandson of a rabbi and the nephew of a Hebrew poet, this sometime amateur boxer was raised on New York's Lower East Side. He began his theatrical career there, writing and directing a number of successful political plays in the thirties (including, in 1932, "Steel," produced by the *Daily Worker* as a fund-raiser) before coming to Hollywood. Rossen's script-writing high points included *They Won't Forget* (1937), a courtroom drama about a false accusation of murder in the South, with Lana Turner in her first dramatic role; *Blues in the Night* (1940), a musicians' saga with an extraordinarily strong and independent-minded woman played by Priscilla Lane; *Sea Wolf* (1941), arguably the best Jack London adaptation ever done, with Garfield as the proletarian, Ida Lupino as the hardened girl, and Edward G. Robinson as the totalitarian ship's captain (now noticeably fascist); *Out of the Fog* (1941), a proletarian saga from an Irwin Shaw play with Garfield as a hoodlum who nearly destroys the lives of a Brooklyn family (including Ida Lupino as the daughter, Garfield's sometime girlfriend trying to break away from her slum life) before fate gives them a second chance; *Edge of Darkness* (1943), a classic antifascist film marking Norwegian resistance against Nazi occupation; *A Walk in the Sun* (1946), perhaps the most realistic major war film to that time; and *The Strange Love of Martha Ivers* (1946), a taut postwar drama with Barbara Stanwyck as a factory owner hiding an old secret, Van Heflin as the childhood pal who comes back to wreck her, and Kirk Douglas, in his starring debut, as Stanwyck's weakling partner-in-crime.[24]

Rossen's directorial debut, *Johnny O'Clock* (1947), was less noteworthy, hardly more than a gambling caper with Dick Powell as a lone-wolf, slightly existentialist gangster. But Rossen had talent to burn, and demonstrated an obvious love of downbeat themes in his best later film, *The Hustler*. That 1961 triumph unfolds in the miserable destiny for the protagonist that Rossen preferred for *Body and Soul*, but then unexpectedly adds a second, near-Polonskyan ending of individualist, albeit proletarian, defiance. Back in 1947, Rossen was still close to the Communist Party but was jaded by the postwar world and, no doubt, also by life in Hollywood. In making a populist outsider into the villain, his Oscar-winning *All the King's Men* (1949) adroitly pulled back from the 1930s aesthetic's radical implications; Polonsky, on the other hand, held to those implications, albeit in changed form.[25]

In commercial terms, Rossen had been known for most of his career as a good Warner Brothers writer, capable at melodrama but rather uninterested in raising his artistic level or, perhaps, denied the freedom to do so until his directorial opportunity. In that sense, he had worked in virtually nothing but genre, which gave him a narrower (or more commercial) understanding of genre than Polonsky, in whose hands the project became something that as yet had no name.

But Polonsky had a well-considered intention in turning to genre. In one of his more reflective interviews during the efflorescence of interest in his work during the early 1970s, he meditated at length on the nature of stories. Genre, like myth or religion, offers ordinary people as well as artists ways to "systematize our relationship to society and . . . to other people." The development of genre in art forms, therefore, was not accidental or faddish but inescapable and, indeed, "fundamental to the way art operates." As art advances, new genres rise one after another to replace the old ones.[26]

No Hollywood director had ever been so thoughtful and articulate on the subject; few Hollywoodites had the literary training even to make the attempt. Polonsky's comments show that his grafting of myth onto genre in *Body and Soul* was entirely conscious. The genre tale, as film scholar and interviewer William Pechter put it, is the "story's rigid central structure" around which the myth is constructed. In *Body and Soul,* as in a few dozen others, some before but many since, the genre is this: "ambitious slum boy battles way up to success." Pechter sensitively describes this myth as empowering, under certain conditions, not the stale Horatio Alger story but instead a "sense of flexible and sensitive human relationships" among the experience-worn boy and his intimates.[27]

The central story line in the great bulk of Polonsky's fiction, whether films or prose, runs unmistakably through *Body and Soul.* It is at heart the story of an immigrant or, better, the story of an immigrant's son, an individual who has turned his back on his working-class background for personal gain. Later, he discovers a moral and (in the broadest sense) political need to rejoin the working class, regardless of the personal price. The broader arc of the Polonsky story encompasses anyone who has left behind a family (or a lover who holds out the promise of a family), or coworkers, neighbors, political colleagues, or even a class or a tribe—in short, his community of human beings—to pursue a goal that alienates him from them and makes him yearn for a reunion.

The archetypal Polonskyan story reaches its critical moment when the protagonist must make a choice. He is not trapped in his fate. After a crisis or other circumstance forces him to choose, the hero decides to return, that is, to recapture the conditions necessary to his humanity. He may pay for this knowledge with his life or escape with no more than the threat of losing his life. But the higher price of a clear conscience is clear. "These things get to reach a limit," says the character in *A Season of Fear,* Polonsky's 1956 novel, refusing to cooperate with a blacklist at his job in the Los Angeles Water Department:

> There has to be a limit to what you will do because you want something, and I think we've reached it. We're hitting the limit. We're getting so that nothing counts except survival and I say the hell with survival. I say the hell with it. I don't want it. I don't want to be around and see the survivors. They're not my kind. I belong to a different species. Wipe me out.[28]

From the opening shot to its final frame 104 minutes later, *Body and Soul* develops with a narrative authority that is rare even among the many extraordinary movies of this extraordinary period. Although it appeared in 1947, it easily could be described as the last film of the 1930s. The opportunity to treat the Depression in film did not arise until after the Second World War. Then, many films on the subject were released, but in some sense *Body and Soul* stands as the final word, a revision of the Group Theater's *Golden Boy,* with none of that film's sentimentality or social ambivalence. In the 1939 production of his theatrical piece (actually played by the Group before the camera), playwright Clifford Odets had related everything to the boxer's violin, his symbolic claim upon another kind of life. Polonsky quietly ribs Odets's sentimentalism with a casual remark about fiddles in *Body and Soul,* but his Charley Davis is in fact too poor to buy a gun, let alone a fiddle, and in the end he is armed with something far more dangerous than his predecessor: an understanding of class in America.

From another angle, *Body and Soul* shares with the finest music a sense of inevitability. From its first notes, it strikes a series of surprising hammer blows. At night, on the grounds of a training camp, a boxer's heavy bag sways in the wind, startlingly like the corpse of a hanged man. The camera pans to the darkened windows of a training shack, and we see through the glass in close-up, as though he were watching the bag, the scarred and swollen face of Charley Davis. The face is John Garfield's, shriven of its 1930s optimism and possessed now of a postwar familiarity with death. Suddenly, boxing champ Davis gets up from his bed, dashes outside to his car, and speeds away. His training coterie rushes to the driveway too late to intercept him, vexed that his next fight is just hours away.

After a montage of the drive back to the city and his old neighborhood, Charley is seen coming through the kitchen door of a small apartment. "Hello, Ma," he says laconically. His mother, played with a virtual Greek death-mask by future blacklistee Anne Revere, betrays her only twitch of emotion in the next shot, past her full-length profile to Charley's at the door, as she slowly lowers a cup and saucer toward the kitchen table without looking and drops them on the floor. Finally, a beautiful young woman about Charley's age enters the kitchen. "Peg?" Charley utters. After a faltering, tearful embrace, the young woman turns her back on him. She is played by Lilli Palmer, one of the secrets of the film's success, as a bohemian art goddess who in an early scene frankly admits her sexual attraction to this proletarian shock of muscles (at least by 1940s standards) and thereafter carries the love interest with an elegance too often overlooked.

The vision Charley Davis seems to have glimpsed in the swaying heavy bag was himself as a dead man. To his mother and fiancée, he has already become a walking corpse. Thus the first scenes pose the film's primary question: what evil has Charley done to earn such contempt? The secondary question provides the routine boxing plot to satisfy the casual viewer: will Charley win the upcoming fight and, given the opening shot, will he live or die? But in the Polonskyan social text, the more interesting question must be whether Charley can repair the injuries he has inflicted on those closest to him and rejoin the circle of humanity— that is, regardless of whether he lives or dies, will he make the right choice?

Body and Soul leaves no more real doubt about Charley's eventual moral decision than about his ability to prevail with his fists. We flash back to the story of his rise from the streets after his father, a kindly and bookish owner of a candy shop, is shot down in a crossfire of gangsters. Charley tells his mother that he is going to make a success of himself the only way he can: with his fists. She pleads with him to "fight for something," not just for money and fame, but he betrays his surroundings and turns into a boasting swell, leaving behind mother and wife to take up with chippie Hazel Brooks and deliver his talents to the mob. Literally revisiting his past (and learning that his neighborhood is betting their savings heavily on him), he turns away again in one last bout of cynical individualism and agrees to throw the biggest fight of his career. Realities begin to strike home when his sparring partner, Ben, who is punch-drunk from previous fights, rebels. Played by African-American Canada Lee (in real life, virtually blacklisted until his sudden, premature death), a dazed Ben throws punches into the air and drops dead of a stroke.

Shocked by Ben's death (and, perhaps, to his own surprise), Charley punches his way to victory, in the process losing the savings he had bet on his own defeat. In the final moments, he scoops Peg under his arm and confronts the boxing boss. "Whaddya gonna do, kill me? Everybody dies." Earlier in the picture the boxing boss, played with dry precision by Lloyd Gough (still another future blacklistee), had said almost the same thing about Ben ("Everybody dies") to encourage Charley's moral drift.

The prospect of this Hollywood happy ending left director Rossen dissatisfied.[29] He wanted Charley to be killed in revenge for betraying the boxing mob, and his version called for a final shot of Charley lying in an alley with his head in a garbage can. Both endings were shot. But in the collaborative atmosphere of Enterprise, where nearly all of the film workers on both sides of the camera were leftist comrades or sympathizers, the writer's view could prevail over the director's, at least if he had the artistic respect of both the producer and the star. Polonsky got his way.

Polonsky's insistence on using the closing scene of *Body and Soul* as he had written it, despite its superficially happy ending, was emphatically political. Charley's recognition of the need for a sense of decency in human affairs begins with the unmistakable suggestion that the boxing business had lynched Ben. Narratively and politically, Polonsky's need for a defiant ending with a shout of hope derives in part from the social context of Charley's awakening at the moment of Ben's "lynching" as expressed metaphorically in the swinging body bag.

With Rossen's ending, the only meaning in Charley's awakening is personal: Charley glimpses his likely future as a discarded fighter who dies penniless in the ring. His awakening is the American individualist's realization that it is time, in the lingo of another genre, to strap on his guns and clean up the gang that has taken over the boxing business. For Charley to die in a hail of bullets is entirely logical from that view. But that would be mere naturalism, little more than an inverted happy ending suited to the weary wisdom of the postwar audience, a knowing noir grimace.

For Polonsky, the scene evidently had another meaning. In Ben's death, Charley for the first time glimpses something beyond himself and comes to terms with the pain of another human being. From that moment, he begins to repair his relations with his family and his community, and his decision not to throw the fight is rooted in his dawning comprehension that he is fighting not only for himself but for Ben and for his neighborhood and for everyone else the system has ground down. That is the meaning of the final "Everybody dies." It is not the defiance of the genre hero who has just killed his enemies but the serene utterance of a soul at peace with itself. Now that he has done the right thing, he is prepared to die—even, in a sense, for Rossen's ending, should that become necessary.

What matters most is the clarity of understanding that Charley attains at that moment. For Polonsky this was nothing less than the hope that all of the world's Charleys one day would make the same declaration. Hence Polonsky's frequently expressed frustration with Rossen's ending: this is not a fable about Charley Davis, it is a fable of the working class; it would be "crazy," as Polonsky once said of Rossen's ending, for a group of left-wing storytellers to conclude their finest work by killing off the proletariat!

Ultimately, the question of the ending evolved into a much larger dispute over the social control of film production and of creative differences among artists on the Left. In 1946, the atmosphere on the set of *Body and Soul* remained one of mutual respect and creative collaboration. By 1948, however, a nervous Rossen had written a letter to Harry Cohn, the president of Columbia Pictures, declaring that he was no longer a member of the Communist Party. Appearing before the House Committee on Un-American Activities on June 25, 1951, exactly two months after Polonsky, Rossen admitted his former Communist Party membership but refused to answer certain specific questions. Like a number of others, he left for Mexico, where he suffered repeated symptoms of heart disease. On his second appearance before the committee, May 7, 1953, Rossen answered every question. Polonsky insisted that Rossen essentially had always been an individualist willing to give the studios whatever they wanted. (Rossen was said to have told a younger Robert Penn Warren on the set of *All the King's Men* in 1949, "Son, when you are dealing with American movies you can forget, when you get to the end, anything like what you call irony—then it's cops and robbers, cowboys and Indians.")[30]

For Rossen, production would trump art. As Polonsky later described popular reaction to the film, the viewers at a sneak preview began taking sides aggressively at the crucial moment when Charley makes up his mind. Enterprise president Arthur Loew, sitting with him in the theater, exclaimed, "It's a hit!" And it was, several million dollars' worth—not *Gone with the Wind* scale, but big money for the time. An Oscar went to the film editor, nominations to Garfield and to Polonsky for best original screenplay. Unity Awards, a special left-liberal ceremony of the later 1940s, further honored the film for having "presented its featured Negro player in a manner highly sympathetic and complimentary."[31]

Decades later, when French critics pressed Polonsky to explain how *Tell Them Willie Boy Is Here* was a "western myth," as he had called it, they asked him further if he had not in fact written *Body and Soul,* along with *Force of Evil* and *Willie Boy,* in the naturalistic style of Odets. Rather sharply, Polonsky replied, "they were not. They were very classical."[32] Again, a 1969 interviewer with *Cahiers du cinéma* invited Polonsky to comment on one critic's remark that the "moral awareness" of *Willie Boy*'s protagonist began where that of *Force of Evil*'s numbers racketeer left off. Polonsky rejected the comparison, repeatedly casting about for a simple narrative analogy that might at last make his point:

> "En fait, je crois que 'Willie Boy' a plus de rapports avec 'Body and Soul' qu'avec 'Force of Evil.' Celui-ci est un film réaliste, dont l'écriture peut-être est moderne, mais 'Body and Soul' était un conte de fées, un mythe sur la vie dans les rues du New York, comme 'Willie Boy' est un mythe, une parabole. . . . [J]e me suis servi de structures musicales, des structures de la fugue, par exemple." (In fact, I believe that *Willie Boy* has much more in common with *Body and Soul* than with *Force of Evil*. [*Force* was] a realistic film and the writing is, perhaps, modern. But *Body and Soul* was a fairy tale, a myth of the streets of New York, just as *Willie Boy* is a myth, a parable. You could say that [in these two films, I used] musical structures, the structure of a fugue, for instance.)[33]

Elsewhere, Polonsky often referred to *Body and Soul* as a "fable of the empire city." Audiences loved *Body and Soul,* and critics ate it up. Bosley Crowther praised it to the skies in the *Times,* concluding, "Altogether this Enterprise picture rolls up a round-by-round triumph on points until it comes through with a climactic knockout that hits the all-time high in throat-catching fight films."[34] Crowther, a film critic, had judged *Body and Soul* solely on its artistic and entertainment merits. A few years later, however, the blacklisters found in it all that they despised. Columnist Ed Sullivan—who began his newspaper career in the early 1920s writing for New York's socialist daily *Leader* and three decades later edged toward his impresario status on television with a raft of red-baiting—pinpointed *Body and Soul* in 1952 as the subversive media production incarnate. It set "the pattern that the Commies and their sympathizers in TV networks, agencies, and theatrical unions would like to fasten on the newest medium." From "the director down," those who "are on the American side of the fence" had been frozen out, replaced by "Commies and pinks."[35]

3

Polonsky recalled that he was, for a moment, "God" at Enterprise, whose executives made him at least nominally a vice president of the studio. Ginger Rogers practically demanded to see him and invited him down to her basement where, dressed in a fur bikini, she served him a "black and white" ice-cream soda. Never a progressive, in a few years she would become (with her mother) the star witness against the Hollywood Left. But she had a near-hit in *Tender Comrade* (1942), written by Dalton

Trumbo, and she saw another hit-maker in Polonsky. He had different plans. Enterprise's great star, Garfield, expostulated to Polonsky, "You want to direct, so direct!" Garfield's longtime secretary, Helen Levitt, a left-winger and the wife of screenwriter Alfred Levitt, then working for Joseph Losey on the 1949 *The Boy with Green Hair,* may have influenced him, but Garfield nonetheless recognized in Polonsky the best director for his talent and persona. Only a "meller" (melodrama) would do, however, and Polonsky began looking for a vehicle.

Force of Evil (1948), the result of prodigious adaptation, acting, camera work, and perhaps above all, direction, has often been more admired than loved. *Body and Soul*'s box-office success could make *Force of Evil* possible, but it could not make it successful. Its disappointment due only in part to the studio's impending collapse, lesser critics long passed it off as a B film beloved of aficionados. A general view—even among some admirers—has been that it attracted, in Robert Sklar's phrase, "a certain excess of praise." Sklar attributes this to "the film's special status in postwar movie history. . . . the last movie made by figures on the Hollywood left before their repression and exile." Sklar asserts, "Polonsky's articulate and intellectual commentary in later years may have made it seem so: if not the last one, then the only important one."[36] According to this view, the film's admirers had thus seized on it to pay homage to Polonsky's talent, clutched by the sense of the loss of never-to-be-made but presumed masterpieces by the industry's best writer of that moment.

Ample reasons for this view would have existed even if Polonsky had dropped dead in 1950 instead of living on to become chief raconteur of the Hollywood Left's dear, dead days. The sense of political struggle touches everything in *Force of Evil,* from script to production and even to historical context. As Sklar notes, the plot aims directly at the throat of monopoly, not only in the numbers rackets in New York but, by implication, in the major studios themselves. Only a year earlier the Supreme Court had found the studios guilty of violating the Sherman Antitrust Act and compelled them to divest themselves of movie chains—creating the economic possibility of the art film in the bookings of independent-minded movie management. *Force of Evil* was perfectly suited to this new film constituency.

The movie's opening shot is of Trinity Church on Wall Street, squeezed into a narrow profile by the slot-canyon walls of office buildings. The camera pans down to the busy street, and we hear the first line of John Garfield's voice-over narration: "This is Wall Street, and today was important, because tomorrow, July 4, I intended to make my first million dollars. An important day in any man's life." The screen dissolves to an interior of one of the office buildings, where we see workers placing small numbers bets at a newsstand and speculating on the value of "the old Liberty number," 776, for the coming Independence Day. Garfield, looking polished and walking with a spring as young lawyer Joe Morse, explains the arcane science of amassing wealth from the collective tiny hopes of suckers who play against overwhelming odds, and for a disorienting moment the viewer wonders what in the world that has to do with Wall Street, where the nomenclature of financial instruments is much more refined. But soon it dawns that the clash between appearances and realities *is* the point: these cheap hoods, including Joe, might have law degrees from elite institutions, wear silk hats, smoke pipes, and have offices "in the clouds," but they are still cheap hoods.

In one sense or another, everyone in *Force of Evil* is a cheap hood. Here is a world unlike anything ever seen in Hollywood. No colorful, redemptive poor people hold out hope for humanity with swelling speeches, no grandfatherly voices resound with reassuring clichés. Only illusion and disillusion exist for a gaunt population, and anyone who tries to draw moral distinctions plunges deeper into despair. This hopelessness, which emphatically includes the world of law enforcement, destined *Force of Evil*'s production for interference. The Breen Office literally rejected the original script, and Polonsky had to rewrite the ending and add some dialogue before shooting could begin.

The story turns on the relationship between Joe Morse and his brother Leo, played by Thomas Gomez. Leo runs a small numbers bank that is going to be forced into bankruptcy when the Liberty number hits on the Fourth of July through a fraud created by Joe's mobster boss, Tucker. Because of the huge odds against the number's actually hitting, Leo will not have laid off his bets (that is, made offsetting bets with a larger bank to hedge against loss); he has, logically speaking, no choice but to accept being swallowed by "the combination" or go broke. Younger brother Joe, for whose college and then law school education Leo scraped and saved, has cooked up the entire scheme to consolidate Tucker's combination. En route to riches, Joe makes every effort to relieve his conscience by persuading Leo, whom he has not seen in years, to come into the combination before he loses his business involuntarily. When Leo refuses on moral grounds, Joe tries to force him into the plan by calling the cops to raid his brother's bank.

At this critical moment it appears that Joe will succeed in defrauding everyone without harming his proud but oddly principled brother, who believes firmly if irrationally that small-time crooks are more honest than big-time crooks. It seems that Leo has been forced in and will become rich against his better instincts, and it hardly matters that Joe's expression of fraternal piety was contained in an act of betrayal and coercion. What matters, in a world like this, is that Joe is going to get rich even while his last scruple is appeased. In a delightful exchange, Joe begins to flirt with Leo's pretty secretary. She asks why he is in such a good mood. He answers, "I'm celebrating a clear conscience."

"Oh?" she responds with a musical sarcasm. "Whose?"

The secretary is played by Beatrice Pearson, an ingenue with a soft soprano voice and a knowing look. She is a lot like her boss. She has worked for Leo for years, but with Joe's sudden appearance, she develops both a new understanding of the numbers racket and a pair of cold feet. Like Leo's streaks of decency, hers are not very convincing. She is torn between fear and disgust for Joe on the one hand, and sexual attraction on the other. Like the Lilli Palmer character in *Body and Soul*—and uncharacteristically for Hollywood—she is a woman with complicated sexual feelings. Pearson has declared that she wants out of Leo's operation, but moments after Joe drops the dime on his brother, she is swept up in the police raid. She fears that her reputation is ruined, but still she cannot give up her fascination for the worldly and about-to-be-rich Joe. The stage is set for the most beautiful piece of dialogue in the movie and one of the most lyrical in all of American film. Pearson, as Doris, begins coquettishly:

"You're a strange man, and a very evil one."

"And you're a sweet child, and you want me to be wicked."

"Now what are you talking about?"

"Because *you're* wicked. Really wicked."

"What are you talking so crazy for, Mr. Morse?"

"'Cause you're squirming for me to do something wicked, make a pass at you, bowl you over, sweep you up, take the childishness out of you. To give you money and make you sin. That's real wickedness."

"What are you trying to make me think, Mr. Morse? What are you trying to make me think about myself. And you?"

"Do you know what wickedness is? If I put my hand in my pocket [he makes the gesture] and give you a ruby, a million-dollar ruby, because you're beautiful, and a child with an attitude, because I wanted to give it to you, without taking anything for myself, would that be wicked?"

"Have you got one?"

"No." [He opens his hand.]

"When I was a little girl, magicians used to fool me, Mr. Morse, with their high hats and their black capes, and their ruby words, because I listened to what they said—they talked so fast—instead of watching what they did. But I'm a big girl now, with a police record, thanks to you, and I know it's not wicked to give and want nothing back."

Joe protests.

"It's perversion. Don't you see what it is? It's not natural. To go to great expense for something you want, that's natural. To reach out to take it— that's human, that's natural. But to get your pleasure from not taking, by cheating yourself deliberately, like my brother did today, from not getting, from not taking, don't you see what a black thing that is for a man to do? How it is to hate yourself, your brother, to make him feel that he's guilty . . . and I'm guilty. Just to live, and be guilty."

Joe's voice trails off and the scene ends. What began brightly as a love scene ends in a confession, as though all of Joe's thoughts, no matter what the topic, finally gather in the same gutter. In the same way, all of the plot threads lead to the same conclusion: Joe's guilt over his betrayal and how it comes to drive all of his actions. We know that at some point he must reconcile himself with Leo, not merely as a corrupt businessman with the generosity to share his loot, but in some larger sense. The film never indicates what this reconciliation might be, and in a world so corrupt such an act might not even be possible. At most, the story suggests, the increasingly desperate brothers might express their love by covering each others' backs in the intragang violence that will introduce the final confrontation between the rival blocs of crooks and politicians. But even this is not enough to save Leo. Still unaware of the depth of Joe's guilt, Leo dies protecting him.

In true Polonskyan style, the ending is a jewel case containing the film's meaning. The Breen Office insisted that Polonsky open the closed world of corruption enough to suggest that the district attorney and the law would eventually redeem it. Joe makes that suggestion when he vows to turn himself in after finding Leo's body broken on the rocks under George Washington Bridge. "I turned back to give myself up [to the district attorney], because if a man's life could be lived so long and come out this way—like rubbish—then something was horrible, and had to be ended one way or another, and I decided to help." Not everyone was convinced that Polonsky had really given in, not even the FBI man who had ordered the tapping of Polonsky's phone and the transcription of his conversation about the film with Ira Wolfert, author of *Tucker's People,* the novel on which *Force of Evil* was based.[37]

The narrative weight of the film and the characterizations are so strongly felt that the last line's concession to the Breen Office is of little aesthetic consequence. Following a breathtaking sequence of ten shots in which Joe descends from the urban landscape into the rubble under the bridge to locate Leo's body, with composer David Raksin's "Regeneration" theme building behind him, the concession is at most a shrug. But the studio monopoly (by this time, a virtual bankers' monopoly over Hollywood decision-making) undeniably had its revenge upon a film about the power of monopolies. The final line of the film would haunt it as the HUAC hearings haunt the period in which it was made. As Sklar put it ominously, "In 1948, neither Garfield nor Polonsky had yet faced the decision that the fictional Joe Morse, by the authority of the Breen Office, had been forced to make."[38]

At the time, even friendly reviewers barely knew what to make of *Force of Evil.* The *Times*'s Bosley Crowther assessed it as "a dynamic, crime-and-punishment drama, brilliantly and broadly realized," revealing "a real new talent in the medium, as well as a sizzling piece of work." Yet its artistic and political implications obviously eluded him.[39] The *New Republic* judged the film "fair to maudlin," a potentially "great picture" ruined by "the smallness of the narrative framework," with too much Odets flavor for its own good.[40] *Time* complained of "lame techniques" that robbed the film of "most of its force."[41]

In the long run, critics were far kinder, and not only for the reasons that Sklar suggests. French critics, among them the surrealists trained by the study of early cinema's unrealized promise, adopted *Force of Evil* as one of their favorite postwar American films.[42] British enthusiasts, who made considerable heroes of the blacklistees (indeed, a handful of blacklistees spent their happiest years around London), adopted the film in a serious way two decades after its appearance.[43]

On the basis of *Force of Evil* more than any other film, critic William Pechter made it his mission to recall Polonsky from obscurity in 1962, arguing that prejudice against *Force of Evil* was proof that "we are still not entirely free of the tyrannical dogma that language is not properly an element of film." With the language in *Force of Evil,* "the impression . . . is of for the first time really hearing, on the screen, the sound of city speech, with its special repetitions and elisions, cadence and inflection, inarticulateness and crypto-poetry."[44] As in Odets's theater, the necessary effect was "achieved by an extreme degree of mannerism, artifice and stylization," but in *Force of Evil,* "the image works with the word" in ways that Odets had never been able to achieve on the screen. Here, Pechter noted acutely, "the language takes on the quality of incantation, and imports an almost choric resonance to the Cain and Abel myth which lies at the film's center."[45]

When Pechter pressed him on these points, Polonsky confessed that he had engaged "in an experiment in which each of my resources was freed of the dominance of the other two." Image, actor, and word became equals. "I varied the speed, intensity, congruence and conflict for design emotion and goal," liberating the language from "the burden of literary psychology and the role of crutch to the visual image." It was, Polonsky laments, "a method I would have tried again and again until solved" had not the blacklist's intervention ended the experiment. Thus, "like those bicycle fanatics at Kitty Hawk [a reference to a script of his on the Wright Brothers for the *You Are There* television show] we couldn't wait to waken in the morning, knowing each day would surprise us. . . . Only our plane never flew."[46] Of course it *did* fly, briefly.

In his widely admired book, *Talking Pictures,* Richard Corliss surveyed the accomplishments of Hollywood screenwriters and decided that an architectural system would offer the best way to rank their contribution to the film arts. Corliss thus established for all time—or until someone dares to revise it—an Acropolis of Screenwriters. In the Pantheon at the very top of this Acropolis are the twelve greatest among the thirty-eight screenwriters he deemed deserving of such honors. Eleven tutelary deities are housed next door in the Erechtheion. Ten more bunk down the hill in the Propylaea, and finally, five more stand "Outside the Walls," with Dalton Trumbo last in line. Even though Corliss remained ambivalent about Polonsky's accomplishments as a director, he did not hesitate to put him in the Erechtheion as a writer.[47]

From Corliss, a champion of screenwriters against the reigning auteurism, this was tribute indeed. Only Preston Sturges and Billy Wilder in the Pantheon had also made names for themselves as directors, and in the Erechtheion stood but one other writer-director. Of most interest here is not so much Corliss's playful taxonomy but that Polonsky looks so much at home in the Greek architecture. In ways that can be appreciated only by closely attending Polonsky's writings about his artistic intentions, his stories' shapes are closer to the didactic narratives of Greek culture than to any tradition other than those of the already established American film genres. Again and again *Force of Evil*'s narrative is

unmistakably classic in style. Like the choral lyric of the earliest Greek
drama, used primarily for public religious ceremonies, the strophe and
antistrophe of the dialogue are marked by a mainly elevated tone and by
the presence of myth.[48] As befits a scholar who learned his Greek and
Latin early but remained close to his boyhood neighborhood vernacular,
Polonsky appears to have wanted to establish an equivalence between the
two or to recreate the former's universality in the latter.

4

Polonsky's two great films bring us back to one of the ironies of the
blacklist in Hollywood. Only conservative critics believed that American
leftist filmmakers got their political message through to the moviegoing
public. Liberal apologists for Hollywood criticized the blacklist as unnecessary because the medium's collaborative nature effectively prevented
the insinuation of subversive material. Even if a rogue director accumulated enough power to push through an unacceptable political message,
an impermeable line of defense was provided by the producers, and the
"top studio executives" retained "ultimate control of the medium" and
posed an impermeable line of defense, according to the authoritative liberal study of the subject. [49]

Abraham Polonsky shared that view partly, at least in light of what his
colleagues otherwise might have accomplished even in the face of censorship. In a 1970 interview with the British film journal *Screen*,
Polonsky observed that the studios had permitted only liberals and conservatives the self-confidence to make strong political films. Frank Capra
could do "anything he felt like," and "John Ford might do something
tremendous" like *Grapes of Wrath* (1940). The Left, by contrast, was
carefully watched and knew it, understanding better than liberals the limits imposed by the studio system's economics and management.
"Leftists," Polonsky observed, knew "that you can't get any radical
activity in films. People who aren't radicals don't know that."[50]
Polonsky, as so often, could easily be misinterpreted because he was half-
joking. It would certainly, he added, "be a lie to say that American left-
wingers didn't do [any] pictures with radical activity. They did pictures
with humanist content and the flavor of democracy."[51] In the Hollywood
climate, that was radical.

The larger question, however, remains largely unanswered. To what
extent did the political thought of Polonsky and those he called the other
"social radicals" of his generation find its way into their films? More

than forty years after Dorothy Jones's 1956 essay, "Communism and the Movies: A Study of Film Content," found that the "self-regulation" of the film industry "prevented . . . propaganda from reaching the screen in all but possibly rare instances," the answer remains elusive.[52] One of the best scholars of the Hollywood Left's films, Brian Neve, wrote as recently as 1992 that if "notions of communist propaganda in film have rightly been dismissed, the impact of the more politically conscious members of the Hollywood community on the films that they worked on has generally been under-researched."[53]

The rediscovery belongs to the present and to the drastically widened access to hitherto obscure films that cable television has made possible. Since *Willie Boy,* critical writings on Polonsky have gradually increased.[54] Meanwhile, a rudimentary theory of the political aesthetics among 1930s and '40s Hollywood filmmakers belatedly appeared during the 1990s. In a 1995 PBS documentary series, Martin Scorsese credited both *Body and Soul* and *Force of Evil* as strong influences on his own movies, which practically dominated film in the United States during the 1970s and '80s. At the same time, Scorsese made the unusual gesture of sponsoring the rerelease of *Force of Evil* on video tape and appearing in a three-minute introduction, in which he discussed the film's effect on his own work.

If there had been any doubt before then, none remained: Polonsky's reputation was secure, however circuitous the route. Scorsese's praise struck themes that have come to be the accepted contemporary view of Polonsky: "*Force of Evil* appears on the surface to be a tightly structured, 90-minute 'B' film, but has so much more going for it. The moral drama has almost a mythic scale; it displays a corrupted world collapsing from within. In this respect, *Force of Evil* is very different from other film noir. It's not just the individual who is corrupted, but the entire system. It's a political as well as an existential vision."[55]

By then, Nora Sayre's older assessment that "very few films were as radical as *Body and Soul* . . . [or] *Force of Evil*" and Keith Kelly's that Polonsky made "one of the strongest, continuously radical political statements in commercial American film" had become the generally accepted view.[56] *Force of Evil* in particular has fairly come to stand for that class of films that had used the already highly stylized conventions of crime stories, westerns, and other familiar American film genres to create critical social messages. Often, where their complex camera work, subtle dialogue, and indirect plot development raised them to high art, the films demanded much from their audiences. At their best, however, they were now seen to have been designed to work at several levels and to be taken at their face value as genre stories only by the most hostile of viewers.

Against their narrative lines thus emerges a dialogue far removed from the familiar conversational lingo of other urban film noir dramas. It is so compressed that, according to a famous but possibly apocryphal incident, an early British critic complained that Polonsky had composed *Force of Evil* "in blank verse."[57] That is one measure of the degree to which Polonsky had tweaked the language of Hammett and other advanced genre writers out of the familiar distich of wisecracks into a higher order of cinematic patter, characteristic of an artist working so consciously within the formal limits of genre films.

In many scenes of the written screenplay, Polonsky achieved the poetry he later described in a cinematic manifesto. A good example (quoted admiringly by Corliss) can be found in the extraordinary spondees from *Body and Soul,* snorted in disgust by a contender for Garfield's boxing title as he eyeballs the champ: "All fat. Night-club fat. Whiskey fat. Thirty-five-year-old fat." These lines hold no exaggeration, no naturalism. They are language reduced to hard objects, poetry as fact. They rake across the screen in images with a power that dares to compete with Garfield's voice-over narration. Like the best Polonsky dialogue, this language arises from the conflict between fully realized characters, the progress of whose emerging self-consciousness is the true subject of the drama. Hence this remarkable passage in *Force of Evil:*

Garfield: "I could feel money spreading in the air like perfume. Tucker opened his pocket and I dived right in. I wasn't strong enough to resist corruption, but I was strong enough to fight for a piece of it." (In a subdued voice:) "I'm dead. I'm finished."

Pearson: "When did this happen?"

Garfield: "The day I was born."

The rhythm and the simplicity of these exchanges informs Polonsky's character development. This technique, to which he alluded occasionally as dialectical, was in practice more a theatrical device than a philosophical principle. Save in novels, where he could develop Marxist principles more overtly, Polonsky's dialectics remained narrative, contained in the contrary movement of his characters.

5

When asked about the continuing Yiddishist themes in his work, Polonsky made jokes. He was eloquent and precise about his work's political content, yet he begged off discussions involving themes closer to home (or *haym*). He was preoccupied with universal issues that go to the heart of Western culture and history, of capitalism and revolution, of loyalties and betrayals that have less to do with ethnic identities than with the rise and fall of cultures and states. No doubt he long regarded the Jewish elements in his work as incidental, the necessary accretions to any story line that grows out of personal experience. In that reticence as well, he was not so different from others from a similar background in his generation of New Yorkers who so often directed their interests toward the New World's secular blessings, most particularly jazz, radio, and the movies. If the form of his genre work was arguably Attic (as he so often implied), the content, that is to say the humanity of his characters, nevertheless derived from the political and social concerns of *Yiddishkayt* (literally, Yiddishness).

As the linguistic memory of seven hundred years of Jewish life in the pale, Yiddishkayt simultaneously embraced the secular and vernacular qualities of urban America's *yiddishe gossen* (Jewish streets). Not at all the self-hating souls contemplating their alienation from Jewishness (as Jewish conservatives so often later charged), the left-wingers of Polonsky's generation arguably conducted their dialogue on Jewishness in the English language and in the manner accessible to the majority of American Jews, whose engagement with popular culture and simultaneously with the paradoxes of American identity was a virtual self-definition.

None of Polonsky's major works until *Romance of a Horsethief* are concerned with specifically Jewish themes. But they draw on the values of Yiddishkayt so often that Polonsky has often been described as the filmic counterpart to the Jewish theater's most famous dialogue-writer during the Depression, Clifford Odets. A near contemporary of Polonsky, Odets made his name early when he wrote both *Awake and Sing!* and *Waiting for Lefty* in 1935. Overnight, he thereby made left-wing drama a paying proposition, at least in Greater New York, and he almost single-handedly provided a theatrical set piece for local amateur and professional actors across the country to publicize strikes and union organization.

As critics have noted, Odets's real genius lay in sympathetically exposing the hopes and frustrations of lower-class and lower-middle-class Jewish families through his portrayals of their intimate lives. No one had previously given English-language audiences the feeling for immigrant and second-generation vernacular in a community where capitalism's ravages were most likely to be interpreted in political terms and where a familiar uncle could be expected to articulate broadly socialist (but also deeply Jewish) moral alternatives. *Golden Boy* (1937) and *Rocket to the Moon* (1938), Odets's last two great stage hits, fully expressed these strengths; the former, a boxing drama of the ghetto-raised fighter who must choose between fists and the violin, is the closest thing to *Body and Soul* in Jewish drama. In Odets's plays, if anywhere, the gnomic words of class and family conflict familiar in Polonsky's films flow out of actors' mouths as if theater had been created to express them.

Odets's failure and disillusionment in Hollywood contained a monumental lesson, or perhaps offered a series of puzzles, in the history of popular culture. The studios gave him no raw material with which he could work effectively, and almost without exception he hated what they made of his work. One of his final plays, *The Big Knife* (1949, filmed in 1956 by Robert Aldrich), with its artistic-minded Hollywood protagonist driven to cynicism and finally suicide, marked his exit from an era. Although he achieved revenge and a measure of personal redemption in *The Sweet Smell of Success* (1957), Odets never recovered the momentum of his early work and, like John Garfield, his testimony to the House Committee on Un-American Activities (albeit limited) broke him.[58]

In another sense, the theatrical quality of Odets's plays ill suited film. The action is not only offstage but almost nonexistent, an additional burden to the demand for close attention to language that his scripts shared with Polonsky's. With a rare partial exception or two (above all *None but the Lonely Heart*, the only film he directed), Odets could not make himself into a screenwriter, although his theatrical work has served occasionally and might have served more widely as a marvelous basis for adaptation. Nor could he successfully quit the Depression setting and psychology, where his insights were most profound. In utilizing some of the same stock of experiences, Polonsky's task was to render the quasi-Yiddish of Odets's English more universal, to place characters in filmable circumstances, and to add one more crucial distinctive element.

With all their strength, Odets's treatments never strayed far from the sentimentalism that had pervaded Mike Gold's *Jews without Money* and was common in socialistic Jewish literature. A conflicted but self-sacrificing mother, like the beloved uncle, seemed destined to play her expected role, usually more as a projection of the protagonist's emotional state than as a figure in her own right. Moreover, by pitting art against commerce (a nineteenth-century view of uplift) and counterposing a young boxer's choice as either classical music or blood sport, Odets shrank from the real terms of twentieth-century culture.

In contrast, Polonsky's women are his characters with the most modern impulses, holding too little power but more hard-headedly political than the men they advise. Nor do his slum boys have any knowledge about, let alone prospects within, the world of high art. Polonsky's Jews had pulled out of the Depression without yet leaving their neighborhoods for the suburbs. In the new world before them, rife with new forms of race and gender conflict, a rejection of capitalism and a renewal of artistic aspirations would not be enough. They had to solve their problems in fresh ways. To realize Yiddishkayt's potential, they had to broaden the subject to the Great City, that is to say, New York itself.

So many decades later, it is not often remembered that until the end of the 1940s New York was a major manufacturing center and a hub of working-class urban institutions. In the extraordinary vitality of its working-class life, even amid masses of immigrants from every nation, Jews had their own unique role. They played both the exploited and the exploiter in every variation: the baker, the bookie, the aesthete, the athlete, the mass consumer and the mass producer, the labor organizer and the strikebreaker. In this world, which had survived in one form or another for three generations, American working-class Jews could, with no sense of contradiction or cultural discontinuity, read the Yiddish press and belong to left-wing fraternal groups, dance to black jazz, cheer on Charlie Chaplin and the Dodgers, follow radio serials, read tough detective fiction, and join militant labor movements. Looking back at it from the 1970s, Polonsky described it as "That world of want," of "poor New York Jews, the Enlightenment, and Utopian Socialism, the Life of Reason haunting the glorious future."[59]

Critics writing about Yiddish litterateurs of New York from 1900 to 1930 almost could have been describing Polonsky and the artists who had migrated to the Hollywood of the 1940s. As a generation, the immigrant intellectuals from Eastern Europe had believed themselves emancipated from the Old World's spiritual values, but they nevertheless renewed those values, giving them fresh relevance and meaning. They often said that Yiddish itself was the true homeland, a spiritual homeland by necessity socialistic and truly international from one Jewish linguistic island to another, all across the earth.[60]

To ask how that uniquely Jewish popular culture affected these New Yorkers, the usual form of the question, is to miss the point. In an important way that generations of suburban grandchildren would find virtually impossible to grasp, these Jews *were* popular culture—as observers, participants, and creators. At the same time they entered fully into

American city life, they took the measure of their own legacy. Take, for instance, Sholem Aleichem, popularly and significantly known as the Mark Twain of Yiddish literature, who made his name in Europe but died in the Bronx. The perpetual credulousness of the Yiddish author's Jewish masses, the rebellion of his young people, and the philistinism of his wealthy classes would become familiar story lines in the Jewish-American novel, as well as in films and television dramas. From the one-column Yiddish short story in the *Forverts* of the 1890s to *The Rise of David Levinsky* by *Forverts* editor Abraham Cahan and *The Generations of Noah Edon* by David Pinski, the story is the same. The Jewish immigrant or immigrant's child in America grows wealthy but realizes that in the process he has lost his soul. In another version best articulated in David Ignatov's modernist Yiddish trilogy *Af vayte vegn*, a searcher after truth strives to escape the gross materialism encompassing successful American Jews and in the process rediscovers ancient secrets. An occluded Jewish leftist tradition, he learns, is simultaneously Jewish and universally human, offering a precious lens—indeed, an optical principle—through which to understand the entire world. Or again, particularly in the popular vernacular, a poor Jewish family understands itself comically, but the jokes turn on tolerance and survival, as in the weekly radio scripts of *The Goldbergs*. Generations from Manhattan to Los Angeles have worked and reworked these themes, deepened and enlarged them to include alienation and gender conflict.

This was the atmosphere in which movies became so significant to Jews in their contact with the world at large. Jews could rewrite, popularize, and to some degree contribute to the evolution of jazz, the essential American music; they could become a business force and the subterranean talent behind more obscure outlets of popular culture like comic books; as authors, they could write one best-selling novel after another; and they could virtually dominate Broadway behind the sets. But film was the medium in which moguls, writers, scenarists, and even stars would bring into focus the Jewish view. From this New York stew of rude experience, idealism and weltschmerz, gangsterism and socialism, an actor like John Garfield could arise from the thousands of others who preceded him, in Yiddish and English, on the city's proscenia. No one would have to invent the familiar figures that Garfield embodied, but such characters needed a Polonsky to refine them and give them form not as archetypes or even as types but as living characters.

For these reasons, it is fascinating to contemplate Polonsky's blacklisting along with Garfield's death. (Polonsky neatly summed the actor's saga: "The Group trained him, the movies made him, the blacklist killed him.")[61] As twin exiles from their proper moment in time and place, the two had a close intuitive relationship, in no small part because of Polonsky's sensitivity to the fact that "Garfield felt himself inadequate as an intellectual." Polonsky tried to convince Garfield that he was mistaken because "being an intellectual and being an artist aren't genetically paired, any more than being an artist and being a good character." But even as he suffered unnecessarily,

> as an actor Garfield was total, and he could play an intellectual with the same vigor and astonishing rapport as a cab driver. Regarding *Force of Evil* he told me before we started that although he didn't understand some of the meanings, the minute he hung that Phi Beta Kappa key on his watch chain he was in business. And so he was. He had the true actor's genuine wisdom for the human, and he could play his kind of intellectual just as well as he could play his kind of cab driver. You won't meet either in New York, but you wish you could.

What made Garfield important, far more than his overall brilliance as an actor, was his presence as "a star who represented a social phenomenon . . . without contradiction in the imagination of those who loved him for something that lay in themselves." It spoke to the time when lower-class "Jews who didn't join the money system gravitated to socialism . . . rebellion . . . and self-consciousness, harsh or neurotic."[62] Some became outright gangsters; more became gangsters in gray flannel suits; but others remained just what they had been all their lives, neighborhood men and women who continued to believe that something better than a dog-eat-dog society was still possible, if no longer inevitable. Only a few years later, when the whole radical era had become an embarrassment for cold-war America, Garfield was crushed for being the exemplar of an ambiance. On Garfield's returning to his home neighborhood while the Committee hounded him, Polonsky eulogized:

> wandering around New York [until his death], talking to himself with a voice from the grave, really with no place to go, rejected, [Garfield] saw far off on those screens his own face, which had become the face of a generation of New York street kids. [Now] I joined those New Yorkers and we stood across the street from the funeral parlor watching the tumult and fifty policemen with white gloves. Later, the papers said ten thousand people had come to Garfield's funeral, nothing so big since the death of Valentino.[63]

This was, more than anything, a Jewish homage to one of their own.

Polonsky later confessed to the limitations in *Force of Evil.* If he and

Odets both derived their creativity "from Jewish jokes and street quarrels," then Polonsky (not unlike the tortured friendly witness Odets) continued to "live dangled between the formal and argot without solution," a Jewish artist seeking something more than contrived and conventional art. Like so many other genuine intellectuals in Hollywood then and now, Polonsky had trained himself well to write "the standard American Movie Dialogue" for a living but remained personally unsatisfied by it. That was the dilemma of the serious, popular artist in a world of moguls and lesser hustlers; over the rest of his career little would change.[64]

6

In retrospect, the cold war's outbreak foreshadowed the ruin of Polonsky's body of work as a touchstone for the immediate future for the American art film. But as Polonsky observed dryly on another occasion, the artisans of the middle 1940s did not yet foresee their gloomy future. Therein lay the difference. The bitterness that swept over America in the years immediately after the war was directed far less at communism or communists than at the disappearance of wartime idealism and the return to business as usual—including the most unsavory business—in American life. Massive strike waves—the largest since the early days of the CIO—expressed rebellion this time against unions as well as employers; popular music echoed with embittered themes of alienation and betrayal; and President Harry Truman's ratings dipped steeply during 1945–46. All this anger formed the context for the film noir, of which Polonsky was one of the finest practitioners.

Polonsky's artistry might be compared, for instance, to that of left-wing director (and later friendly witness) Edward Dmytryk. Closer to the contemporary middlebrow (or middle-class) left-wing view of both political art and morality, Dmytryk fashioned "theme" films and genre features alike with great success. His smash hits, *Hitler's Children* (1942) and *Murder, My Sweet* (1944), facilitated other remarkable productions, including *Till the End of Time* (1946), a returned-GI epic with an antifascist barroom brawl; and *Crossfire* (1947), perhaps the strongest contemporary condemnation of anti-Semitism. Famous for a certain visual sadism (often realized through the direction of Robert Ryan, who, along with Garfield, Robert Mitchum, and Barbara Stanwyck, must be considered the noir auteur's preferred repertory), Dmytryk could count on heavy backing for his productions and confidently expect to reach huge audiences that Polonsky could only imagine.[65] Along with Dmytryk could be included the more avant-garde Nicholas Ray—*They Live by Night* (1949), *In a Lonely Place* (1950), *On Dangerous Ground* (1951), and *Johnny Guitar* (1953)—who wholly escaped the blacklist, thanks to his never joining the party and to the protection of his studio chief, Howard Hughes. Ray went on to direct *Rebel Without a Cause* (1955) with his spiritual mentor, Clifford Odets, on the set, pointing the way to a new kind of cinematic outsider. Polonsky's merger of the low-budget feature and the "art film" would never be possible or necessary for either of these heavily bankrolled figures.

Closer parallels can be found in other directions, not in finished products but in limited portions of specific efforts and their underlying artistic intentions. *Deadline at Dawn* (1946), scripted by Odets and directed by Harold Clurman, perhaps comes closest to Polonsky's gnomic dialogue but fumbles through an overly complex plot and unbelievable blue-collar characters. *Clash by Night* (1952), director Fritz Lang's overwrought blue-collar melodrama based on an Odets play, renders earlier class and ethnic themes into a struggle over adultery. (It starred both Ryan and Stanwyck, along with a little-known, ardently left-wing supporting actress named Marilyn Monroe.) Jules Dassin's *The Naked City* (1948), written by Maltz, has some of Polonsky's grittiness but finally is a pseudo-documentary police-action film. Many similar good points can be found in John Berry's *He Ran All the Way* (1951), a boy's night of terror and self-searching with revenge in mind and gun in hand. Exceptionally well made, it, too, is unable to escape the limits of the genre.

Behind these films stands a small army of further forgotten 1940s noir or noir-influenced films and their creators, including Sylvia and Robert Richards, John Bright, Adrian Scott, Sidney and Harold Buchman, Bernard Vorhaus, John Wexley, Cy Endfield, Guy Endore, Gordon Kahn, Ben Maddow, Irving Pichel, and Leonardo Bercovici. Occasionally successful in big productions, most of these Left writers and directors spent their time urgently trying to turn small-to-minuscule budgets into something approaching an artistic rendering of everyday struggles. Sometimes they succeeded grandly—in a scene or two, or even for just a few moments—before being overwhelmed by imposed limitations. Whether these works succeed or fail as whole films, they offer the careful viewer insights into the pre-ideological (that is, unarticulated) content of the protagonists' actions. Again and again, in the most optimistic moments, these protagonists act and then they "know" what they have merely glimpsed all along. On the dark side, however, they are crushed or can make no use of their knowledge.

To note that these filmmakers' collective effort—itself never quite thoroughly or coherently articulated—could not be sustained beyond certain vivid moments is not to deprecate their work but to comprehend their efforts as the products of material conditions. The relative philosophical fullness and stylistic completion of Polonsky's work can be seen better as the culmination of a remarkable moment in film and cultural history. This conclusion echoes a point that the blacklist survivors themselves have repeated so often when discussing their craft and the work of their time: Polonsky's leading role both as intellectual and as artist.

7

Polonsky told a *New York Times* reporter in 1947 that he had a play in the works titled "Woman in Arms," scheduled to be directed in either New York or London by the famed Harold Clurman. By any standards but those of a cold war closing in on victims all across the planet, it might well have capped a fast-moving phase of screenplays with a political triumph on the legitimate stage, giving Polonsky another creative direction. An earlier version, "Pièce de Résistance," had that possibility for several related reasons.[66]

"Woman in Arms" grew out of Polonsky's never-produced film script of the Resistance, with some of the same sexual tensions and semicollaborationist characters but simplified technically for the stage set and reduced chronologically to one moment, the day the Liberation of Paris is about to begin. By any standard, Andrée is Polonsky's spokesperson for true emancipation. She has led a double life, organizing the Underground while comfortably surviving the Occupation thanks to her former husband, a collaborator-intellectual. ("In our district, all the young women want to grow up and be like you," her aide says). Albert, Andrée's past and present companion, is an utter cynic who plans to leave Paris with the departing Germans and relocate to Switzerland, safe from harm. Louis, the sixteen-year-old servant, is actually her political protégé and obviously a Communist partisan. (Late in the play, he combines "Vive la France" and crossing himself with calls for the solidarity of the international working class.) Her husband Claude, thought lost at the front—and actually in a German prison-camp—improbably returns to the scene, desperate for her love or, more precisely, for her body.

Much as in Polonsky's earlier effort, the political drama weaves in and out of gender relations. At every step, Andrée insists upon realistic assessments of romance and love, often with aphorisms. ("Permanent adultery is marriage . . . It always begins with love and ends in adultery. That's what men mean by domestic bliss.") She expresses in the strongest terms her recollection of bourgeois marriage, "the desert and wilderness of boredom." When challenged by the insistence that this was only her bored bourgeois *life*, she answers sharply,

> That's what I thought. But during these past four years I've been friends with girls and women who work, with never a moment to breathe or think, and their story is like mine, only worse. They're bored by exhaustion, and when they're lying there, dead with fatigue, the brute climbs into bed and wants to make love because he's rubbed against some stenographer in the subway. Boredom, endless, prolonged, everlasting boredom . . . with the society of our masters. Oh, you dull, dull men, you mindless apes and goats. If only you knew how boring you were. It makes me yawn, just to think of it . . .

After which, her ex-husband grabs her, set upon rape, and she tosses him to the floor with a judo move.

Claude makes the usual statements about war's existential effect on the human spirit; Albert represents the cowardice of the bourgeoisie, young Louis the heroic recklessness and too-fast moral judgments of youth. During the second act the play shifts into a sort of moving tableau of the three men awaiting (for different reasons) the assassination of Nazi officers at the moment of liberation. Now Andrée reveals the spirit of Polonsky's effort. Asked how she could be a leader of the Underground unbeknownst to the man she lived with, she answers,

> Being part of the resistance was easy for a woman. In fact, she didn't have to learn anything new. The French men she loved had taught her all the subversive skills needed for the Germans she hated. How to lie and conceal her real motives, how to be a hypocrite, how to seem docile and weak when she felt rebellious and strong, and especially how to hide every bit of talent, intelligence and superiority she possessed from the eager eyes of male masters. In the resistance all these vices became virtues. I learned all about humiliation and wounded pride long before the first German pinched my behind. You, Claude, my father and Albert, had taught them to me.

At the dramatic conclusion, Andrée is eager for France to live a new life but fears the lingering effects of the violence, especially on those compelled to carry it out, young Louis in particular. The bourgeois male has not changed. ("You want to overturn the relation between the sexes which is the basis of all civilization. Thank god, even the communists are against that.") But the aphorisms remain: "Is it possible for a man and woman to be happy together?" Claude asks. "Not if it's happiness they want," she answers.

Polonsky had told the *New York Times* that he would follow the play with another stint at Enterprise directing one or two projects, the more prestigious being a comedy by Ring Lardner, Jr., "over the problem of faith and reason in which reason wins."[67] As Enterprise tanked and the blacklist settled in, Polonsky's directorial career narrowed to one potential project and then dissolved.

8

The FBI's Polonsky file reveals a fascinating story of relative neglect during the first year or two after the war soon growing into rapt attention bordering on obsession. A report of "known Communists in the Screen Writers Guild" as of July 1945 fails to mention him (factually, Polonsky had not yet rejoined), and only in May 1946, with a document analyzing the subversive content of the *Screen Writer*, does he appear as a studio chair of the Left SWG group at Paramount. Listed here along with non-Communists, the FBI identification grows more definitive in the HICCASP-connected School for Political Action Techniques of the National Citizens Political Action Committee. The school's faculty and sponsors included Polonsky, along with many non-Communists such as UCLA professor Franklin Fearing, screen actors Gregory Peck and Albert Dekker, state attorney general Robert Kenney, and prominent black newspaper editor Charlotta Bass.

The same report lists Polonsky as a sponsor of the *Hollywood Quarterly*—with his name asterisked as a "known communist" for the first time. Polonsky's billing as secretary of the Hollywood Writers Mobilization, a subgroup that agitated against restricted-covenant housing in Los Angeles, no doubt proved especially troubling to the FBI director J. Edgar Hoover, who saw Communist subversion and movements for equal rights for African-Americans as more or less the same thing. From 1947 to 1949, Polonsky's profile had emerged and sharpened astonishingly. A typical FBI report noted that he had previously been identified as a CP member in Hollywood, but by the later 1940s, this "first-rate writer," Communist loyalist, and "arrogant, difficult man . . . disliked by many people in the motion picture industry" had become a figure to reckon with.[68] In contrast to the Hollywood informers' usual wild misjudgments of party members' aesthetics and the political intentions of their films, this assessment is not far off the mark. That studio execs regarded any rebellious spirit as "arrogant" and "difficult" goes without question.

Another FBI document of the era revealed (or mangled) the party's inner struggle in the last few years before blacklisting became absolute. As one of the first nineteen left-wingers called to testify before the House Committee on Un-American Activities in October 1947, and for practically a decade the unassailable section leader, John Howard Lawson was increasingly under local pressure from those who considered his slavish response to Russian (and New York) signals destructive of the Hollywood Left's artistic creativity and political attraction. That they needed all the help they could get made this all the worse. Polonsky, Waldo Salt, and Arnold Manoff argued that screenwriters should spend their off-studio energies on writing, not party matters. One member of their faction (Leonardo Bercovici later claimed responsibility) submitted a position paper arguing that "the Communist Party in the United States should be an American party, stand on its own feet and not 'sneeze whenever STALIN got pepper in his nose.'" According to Bercovici, the paper was presented to the Los Angeles section at large and promptly suppressed. The informer's version, which cannot be authenticated, is that the branch had tried to submit it to the Los Angeles section's annual convention, but as no other Hollywoodite was a formal speaker there, Lawson insisted that only he could speak on such issues. He refused to submit the document or even to read from it.[69]

One more informer offered this particularly knowledgeable recollection and keen observation:

> According to [blank], POLONSKY was one of the real CP leaders in Hollywood, and she believes he must still be. She describes him as one of the really brilliant men in the movement. She recalls that she first met POLONSKY in 1941 in New York, at which time she had no idea he was a CP member. In that year [blank] or [blank] as she was then known, was sent back to New York by Paramount Studios to interview potential writers for the film industry. One of the dozens that she interviewed was ABE POLONSKY, which was the first time she ever saw him. She realized POLONSKY's potentialities as a screenwriter, and he was one of several that she recommended to WILLIAM DOZIER of Paramount Studios. It was not until POLONSKY arrived in Hollywood from New York that she learned that he was a party member. From that time, POLONSKY was always a leader in the CP and one of the few men who could successfully challenge the views of JOHN HOWARD LAWSON on any particular issue.[70]

That more or less wraps up not only the inside view of Polonsky's evolution from the quiet intellectual communist of 1941 to the artist of the later 1940s who was not only a Communist but the one Hollywood Communist with the intellectual and political credentials to press the attack upon the left-wing philistinism of party directives.

Lawson was believed, rightly or wrongly, to be near the end of his screenwriting career in any case. Consciously or unconsciously, however, aesthetics as didactic and limited as his continued, and doubtless would have endured without the enforced pause of the blacklist. But something had shifted in the Hollywood Left, from the temper of the late 1940s films to the *Hollywood Quarterly*. Of course, Polonsky had scarce opportunity to appreciate the change, as the Left's influence on the Screen Actors Guild lay in tatters. To make matters worse, a new wave of HUAC investigations loomed.[71]

The new HUAC investigations' first target was the Joint Anti-Fascist Refugee Committee (JAFRC). Chairman Rankin brilliantly deduced that this already defunct group's militant 1930s propaganda against Francisco Franco was proof positive of Jewish anti-Catholic propaganda. Executive board members who resisted demands for the organization's membership records, including Dashiell Hammett and Howard Fast, eventually went to jail for contempt: the first major precedent for the blacklist. Moreover, 1946 was an election year and California was rightly considered a key state. To top it all, national antistrike legislation demanded by President Truman was in committee, and its fate rested upon the moiling political waves.

The Hollywood Left quickly rallied around Robert Kenney's gubernatorial candidacy against the popular incumbent (and future Supreme Court justice) Earl Warren; however, its most powerful organization, the HICCASP, split over whether to support the left-leaning Ellis Paterson or centrist Will Rogers, Jr., for senator. James Roosevelt, still highly prestigious as the late president's son, came out to head HICCASP, wavered on the senatorial choice, and left town with the organization even more badly divided. California Democrats thus faced the prospect of near-extinction with a Republican sweep in November.

In the picture-within-the-pictures of real-life Hollywood versus Hollywood, the Motion Picture Alliance for the Preservation of American Ideals, like the International Alliance of Theatrical State Employees' Hollywood local, had contributed heavily to the Republican campaign, urged the Tenney investigations, and now stood to gather the spoils. When the strike by the Conference of Studio Unions disintegrated, the CSU itself was as good as dead; HICCASP was most frequently in the headlines for supposed red links; and the Screen Actors Guild leadership was shifting decisively to the right, despite adamant resistance from the likes of Katharine Hepburn and Edward G. Robinson. Then things got even worse.[72]

President Truman's Executive Order 9835, instituting loyalty programs for civil servants, set the definitive blacklisting process in motion. The attorney general used the HUAC files to do far more than check on civil servants; he prepared to issue a list of subversive organizations. Thus HUAC turned, for example, from its attempt to snare the deeply political Gerhart Eisler (who left the United States for East Germany) to his mostly apolitical and estranged brother Hanns, who worked as a composer in Hollywood. The Congressional Labor Committee, guided by Fred Hartley of the future Taft-Hartley bill, raced ahead in Los Angeles, ostensibly to investigate the CSU strike but actually to prepare a political fishing expedition, with headline-seeking congressman Richard Nixon carrying the ball. Ronald Reagan, former ally of the Left, pushed his way into political prominence by attacking the Reds for bringing "disruption" to Hollywood (what Reagan ominously called "one big union" was merely industrial unionism, but for the future president, anything beyond craft unionism demonstrated a subversive taint). By the time J. Parnell Thomas arrived in Hollywood to investigate the *content* of films, the process was well under way. In June 1947, the Taft-Hartley Act became law and union leaders were all but compelled to declare they were not Communists.[73]

Later observers would conclude that the Motion Picture Alliance once more played a crucial role in the investigation, creating fresh opportunities for "friendly" testimony and scandal-mongering journalism. This time, the investigators and their Hollywood supporters declared that screenwriters were the chief enemy and that the films themselves as much as any outright political activity offered the true source of subversion. Jack Warner testified that "communists injected 95% of their propaganda into films through the mediums of writers"—although he added, no doubt in self-protection, that he had never knowingly employed or even met a single Communist![74] The appearance of the first major round of friendly witnesses served notice of tantalizing headlines to come.

Subpoenas to an "Unfriendly Nineteen" well-known left-wing screenwriters and directors set in motion the last Hollywood political movement in which Polonsky played a leading role. The Committee for the First Amendment formed in the spring of 1947, and as FBI documents testify, it was at first larger and more inclusive than anything the Left had organized since the war. Sterling Hayden, Danny Kaye, Humphrey Bogart, Lauren Bacall, Jane Wyatt, Gene Kelly, and John Huston among others announced their support. The famed radio writer, producer, and director Norman Corwin directed several broadcasts with an even

larger array of stars, from Judy Garland to Howard Duff, pleading for
tolerance and for the rights of free speech and association.

As Polonsky liked to tell the story, the First Amendment committee's
initial meeting, held at Ira Gershwin's house, was so successful that
Howard Hughes offered to charter a plane to fly "his" stars and others
to Washington to testify against red-baiting. At the hearings in October,
only eleven (the Hollywood Ten plus Berthold Brecht) were called to the
stand.[75] Uncertain of the best legal or political course until the last
minute, yet convinced that the current hysteria compelled them to stand
on their constitutional rights in general rather than their prerogative to
be Communist Party members, the witnesses met charge with charge,
refusing to let themselves be badgered or to admit to anything but the
right to work as they chose. The press, which at first sided openly with
the studios and the committee, had a field day. If the most sanguine
observers imagined that the writers had won, the long faces returning on
the plane from Washington told a different story. As Polonsky recalled,
his friend Danny Kaye continually wended up and down the aisle, joking, singing, and otherwise cheering everyone as much as possible.

The First Amendment committee put up one last, bold publicity effort,
a "Hollywood Fights Back" national radio broadcast on October 26.
Gene Kelly, Lauren Bacall, Joseph Cotton, Peter Lorre, Danny Kaye,
Richard Conte, Burt Lancaster, Robert Ryan, Robert Young (who only
seven years before had been the foremost celebrity of the isolationist
America First Committee), Van Heflin, Lionel Barrymore, Edward G.
Robinson, Frederic March, William Wyler, Judy Garland, Frank Sinatra,
and Vincent Price let themselves be heard loud and clear. Freedom of
speech, the fundamental right of Americans, demanded that HUAC back
down.[76] But of course, it did not.

The committee's next meeting would be a mere rump Left caucus,
much as HICCASP had devolved from a prestigious left-center coalition
to a small and politically isolated group. In a famed—or notorious—
November 24–25 meeting at the New York Waldorf-Astoria Hotel, the
Hollywood producers announced that the Ten would be sacrificed, dis-
charged until and unless they satisfied the studios as to their loyalty. This
capitulation, meant to delay and soften a full-scale witch hunt, instead
signaled the hunters to charge ahead. Now only a successful legal challenge to the charge of contempt of Congress against the unfriendly witnesses could have changed the situation. After one probable sympathetic
justice retired and another died, the Supreme Court finally settled against
the defendants in 1950, sending most of them to jail for a year.

Meanwhile, the darkness descended. The actual blacklisting of hundreds of others would take time, mainly because numerous producers—unwilling to resist the pressure of the banks or the politicos, but also unwilling to lose their talent—sought to ride out the storm. Even Walt Disney, champion of the industry's Right, kept capable left-wingers on staff, but the blows fell one by one.

Polonsky played no significant role in the last furious years of the Left's backstairs campaign in the Screen Writers Guild. He lacked the credentials of battle-hardened union warriors in any case. The 1947 elections brought defeat to party members Stanley Rubin and Leo Townsend, who had been SWG secretary and treasurer, respectively. Both would soon become friendly witnesses. Along with the further defeat of Left stalwarts in elections for the SWG's executive board, this was a stunning blow. Within a few years, the SWG had agreed to blacklist its own members, denying membership to anyone who refused to testify. A generation would pass before SWG officials, embarrassed by their predecessors' misdeeds, invited the surviving victims to return, with apologies for the organization's inexcusable past behavior and eventually an effort to provide compensatory pensions for those blacklistees who had grown both old and desperately poor.[77]

The early days of Henry Wallace's campaign for president offered the Hollywood Left its last glimmer of hope. Katharine Hepburn gave the former vice president a stirring introduction at Gilmore Stadium, and a crowd of twenty-seven thousand urged him on. But the daily headlines—including the Communist takeover of Czechoslovakia, Russian opposition to the Marshall Plan, and the steady beat of investigations and firings—thwarted the Left's recovery or even resistance to the approaching blacklist. The filmmakers who had put their energy into delivering their last possible noir messages had been the most politically astute after all. That, as Polonsky appreciated, was little consolation.

4

POLONSKY'S FIFTIES

READYING HIMSELF TO BE EXILED in one sense or another, Polonsky never lost his buoyancy. Unlike many others who either became severely depressed or fled to more politically tolerant climes, he quietly changed course. No doubt because he had pursued such varied intellectual callings and regarded filmmaking as merely one choice among many, he could join what amounted to an artistic underground. His closely handwritten notebooks—he titled a section of them "Bourgeois Agony" or "B.A."—suggest far more concern with the increasing personal isolation from the political milieu that had enlivened his past.[1] Like so many other intellectuals active in vital movements of the 1930s–40s, he now had to live without the hope that somewhere, if far away, a counterforce to ravenous capitalism was firmly established and socialism would somehow evolve even, if necessary, from state tyrannies. For Polonsky and those others who could not accept capitalist consumerism as the model for global development, *Force of Evil*'s dark view had triumphed over *Body and Soul*'s bright determination. Polonsky had far from given up politically, but quiet determination now replaced hope. In a way, he had been preparing himself for this eventuality all along.

After *Force of Evil*, Polonsky informed his family, now including two young children, that he intended to move to southern France and write a novel "like all the famous writers do." The Polonskys decamped to Paris, where the former intelligence officer first looked up some old comrades from the Resistance. Within a few months he moved to Cannes to

write what became *The World Above,* his literary masterwork. He went
to Hollywood for a few months' sojourn in 1949 to write the script for
I Can Get It for You Wholesale. The studio there wanted him to pursue
a writer-director's career. Had his Hollywood prospects looked brighter,
he would have been foolish to leave, but he returned to France to begin
arranging a European production of his next script, "Mario and the
Magician." Again, had his prospects brightened back in France with the
actual production of "Mario and the Magician," he might have stayed in
Europe for at least a few years. As it was, when the clouds thickened over
American cultural life and Sylvia asked what they were going to do, he
had no real choice. He would never seriously consider making the self-
exiled group's long-term commitment abroad.

Did Polonsky have more career possibilities than the others? Not really,
although he might have thought himself a more adaptable writer, perhaps
a novelist of popular potential despite the circumstances. But like a handful of other script writers so well known that projects would come their
way early and often, he correctly concluded that he could write under the
table for as long as the blacklist lasted. The moral decision was more
clear-cut: he did not intend to be kicked out of his own country, but he
came back knowing he would almost certainly be blacklisted.

When the cultural iron curtain fell, Polonsky could not have yet
assessed his options. But his past nimble shifts from one occupation to
another and from one form of writing to another now served him well.
No more than a handful of other blacklistees remaining within the
United States adapted to achieve any kind of writing success beyond the
commercial novel. Many more wrote noncommercial novels, financially
unsuccessful if personally satisfying ventures. With few exceptions, those
who made their way secretly into television considered it strictly hack
work. In this way, as in others, Polonsky remained sui generis, no literary giant, not even a credited writer in his other chosen media, but a formidable figure nonetheless, unbeaten and resilient.

1

If Polonsky had few illusions about what awaited him in Hollywood, his
worst fears—short of a jail stretch or the sudden arrest and massive
detention that some of the most repressive laws hinted for thousands of
unrepentant Reds—were quickly realized. When Hollywood's rumor
mill had him about to be named as a Communist, he had signed to write
and direct a film at Twentieth Century–Fox. Somehow hoping that

Polonsky might escape the fate now falling upon so many others, Darryl Zanuck advised him to work at home instead of coming to the studio. For a few weeks before Polonsky refused to cooperate at the HUAC committee hearing on April 25, 1951, the studio faithfully kept him on the payroll. The local press, hungry for victims, hammered at the studio. By Polonsky's account, Zanuck told him, "I'd like to keep you, I'll try—but when the pressure gets too tough I have to let you go, because I can't take it." Sure enough, one day the pressure got too tough and Zanuck let him go. For Polonsky, it was finally time for a separation.[2]

The hearings themselves marked the line in the sand. When committee members pressed Polonsky to admit belonging to assorted Left organizations he pleaded the Fifth Amendment; when they badgered him to reveal who had recruited him into the OSS he declined to answer, on national security grounds, obviously unwilling to mention his brother. When they followed the then-familiar tack of asking whether he would support the United States if he were sent to Korea, he responded that he would obey orders but considered war to have become an impossible way to gain peace in the modern world. Unlike a number of other unfriendly witnesses, Polonsky remained polite, and perhaps for that reason was allowed a scant debate over the Founding Fathers' intention in the Fifth Amendment. Apart from a few details of his career, Polonsky's interrogators asked practically nothing about the movie business that he and his comrades had purportedly subverted. Was he an executive in Enterprise? He admitted to a nominal vice-presidency. Did he know if any of the Hollywood Ten were writing for films again, using fronts? He declined to answer.[3]

In short, Polonsky's appearance came to naught, or might have except for a single phrase and its dramatic exploitation. Congressman Harold Velde complained that "in refusing to answer whether or not you signed a loyalty oath when you went into OSS, you leave me with the impression that you are a very dangerous citizen."[4] Perhaps the remark was a committee member's typical overblown rhetoric, aimed at the only Hollywood writer who had served in the one United States intelligence service that had been full of left-wingers and presumably also could have been involved in something dreadfully un-American. A shadowy figure then appeared in the hearing room to consult with Velde. Polonsky had the impression they were discussing certain unspecified secrets, perhaps even ending this line of questioning entirely. In any case, the *Hollywood Reporter* took up the cry, detailing the testimony and drawing a headline on an inside page, "POLONSKY HELD 'VERY DANGEROUS CITIZEN.'"[5] His career had been in trouble for months or years; now for the foreseeable future, at least under his own name, it was over.

In the first days of March, *I Can Get It for You Wholesale* had premiered in Hollywood. It received affable notices (its solid performances "help to supply a reasonable amount of interest in the Abraham Polonsky script," wrote the *Variety* reviewer) before Polonsky's notoriety and that of his fellow blacklistee, director Michael Gordon, quashed the film's prospects of any wider notices, let alone critical acclaim. Had *I Can Get It for You Wholesale* appeared a year or two earlier, it might have captured the close of the era that considered women's careers socially legitimate, and sympathetically treated the personal dilemmas inevitably arising from those aspirations. Had the film's production been delayed six months, Polonsky might have had to fight for his credits, and he probably would have lost the battle, as did Paul Jarrico with his script for *The Las Vegas Story*, due to the contractually redefined "moral turpitude" of refusing to testify. As it was, the absence of what *Variety* called "sock gimmicks" (dramatic flourishes) made the realism of *Wholesale* seem bland.[6] Its edgy realism did not prove sufficiently attractive to audiences even while it successfully posed the dilemmas of a businesswoman up against the glass ceiling.

Jewish New York, and Jewish contact with the world at large, provided the subtext of *I Can Get It for You Wholesale*. Unlike in *Body and Soul* or *Force of Evil*, it provided the text as well. In its complex mixture of idealism and weltschmerz, gangsterism and socialism, actors embodied familiar figures whom no one would have to invent but whom a Polonsky would have to refine and complete in ways that the screenwriter could almost draw from memory.

An hour into a film that some critics regard as a cinematic high point in women's resistance to postwar redomestication, *Wholesale*'s most memorable scene begins with the male protagonist's paroxysm of jealousy. Harriet Boyd (played by Susan Hayward), the designer and part owner of a new fashion house in New York's garment district, is seated at a table with a buyer from the heartland who has just placed an order for 1,500 dresses. Boyd's partner and suitor, Teddy Sherman (played by Dan Dailey), has just deposited two attractive dates at the bar, having planned a night on the town with the buyer. Now he discovers to his horror that Harriet not only has beaten him to the order but has agreed to spend the evening with the buyer, a properly named Mr. Savage (played by Harry Von Zell, soon to become a famous straight man on television's *Burns and Allen Show*). The clear implication is that Harriet has agreed to sleep with Savage in exchange for the order. That practice, in which Teddy is known to indulge routinely with female buyers, is one of the keys to his considerable success as a salesman.[7]

But this is also the night that Teddy had intended to propose marriage to Harriet, and her apparent willingness to barter sex for business shocks him. When he confronts her, Harriet says, "Don't you take your buyers out, wine them and dine them and amuse them?"

"It's different," Teddy responds.

"How?" she asks.

"Because I'm a man, and you're supposed to be a lady. It's different." When she presses him again, he evades the issue. "I'll write you a letter. Meanwhile, let's go."

A moment later, Teddy socks Savage in the jaw and follows an enraged Harriet into the street as she attempts to hail a taxi. He begs her to understand his motives and reveals the special significance of the evening to both of them. In most Hollywood movies, that moment might begin the denouement, but now the dialogue turns to ice.

"What do you expect me to do?" Harriet seethes. "Throw my arms around you? Listen, when you marry someone it will only be so you can rope her off, while you go on playing the field. Well, I'm not having any."

Teddy puts his hand on her arm in familiar Hollywood fashion. "Can't you get it through your head? I love you."

"You love me?" Harriet responds. "You mean you want to own me! I worked and schemed to get a business started just so I could be free of men like you, so I could belong to myself. Do you understand that? You love me so much that for the sake of your crummy male ego you're ready to take something I've worked for and dreamed about all my life and kick it under a barroom table. That's how much you love me."

The speech earned *Wholesale* a permanent place in film history.[8] One would be hard-pressed to find a comparable declaration of sexual independence or rejection of the sexual double standard in a commercial film. It is not, however, the speech Polonsky wrote before leaving for Paris. His original was far more pointed and considerably more dangerous than Oscar Saul's revision, less about Harriet Boyd's personal anger than about women's rage in the largest philosophical sense. Indeed, in this scene and in a few others written for her in the original, Harriet is much darker and more complex than the merely ambitious professional woman played on the screen so expertly by Susan Hayward. In the original, Harriet does not merely reject the double standard, she claims the male standard as her own:

"I'm proposing to you."

"What for, another brawl? You want to own me? Let's be very clear, General Sherman. I'm exactly like you. Sex is part of my stock in trade along with my talent, my brains, and the five thousand dollars I put into the business."

A cab rolls up and she steps in. Teddy leans in the window and says, "I don't like your idea of our business."

HARRIET

And I don't like your man's world where the woman is supposed to keep her eyes closed, her brain half-soaked in alcohol and not know that everything in pants, including the loving husband and father, is two-timing the woman he's supposed to be in love with with every other woman that comes along. When he can. And when he can't, he's thinking of it. I'm not grateful for the vote, mixed bathing, community property and a black negligee on Mother's Day.

CLOSEUP: I believe in the single standard, even if it's yours, and you know what that is.

This is no longer the talk of a tough-minded, unsympathetic professional woman with a career-related grievance; it is the language of someone who has reflected carefully on the condition of women in general. Harriet Boyd sounds more like Emma Goldman than like a woman who works a stone's throw from Wall Street. She was as much at home in the world of high fashion and high finance as Joe Morse, whom she resembles more than a little.

Of the many dramatic questions in *I Can Get It for You Wholesale*, the dilemma of Harriet's character is central. As Polonsky himself put it in an interview, "There's a problem [with *Wholesale*] because in the end she pulls back. She has to like this guy. It had to be suitable for Zanuck." In other words, the more Harriet's feminism develops along the way, the more unlikely her conversion will seem at the end. Just as sharp is the conflict between her rich social understanding and her willingness to ignore it for personal advancement. At some point she might become so unattractive that the contemporary viewer, even the sophisticated viewer, would find it difficult to understand why Teddy Sherman would cling to any feeling for her at all.

Another scene in Polonsky's script established Harriet's character much more clearly than the screen version. In the shooting script, Harriet wheedles five thousand dollars of potential investment in a clothes business out of her younger sister, Marge. After first offering to finance a

honeymoon for Marge and her fiancé, Ray, Harriet fakes a phone call
from her business partners, who supposedly tell her she must immediately raise five thousand dollars in capital. She reneges on the honeymoon, but after she has demonstrated such willing generosity to them,
the couple can hardly refuse her the capital to become a partner in the
new business. Although that scene pointedly establishes Harriet's ruth-
lessness, it again is not Polonsky's. His original is more ominous. After
Marge and Ray enter the apartment, we gather by indirection that Ray
and Harriet were once somehow romantically connected. Harriet correctly believes that the old flame is not dead, merely guttering. Polonsky's
stage directions are exacting:

FULL SHOT — ON HARRIET
(*Standing at the threshold of a small hall that leads, let us say, to the bath
and dressing room. There is strongish light behind her and the living room
is not too bright. The negligee is thin and there is a lot of Harriet silhouetted
there.*)

HARRIET (*in the song sirens sang*)
Why, hello Ray.

(*She starts forward and does not forget that model's walk . . . Marge's face
has grown sullen.*)

The entire scene is played out unambiguously as a seduction. The point
is reached after Ray leaves and the two sisters, sharing a bedroom, prepare to turn in.

HARRIET
I want you to be happy, Marge, and married to Ray, with kids and a neat
little apartment in Queens. That's fine. But I want that five thousand dollars
that Mom is saving for your marriage. I need it for my plans.

CLOSEUP — MARGE

MARGE
It's for me. You can't have it.

CLOSE TWO SHOT
(*Camera moves with* HARRIET, *losing* MARGE. *She moves off and crawls into
her couch, lies back and looks dreamily at the ceiling.*)

HARRIET
If you asked Mom, if you told her you wanted to invest it in the business
I'm starting, she'd give me the money.

(MARGE *enters the shot.*)

MARGE

No. People like us'll never see five thousand dollars in one piece again as long as we live.

HARRIET

I'll turn it into fifty thousand.

MARGE

You'll turn it into zero. You never think of anyone but yourself. You can't. (*There is a pause.*)

HARRIET

Turn out the lights, won't you? I'm sleepy. And I've got a lot of things to do tomorrow.

MOVING SHOT — ON MARGE

(MARGE *walks over and snaps off the lamp. The room is in semidarkness and she stands there at the lamp, thinking.*)

HARRIET'S VOICE
(*dreamily*)

Ray was telling me about his law class reunion dance. I might ask him to take me.

(MARGE *turns her back to her sister, her bearing frozen; anguish burning to the surface. She walks back to the bed as if hypnotized, into a* TWO SHOT.)

MARGE
(*desperately*)

He's taking me.

HARRIET

He could change his mind.

(*And as* MARGE *breaks into tears,* HARRIET *sits up.*)

HARRIET

You really want that poor fish, Marge? I could help you.

MARGE

You wouldn't, not you.

HARRIET

I could, but I want your help. The two of us could get Mom to lend me the money. There's no risk at all.

MARGE
(*with a sudden shock*)

Blackmail?

HARRIET
(*coolly*)

You want Ray, don't you?

(There is silence and then MARGE *turns and with slow steps moves through the darkness of the room, while the* CAMERA PULLS BACK INTO A FULL SHOT, *holding her until both she and Harriet are lost in the blackness of the* SLOW DISSOLVE.)*

There is no mistaking in this the outline of the femme fatale, created from the familiar clay of 1940s noir conventions. But this is a "women's picture," closer in spirit to Joan Crawford in *Mildred Pierce* (1945). As critic Elizabeth Cowie has pointed out, the women's picture and the "male melodrama" of the noir world share many of the same characters and motivations, with the expectable difference in gender emphasis. In both genres, "the classic story relates to the emphasis in film noir on contractual relationships, governed by money."[9] This was about as far in that direction as the femme fatale could be developed by 1950. Such characters seem to have died with the B film, or perhaps they only went into hibernation for the television film decades later.

That Polonsky could find some political salvage in *I Can Get It for You Wholesale* in the first place is remarkable. It is also a measure of how Left screenwriters managed to inject moments of cinematically historical significance into the most commercial studio projects. Still, *I Can Get It for You Wholesale* was a stretch for the man who made *Body and Soul* and *Force of Evil*.

Wholesale was based broadly on Jerome Weidman's widely read novel on a popular theme. The novel was eventually turned into a musical with Barbra Streisand and Elliott Gould, yet Jewish circles, and not merely those on the Left, widely regarded it as an embarrassment. The novel's view of the labor movement could only be described as low and naive. In brief, it tells the story of a young Jewish hustler who organizes the shipping clerks in New York's garment trade and persuades them to strike. He then makes a fortune by hiring them and contracting with their former bosses for their labor.

Hailed at the time by some critics for its satirical brilliance, the novel is more likely to strike contemporary readers as humorless, cartoonish in plot, and unappetizing in its characterizations. In his 1986 memoir, *Praying for Rain*, Weidman himself recalled a story that raises more questions than he cared to answer. One day in 1938, some months after Simon and Schuster had published *I Can Get It for You Wholesale*, publisher Richard Simon summoned Weidman to his office in Manhattan. Simon, by then a close friend, introduced Weidman to Nate Spindgold, a vice president of Columbia Pictures. Spindgold had been appointed as a spokesman by "a small group of Hollywood studio executives" who wanted to see what they could do "to fight the acceleration of anti-Semitism in this country."[10]

"They had made an agenda," Weidman wrote, "and they had sent Mr. Spindgold to New York to see what he could do about the first items on it. These were three books, all published by Simon and Schuster, that these Hollywood executives felt should be withdrawn from publication." The first was Richard Simon's own volume about the Leica camera. The group objected to it on the grounds that by promoting a German product it helped to increase that country's dollar credits in the United States. "The other two books Mr. Spindgold and his colleagues had decided should be suppressed were my best-selling novels *I Can Get It for You Wholesale* and its sequel, *What's in It for Me?*" When Weidman cross-examined Spindgold on his views of the books, the movie executive confessed he had not read them. Weidman then left the room with a pungent exit line.

When Weidman and Simon discussed the incident over the phone, Simon said he had explained to Spindgold that a clause in the contract prevented him from pulling the books off the shelves without the author's approval. Nonetheless, that very day, the late editions of the *New York World Telegram* carried a front-page story that Simon and Schuster had withdrawn three of its best-selling volumes under pressure from Hollywood executives who were "determined to stamp out anti-Semitism in this country." In actuality, the books had not been pulled, and afterward the *Telegram* and others that had followed its lead retracted the story. For years to come, however, many in the literary world would believe Simon and Schuster had withdrawn the books.[11]

For whatever reason, Weidman seemed to find his friends and admirers in largely conservative circles, including John O'Hara, Somerset Maugham, and even the red-baiting Walter Winchell, or among the cultivated second-generation German Jews such as Simon who had enlivened American publishing since the 1920s. Weidman generally lived a life remote from the concerns of the New York or Hollywood Left, at one point taking an executive position with Simon and Schuster. Indeed, his only recorded admirer in the film capital appears to have been F. Scott Fitzgerald, who observed in a curious letter to a friend about writers at the time, "As for Americans there's only one [Jewish author]—Jerome Weidman, whose two books . . . have been withdrawn as too perspicacious about the faults of his own race."[12] Weidman did not record his own reaction to this remark. For all of the New York literati's disregard for Hollywood screenwriters, many of them shared similar backgrounds.

Weidman (born in 1912), Polonsky, Rossen, and so many other story-tellers came up from the Lower East Side at nearly the same time and from roughly the same background.

Why would Zanuck and Twentieth Century–Fox even bother with a property that carried so much baggage? The answer is deceptively simple: Simon and Schuster's advertising account with the *New York Times* in 1937. Well known for its heavy ad schedule at a contract rate, the publishing house got a sizable discount for agreeing in advance to buy a set amount of lineage every year. "Just before *I Can Get It for You Wholesale* was published, Dick Simon discovered that the [Simon and Schuster] list for the balance of the year was smaller than his firm had anticipated when they signed their last contract with the *Times*." If they could not use the space for which they had already paid, they would lose the lower rates that the *Times* had quoted. Simon therefore "decided on a gamble. Instead of spreading out the paid-for space on all the books he thought they would be publishing . . . he shot the works on the only book Simon & Schuster then had ready for publication: *I Can Get It for You Wholesale*."[13] Not unexpectedly, the market took a huge interest in the book, or more precisely, in the title.

Variety reasonably complained that the resulting film "hides behind a title that suggests comedy rather than drama." The title unmistakably promised a story that would treat then-popular ethnic stereotypes, the source of so much American humor (and so much of it hurtful). But the humor in this particular cliché, like that in its obverse, "retail is for gentiles," would depend greatly on the amount of affection to be found in the mockery. Hollywood left-wingers certainly found very little. When Zanuck first discovered that someone at Twentieth Century–Fox had bought the rights to the book, he recoiled from the project: "I'll be damned if I'll make a picture from an anti-Semitic book."[14]

After reconsidering, Zanuck asked Weidman to change the story. Weidman refused but said he would not object if the studio made its own changes, and he even contributed the idea of making the protagonist a woman. Polonsky later recalled that he took up that idea with a provocative proposal, "Let's make it on the woman question." Although this would be Polonsky's first film project after *Golden Earrings* over which he had no control—not even his limited leverage over Rossen in *Body and Soul*—he did have influence with the director, fellow left-winger Michael Gordon. Beyond the scenes and dialogue already described, little of Ponlonsky's script was changed.

Polonsky cleaned up the book with several sweeping strokes. He eliminated the labor theme as unworkable and transformed the protagonist from a Jewish man to a beautiful young Irish-American fashion designer (and not industrial worker) who wanted to organize her own fashion house. He thereby sublimated the theme of class betrayal into a love story revolving on Harriet Boyd's opportunity to marry a merchant prince whom she does not love.

But the issue of class by no means disappeared. Finally, and most importantly, Polonsky created a new character, Sam Cooper, one of Boyd's partners. Played by future blacklistee Sam Jaffe, Cooper is a kindly, aging, Yiddish-accented *zeyde* (grandfather). At every turn in the plot, Cooper is there to console and guide Harriet's and Teddy's affairs in a judicious and morally proper direction.

Polonsky uses Cooper to give an edge to the otherwise maudlin ending, a studio-required dissolve from the predictable tearful embrace. As Harriet returns to the fashion house but continues fretfully to deny that she loves "that baboon" Sherman, Cooper's explanation to Sherman ties everything together and also binds him to a moral bargain: "It's very simple why she came back. . . . Maybe Seventh Avenue is a jungle, but that doesn't mean you have to live like a wild animal in it. That's all. She knows, so she came back."

Sherman is "moved" in spite of his anger at Harriet, and as her tears begin to brim in close-up, we hear Sam in voice-over, "And it's not easy to say, please come back. . . . Besides, all love affairs are a mess from the word go. What else can you expect from two strangers?" Thus, Sam apologizes on her behalf, and Polonsky solves the credibility problem that any such speech would present coming from the mouth of the practiced deceiver Harriet. As Hollywood endings go, this one is very serviceable; the quality of the writing rescues it from the formula Hollywood ending.

But Polonsky also deployed another narrative trick, namely, a second ending. Preceding the Hollywood embrace by only a few scenes, this second ending points to the tale's political moral. Boyd has betrayed her two business partners by selling their interest in the shop to a competitor. Or at least she thinks she has. Although the deal violates their three-way contract, it will make Sam and Teddy wealthy, so Harriet sees no reason that they can possibly object to it. There follows a long, bitter exchange about the relations among people who value commodities more highly than loyalty. Like the ending of Polonsky's *Body and Soul* and *Force of Evil*, the dialogue evokes an almost eerie sense of the situation of the Hollywood screenwriter whom producers routinely tell to shut up in exchange for large sums of cash. The curtain falls on the film's political story with Sam's lines, "We are going bankrupt. We are closing up, even though it means a terrible blow to all our plans and hopes. But not because we hate you. With Teddy and me, when it comes to choosing between people and money, we'll go bankrupt every time. That's all. Have a nice trip."

With all its virtues (especially in the original script), *Wholesale* was written to order, nonetheless. All the time he worked on it, Polonsky had something different in mind, something closer to *Force of Evil* in artistic symmetry. He hoped that Zanuck would repay him for *Wholesale* with a chance to write and direct an A film as different from the standard Hollywood product as *Force of Evil* had been from hundreds of other B films.[15] "Mario and the Magician," unrealized on the screen but marvelous on paper, approaches the ideal, poetic film that Polonsky would call for in his later manifesto on cinema. Only an extraordinary production, in Europe more likely than in the United States, could have made such a script bankable. "Mario" represents, in short, the last burst of the art cinema that had begun to flower under cover of dark (noir) in the vicinity of Hollywood. It would not blossom again until the 1960s, and by then it would be but a pale imitation of its European models.

Thomas Mann's 1929 story is written in the first person as a German intellectual's travel diary. The narrator is vacationing in Italy with his wife, who is a cipher—quite unlike the character in the film script, as we shall presently see. The magician of the title appears only in the final scene, with motivations that can merely be guessed. The discomforts of a disappointing holiday in Torre di Venere dominate most of the story, along with the events around the magician, whom Mann's narrator calls "that dreadful being who seemed to incorporate . . . all the peculiar evilness of the situation."[16] The story is by no means a simple political allegory of the day, but neither was it written in a political vacuum, as Mann admitted two decades later from his exile in Hollywood, where he knew Polonsky casually. Italian fascism and its rising German counterpart, years before Hitler captured power, revived all the worst memories of the "Great War" and inevitably provoked an uneasy sense of potential crisis in Mann's circles.[17]

Polonsky abandoned the travelogue perforce to invent dialogue, which is virtually absent from Mann's work, and to create a dramatic situation with strong sustaining characters—including something like a romance—and give the narrative finale a substantial, explicit meaning. In Polonsky's rendering, summer's end in a resort town and fishing village on Italy's southwest coast recreates the seaside ambiance of the also unpublished "The Discoverers." The beach, the playful children, and the birds overhead produce an otherworldly ambiance that critics have recently come to call a border situation.

But in this setting of Old World cultural continuity and authentic fascists, Polonsky explores the thematic possibilities of a psycho-poetic drama with stronger political undertones than in Mann's original. Polonsky opened by bringing forward and politicizing a minor incident from the story: feeling uncomfortably sandy on the beach, eight-year-old Marie von Hoffman, daughter of a famed German novelist and visitor, has innocently taken off her bathing suit as if she were visiting Norway, where "they all do it." When a bunch of rowdy boys promptly howl at her, she and by extension her father suddenly represent not only a new and unwanted moral daring (as in the story) but a disruption of Italian order under the duce. A man in a bowler hat, not a mere small-town moralist as in the story, becomes a threatening braggart who assures listeners that he marched with Mussolini in the storming of parliament.

The Mario of the title is a handsome young waiter, the lowly son of a municipal clerk. He tries to assist and reassure the girl's mother, Helga von Hoffman, who has long since tired of playing the great man's wife and hungers for her own life. The hotel maid Silvestra, who is herself in love with Mario, tells Helga that he is the kind of fellow parents like, similar to Italy itself in these days, unrebellious on the surface but boiling inside with aspirations that are unfulfillable under present conditions. Italian officials, famed both for their formal courtesy and bureaucratic inefficiency made worse by the assorted privileges allotted to fascists' friends, continue to make matters difficult for the visiting family. But the proprietress of the little inn to which they have moved lifts their prospects. The proprietress is a former helper and intimate of Eleanor Duse, the great Italian actress, who decades earlier had been a sensation in America. In the ubiquitous theatrical atmosphere, the village is about to stage a little annual festival for itself and for its tourists.

Fascinated with the handsome waiter and impressed that he knows the great plays from Sophocles to Ibsen, Helga draws him into her confidence. In typical Polonskyan dialogue, he says, "your husband . . . I hear he's a great man," and she answers, "You think a woman married to a very great man has fulfilled herself? [Besides] He wasn't so famous when I married him."[18] While Mann's protagonist naively pictures himself as interested exclusively in the cultural scene and the growing children, Polonsky's is indifferent. Learning that the family is returning abruptly to Germany, Polonsky's Mario pours out his hopeless love for her. This serves the screenwriter's impulse to explore the social contradictions between "civilized" Western Europe and the poor (but spiritually rich) South, as well as the world's disappointments for two potential lovers.

Real magic takes place in the carnival performance, a bit condensed from the story's lengthy passages but true to their form, with one significant switch. After bedazzling the audience through all sorts of trickery, Cippola, the hideous old magician who as in Mann refers to friends high in Mussolini's favor, first unites Mario and Helga in a sort of mutual trance. Then, as in the story, Cippola hypnotically compels Mario to see him as Silvestra: "this strange man, through sheer power of personality . . . becomes more and more a caricature of Silvestra . . . despite his face, his age, his sex."[19] The magician then suddenly and cruelly reveals himself to Mario. Mario pulls a pistol out of his jacket. (In Polonsky's version, von Hoffman has earlier pressed him to take the pistol and keep it for him.) Without ceremony, Mario shoots the magician dead, as in Mann's original. But Polonsky's magician dies almost in gratitude, released from his own cruel inner drama. The weight of modern history shapes a new and terrifying artistic terrain. The play within the film play ends with Mario on the stage alone, a survivor who is not really a survivor at all.

In the film script's political background, blackshirted fascist special police have appeared earlier, at just the moment when von Hoffman insists that the waiter take his gun. They are pursuing an elusive rebel hiding in the hills above the resort. Metaphorically, Mario, with his yearnings to be free, is that rebel; the magician Cipolla, who seduced an audience (that is, a nation) with tricks, is the buffoon Mussolini; like the dead Mussolini in 1943, the dead Cipolla is seen hanging upside down, albeit on the stage.

Polonsky subsequently said from time to time that he had wanted to make a film like those of famed French director Jean Vigo. Indeed, until Vigo's 1933 *Zero de Conduite* finally appeared in American theaters in 1947, Polonsky had hardly considered film to be an art form. Panned by and probably incomprehensible to United States film critics of the time, *Zero de Conduite* was for Polonsky "a picture about a revolution and [Vigo is] telling that story using the kids symbolically," proof that "most pictures are *incidentally* significant."[20] *Zero* was, however, more experiment than film, a succession of images of a wild classroom rebellion against tyrannical school officials. If *Force of Evil* partially realized the artistic possibility in Vigo's film, the ideal production of "Mario and the Magician" would demand the realization of a literally surrealist dream.

The moment was wrong. Polonsky later wondered a bit that he had not pursued the experimental films being made in New York later in the 1950s, but as he said, going from a career (however brief) in major studio productions to one in ten-thousand-dollar experiments did not appeal to him. The door had closed on Polonsky the auteur, and it would remain closed for a long time.

2

Polonsky made a similar artistic decision about the novel he finished in Cannes, straining at the limits of a standard narrative but staying within them, nonetheless. The result is *The World Above,* published in 1951 by Little, Brown, a highly ambitious work that traces the evolving awareness of its lower-class-born protagonist through sometimes jarringly episodic life stages. Polonsky would, no doubt, quite accurately add that these episodes were no more jarring than the real-life conditions of millions of Americans during the 1930s–40s.[21] His leading character evolves from an avid young scientist in the first pages to a lover and paramour, then a distinguished psychologist, a military officer, and a near-existentialist. In the end he has become both a courageous opponent of McCarthyism and a man capable of loving a woman whose personal history and motivations are no less complex than his own.

The occasional difficulty of the plot, however, does not demand the reader's close attention so much as the intricacy with which the character development mirrors historical changes. *The World Above* is a conventional novel, an *Erziehungsroman* in the tradition of Zola, with Goethe's classical humanism implicit. Thus, Polonsky quickly places Dr. Carl Myers in a decisive triangle including his friend David (who has well-concealed but deep homosexual feelings) and his lover, Sandy (David's future wife). Class and political circumstance mark their personal boundaries. David, the scion of a family fortune, is a vigorous New Dealer. Without knowing it, he wants the power and celebrity natural to his social class far more than he wants dramatic social change. That weakness was inherent in the New Deal, but in the novel it becomes evident only as the bureaucracy of economic reconstruction is transformed into a bureaucracy of military victory and postwar hegemony over a suffering world. In the middle, Sandy is a casualty of the limits on the contemporary middle-class woman.

The World Above is scarcely less about the loyalties and tensions of family. Carl has no wish to return home but finally has no choice. His brother, Bill, a CIO organizer assigned to Westchester County, was doubtless drawn from Polonsky's own experience there with real-life anonymous heroes. Carl's sister-in-law Juley is a woman whose pregnancy and life difficulties make her appear both slovenly and contrite. Through Carl's eyes she is at first repellent and later a blowzy war worker whose looks and behavior epitomize the deterioration of home-front life. Struggling with an infant and then a growing child, Juley is in fact more intelligent and more courageous than Carl can imagine for a long stretch of the novel. Carl's dramatically changing perception of Sandy and Juley only gradually reveals what any experienced Polonsky-watcher might have guessed: this is a deeply psychological feminist novel.

Modern feminism and its theories remained decades in the future. But thinkers as diverse as Abraham Maslow, Herbert Marcuse, and Hollywood psychiatrist Judd Marmor were quietly beginning to assemble arguments for a radical approach to psychological development. (Not so incidentally, Marmor was the son of a distinguished Yiddish Communist journalist and a close friend of Albert Maltz.)[22] Polonsky's own determined artistic escape from what he would call the "paralysis of naturalism" led him through a different order of knowledge and insight than either Freud or Marx offered, albeit one owing considerably to both.

After Carl abandons Sandy to study in Europe, she quickly marries David and then grows bored. When Carl returns to take up residency at a distinguished Manhattan research facility, Sandy begins an extramarital affair with him. Carl leaps into the adultery, significantly after a dismal visit to his mother's flat in the old Lower East Side reminds him of what he has apparently escaped. The romance escalates as he moves on to a state psychiatric hospital in a picturesque village up the Hudson from New York. There, his chief patient is a stricken little girl, apparently mute and hopeless despite drugs, shock therapy, and above all, endless hours of his close attention. An insulin-induced coma prompts a surrealistic explosion of speech, if not communication, "a running flow of words, an effervescence of phrases, of run-on sentences, a million poems in one."[23] The truth which she cannot articulate in this overflow is sexual. Hers is the fate of the passive child who, with puberty, regresses and torments herself, unable either to return to childhood or to advance to anything like adult normality. Perhaps this is Carl's and Sandy's metaphorical fate as modern intellectuals whose sexual activity resolves nothing.

Carl is brought suddenly back to one of life's realities when he stumbles into the middle of a strike. Mistaken for his class-conscious unionist brother Bill, Carl is beaten bloody and left for dead in Bill's cabin. Years pass until separate worlds connect again in wartime, bringing another clarification. By now David is a brilliant diplomat facing "his fate, as his destiny, his great opportunity," and Carl is a major in a London-based air force hospital that is under attack.[24] When the old friends accidentally meet, with V-Bombs whistling overhead, the gravity of David's homosexual feelings becomes marginally clearer—perhaps as much as possible when treated sympathetically in 1951. Freed of his various misconceptions about social class, sex, and friendship, Carl now must work out his own fate. With uncharacteristic optimism, Polonsky allows Carl to begin straightening out his life after the war despite all the weight of the past.

For Polonsky, brother Bill's death in combat buries the great radical hopes of the 1930s. He dramatizes this beautifully in a dialogue between Carl and Bill's former union comrade, Sam. When Carl learns to his dismay that Sam is living in Juley's apartment and is obviously her current lover, he is outraged at first but then becomes grudgingly sympathetic as Sam describes the widespread disappointment facing the union movement in a postwar world: "Those days are gone. We've flopped . . . and now it's different." That proletarian possibility has vanished. Juley, however, with all her limitations and with a son to raise, offers a future, nonetheless. Articulating the enduring element of 1930s unionizing among its participants, Sam, the lover who is about to be discarded, nevertheless tells Carl, "You belonged to us."[25]

Most contemporary reviewers considered *The World Above* a realist epic. A *New York Times* writer thus compared it to Sinclair Lewis's *Arrowsmith,* in "a doctor's search for a working philosophy that will reconcile his strictly scientific principles with a broadly humanistic faith." From a broader perspective, this characterization of the novel, like characterizations of Polonsky's films via plot analysis, is an injustice to the qualities of his writing. A *Philadelphia Inquirer* review that praised the book more generically as "fascinatingly rich in psychiatric insights and romantic interest" may more accurately point out the central reason for later generations of readers' enduring interest of the novel.[26]

The World Above might indeed best be described as a tale written from the inside out, its storytelling notably distinct from the artful play on genre in Polonsky's films. As a novel, it is the work of a mind emancipated by its own struggle to create, and its structure is a record of that struggle. It has in common with Polonsky's films the marked use of language, liberated here from the poetry of film to a poetry that aims to do nothing less than describe the political structure of social reality. One remarkable passage follows Carl's realization that he has been offered a bribe of sorts to leave for Europe so that Dave can marry Sandy:

> He wanted money. . . . It was a money civilization and a money time and even science was helpless without money . . . and one could not even invent a theory of the universe without money to prove it. It seemed that all history, the death of the martyrs and the victories of conquerors, the pain and ecstasy of revolution, the repressions, tortures, pains and joys, were nothing but the slow accumulation of money, the creation of the horde which now like a magnetic mountain raised itself in the world; and each thought of man, each dream of nobility that launched itself upon the seas of life, was slowly and then swiftly attracted to this mountain where the thought was wrecked and the dream drowned while the money was attracted to the mountain and there added its tragedy to the mass. . . . He got off the bed and straightened his clothes, already thinking of who could help him.[27]

After Carl emerges from the war with a successful record and extensive experience practicing in a psychiatric hospital, the true novel of ideas begins to emerge. Carl travels from California to New York to deliver his groundbreaking new theory of the origins of mental illness. Derived from his study of the broken veterans of the Second World War, the paper is entitled "A General Theory of Causation." To a lecture hall full of the "pink faces and plump bodies" of established practitioners, he begins with his view of normative psychology:

> In striving to organize a system of cure, we were forced by our investigations to discover an obvious secret. We found out that in investigating the many mental ills we were in fact observing what constitutes social reality. If biology is the science of man as a going physical system in relation to himself and the world about him, psychology is the science of man as a going system in terms of the mechanism and content of his social inheritance. When psychology is less than this it is biology, and when it is more it is history. Since the social inheritance is not the past but what the present is becoming because of the past, we found ourselves attempting to assign the causes of psychic malformation to the specific societies from which our patients came. . . . We were forced to assert the hypothesis that no science of psychology can be founded on what man is, but only on what man is becoming, the general rule being that he is never becoming anything but what society itself is becoming.

As the audience's interest turns into a flurry of shared anxiety, Carl plunges deeper:

> If mental illness is the result, the direct result of the influence of society on the individual, if we accepted this, then we were faced with a dilemma. We could strive to readapt our patient to the society that had made him ill, and this is

certainly possible, if not quite a cure; or we could accept the notion that society would have to be altered if we wanted to cure the patient, and that the patient himself would have to participate in the understanding and alteration of those societal influences which had damaged him.

Then, logically,

> Only when man was looked at not as mind reflecting or inventing the universe, but as an animal in conflict with it, an animal whose consciousness was part of his struggle with society and nature, part of his relation to it, part of his gift to it, in short, only when the mind was not removed from existence but discovered to be its creature, only then was a rational science of psychology actually possible.[28]

In a society where most people are not judged mentally ill, society may still be sick. At least to the critics of postwar American society, this was evident in the reality that a lack of unemployment did not mean the social conditions that caused unemployment had been abolished. A real crisis was still only around the corner, for "when the contradictions and strains occur all together as so often happens, then the organism falters, begins throwing up defenses, finds refuge in symptoms, and becomes mentally ill." Mental illness is not merely a collapse, rather a "form of action, a form of will, a form of struggle, but at the level of accepted social defeat."[29]

Twenty years before R. D. Laing but with none of Laing's cribbing from Eastern religious psychology, Polonsky's characters had articulated social theories that anticipated in many ways the most fluid New Left thinking. For decades, Polonsky told an interviewer, the most determined inquiries about the theory expressed in *The World Above* came from Harvard medical students. The fictional Myers is ostracized for daring to utter the theory in public. By the closing pages, he is hauled before a congressional committee on a manufactured charge. After lengthy testimony, "Carl repeated [to the committee] the statements he had made in New York."

> "You dare to say they are true?" Vaughan [the committee chairman] shouted.
> "Listen to yourself and you can be certain they are true," Carl replied.
> "You are in contempt," Vaughan yelled, and he shook with fury and banged the rostrum.
> "I would indeed be contemptible," Carl told him, "if I did not assert my rights against the gavel and the miseries of the time."[30]

Polonsky had inescapably drawn this form of questioning from the Rapp-Coudert hearings and the early HUAC ventures into Hollywood.

But he insisted that he was not telling the reader what to do, in these circumstances or any others: "I do not write stories which attempt to sell a certain morality to the audience. . . . If we have certain concerns about our nature in [the world], we're going to pay a price for that."[31] Or again, "with a little opportunism the characters I created could have adapted and survived. And so, with a little opportunism, we all can." Speaking for himself alone, "compromise never occurred to me as a possible action. . . . It never even occurred to me as a possibility . . . [in] the same way that it doesn't occur to me to hit someone on the head and take his purse."[32] The alternative, redemption, obviously is possible, too, but it is never painless or free. The fictional Dr. Carl Myers wins it for himself, in his profession and in his relationship with Juley now as husband, lover, and stepfather of her child. In postwar America everyone has that option—or responsibility.

Author Polonsky himself avoided moral compromise but needed to make a living. A few got along well (albeit at fees far lower than before) on major scripts of their own devising. Extraordinarily, Albert Maltz provided the script for *The Robe* (1953), Hollywood's most expensive film to date and the template for a decade of high-profile biblical drama. Dalton Trumbo used Ian MacClellan Hunter as his front for the much-admired *Roman Holiday* (1953); when Hunter himself went under the ban, Trumbo quickly delivered *Carnival Story* (1954) under a pseudonym. (In another odd twist a few years earlier, Maltz had written the famed antiwestern *Broken Arrow* under the name of future friendly witness Michael Blankfort.) Hugo Butler's wife, Jean, recuperated her maiden name of Rouverol to script the Joan Crawford vehicle *Autumn Leaves* (1953), her second screen credit. *Executive Suite* (1953), *Ivanhoe* (1953), and *Friendly Persuasion* (1956) were but a few of the larger films whose scripts were rumored or established to have been written in whole or in part by blacklistees. As the cold war began to thaw, *The Brave One* (1956) and *The Defiant Ones* (1958) delivered Oscars to scripters who could not openly share their triumphs. From abroad, *Bridge on the River Kwai* (1957), *Rififi* (1954), and a handful of forgotten films written by Hugo Butler, Ring Lardner, Jr., Donald Ogden Stewart, or Jack Berry and directed by Jules Dassin, Joseph Losey, or Cy Enfield occasionally showed up on American screens. Back at home and close to the bottom of the B listings, some Disney features, forgettable horror films, underrated noirs, Second World War dramas, and a notable western or two also appeared under noms de plume.[33] The real years of renewal, such as they were, lay well ahead.

On his return to Hollywood, Polonsky faced up to the blacklist's reality by working under the table, quickly penning the first rewrite of some fifteen film scripts he would handle under an assortment of names. He cautiously admitted that "major Hollywood directors were involved in some" of the projects, and that "one or two are not bad." Did he merely patch them up or rewrite afresh; did he write noirs, westerns, or some of the social drama of the time? He adamantly refused to say, insisting that only those people whose names he used (with their kind permission and participation) could properly reveal that information—and at the time of this discussion nearly all of them were dead. Instead, he offered the usual jest, "Let us [blacklisted] writers make our usual claims that we wrote all the good pictures and everyone else wrote all the bad ones. In that way the guerilla warfare continues." As if that admission alone would explain the larger scene and its meaning, he would never uncloak that part of the past.[34]

Polonsky redevoted his higher art and his political art to literature. His notebooks reveal that through the early 1950s he was working on the novel about his early childhood that eventually became *Zenia's Way* and was finally published in 1980. He also had at hand a more immediate task. A few of the other blacklisted screenwriters delivered book-length analytic defenses (Gordon Kahn, *The Hollywood Inquisition*) or pamphlets with burning polemics (Dalton Trumbo, *The Time of the Toad*). Polonsky chose the literary medium for *A Season of Fear,* published at last in 1956 by Cameron Associates. The tiny firm's director, Angus Cameron, was a former Little, Brown editor who reputedly had been fired after Arthur Schlesinger, Jr., a prominent antagonist of the blacklistees, complained to the company about its employing a "subversive" editor.[35] Ironically, *A Season of Fear* has been Polonsky's most widely-read novel, thanks to European editions. Within the United States, the book hardly received a review and died without ceremony.

Polonsky happened to have a friend in the Los Angeles Water Department who was facing the blacklist, and that seemed a perfect setting for the Kafkaesque blacklist process. *A Season of Fear*'s protagonist, a likable if by no means strong-minded Charles Hare, is as intensely aware as later *Chinatown* detective Jake Gittes of the role of water control in Los Angeles life. Indeed, Hare and his immediate boss had planned the aqueduct to the Colorado River, assuring the city of water (at the expense of previously widespread aquatic, avian, and other natural life in the newly deprived valleys). If the folks in the water and power building were anything, they were dedicated materialists who "knew it all from the first drip of melting ice to the mapped millions of flowering arterial capillaries that lay in waste beneath the city." As for so many other typically American and Polonskyan males, that order of knowledge is enough for Hare. He never questions it, never draws social conclusions, likes his job as only a devoted technician can. Meanwhile in his personal life he "fell in love, married young, did my job and voted."[36] He asks for nothing more.

But all is not well these days. One staffer at water and power refuses to sign the loyalty oath required of all employees. Meanwhile, Hare's late brother-in-law, an idealist who died in the Second World War, becomes the curious subject of a postmortem investigation. Much as in Polonsky's unproduced forties play, "Out of This World," the inquiry proceeds across intellectual circles with detectives trying to search bookshelves for suspicious titles.

The FBI is actually less interested in Hare's books than in those of his casual friend Professor Strom. As an antifascist refugee the professor is naturally viewed with suspicion. "[A]mong the names of some of the authors" in his possession, the professor confesses ironically, "are Karl Marx and Lenin. . . . I even read Russian and do." Like his fellow German refugees in those days, Strom imagines that he can still smell "the odor of so many millions burned to death on the outskirts of pleasant German towns," and he wonders what particular hell American officials have in mind for their intended victims. He has ceased to want anything but to survive, yet even that is too much to ask in this age.

Unlike Carl in *The World Above,* or Charley in *Body and Soul,* Hare never musters the strength to take a position. He cannot bring himself to sign a petition defending his colleague who refuses the loyalty oath. He ransacks his brother-in-law's belongings and prepares to burn them, growing more uneasy amid the banished ideas, which are not even Marxist but simply reflect the activist 1930s. Reading the titles with a growing dread about his actions' implications, he observes how

each time he lifted a book from this well of a trunk he knew that it would contain upon its pages the hard words that screamed from the headlines of the newspapers, the fiery words of the present wars, the maddening words of revolution and class, the horrible fantastic words that now agitated the country. And besides the words were the names, the German, French and Russian names which had alarmed the continents for ten generations, called up armies, the most extreme passions, and announced for everyone to hear: Life and Death.

The words in these heavy, these too solid books, jumped alive from any page. There was not a line of them free of them. . . . The reaction he had to

the words was not one of knowledge or experience, of interest, even of curios-
ity. His relation to them was the relation he had with the tone of his environment, of the endless days in which these words had become atomic warheads,
diplomacy, secret weapons, the threats and counterthreats, the investigations,
imprisonments, speeches, denunciations, the informing, the vengeance, the
headlines of daily life, iterated and reiterated in radio, television, the press, in
rumors, speeches and election campaigns so that in the end the most isolated
and rarefied mathematician dwelling among its essences, the most amusing
comedian, the mildest schoolteacher as well as union men, respectable women
and respectable business men could be consigned to the machine of public
opinion and there pulped into waste because of these words. The words took
on a reality such as God and the Devil had once had . . . [37]

Over this political-psychological drama, Polonsky layered what can
only be called the California Novel. Detective writers like Raymond
Chandler and Ross Macdonald had probed the corruption beneath the
surface of sun-bleached California prosperity, and heterodox young
Berkeley radical Philip K. Dick produced existential novels with similar
settings and political moods before turning full-time to science fiction.
Polonsky's California was the freeways, the heat, and the dull indifference of the middle class to anything but its suburban privileges, which
now included beach parties and semicasual adultery. Drinking heavily,
Hare drifts into the arms of his neighbor Pickett's wife. Although she
clearly desires him, she feels like lead in his arms, almost literally dragging him down. Eventually, against all his better judgments and his
enormous fondness for his own wife, he has a one-time sexual liaison
with the woman. Her passivity, however, signals that she is no femme
fatale but just one more bored Californian.

Still later Hare learns that Pickett, the husband he has betrayed, is
himself a typical master-betrayer of the day: an ex-radical who names his
former friends and protégés without the least compunction. In fact, he
takes mischievous pleasure in having earlier defied the system and now
making a cleverly timed career move to reconcile with it.[38] Near the
book's climax, Hare finds himself swimming in the ocean, too far from
shore. Given a chance to save the drowning Pickett, he refuses to take the
risk. In the novel's last moment he is at home with his wife, realizing that
in all sorts of ways he has failed her. She generously offers a compromised consciousness, the forgetfulness of history in which "enemies
began to converse and the profoundest crimes lost their horror and the
greatest idealism its martyrdom . . . the common sense of survival."
Unpolitical, not even committed, like the frightened rabbit of his name,
Hare is a coward, but he realizes his unpolitical, uncommitted existence

is not enough. To "force his thoughts to explain his memories" is his obligation and his cross to bear. In the last sentence, he waits "in an unfathomable silence" that the McCarthy era knows so well, and tries to start his life again.[39]

Helen Davis, the only critic of note to review *A Season of Fear*, aptly suggested that the melodrama of the final scenes stemmed inevitably from Polonsky's conscious creation of a limited, weak protagonist. Davis further pointed out that Polonsky fell short in his attempt to effect a supreme symbolic importance in Hare's words and actions.[40] Those failings reflect the difficulty of the blacklist-era novel, which often depicts a cardboard hero resisting the national drift to the Right, rather than a complex contemporary figure torn in many directions simultaneously. Those noninformers who had abandoned faith in Russia and, before that, the uprising of the proletariat, had to cling to their moral stance because they had lost so much else. As Walter Bernstein has said, informing was not finally a political issue at all, but rather a personal, moral choice.

Still, *A Season of Fear* is a definite political and literary statement reflecting Polonsky's enduring commitments. Although Hollywood had provided the venue for his best creative efforts of the period, it no longer offered any place for his family. With the blacklist's ugly publicity and atmosphere all around him, the setting had become uncomfortable even for working under the table. Thus, in 1953 he abandoned a town that, as he said, considered him almost a criminal and returned to New York, where nearly everyone was a criminal of one kind or another and no one thought the worse of them for it.

Almost on his arrival in New York, Polonsky set out on a political-literary attempt to rally the handful of left-wing intellectuals who were neither silenced, reduced to praising American society with faint damnations, nor relegated to the increasingly isolated and constrained world of intellectual-cultural communism. He still had no taste for the regular Communist cultural magazines. Party leaders had torpedoed *Mainstream*, a magazine of fiction and prose launched by independent-minded left-wing intellectuals at the fringes of the Popular Front after the Second World War, because it detracted from the *New Masses* (itself badly reduced from its 1930s glory days). The creative cultural milieu shrank further when the *New Masses* became *Masses and Mainstream*, hard-line in its tone and political bearing.

But some of New York's writers, artists, and critics in the arts, sciences, and professions tried to reestablish a semi-independent Marxist voice on culture. *The Contemporary Reader*, appearing in 1953 and lasting only four issues, claimed the "warm humane tradition of Whitman and Mark Twain, of Artemus Ward and Mr. Dooley, of Carl Sandburg, of Negro and working class folk song," otherwise displaced by aestheticism or brutal pseudo-realism. Neither the ivory tower nor the old left-wing obsession with content would do: "Through the mastery of technique alone can theme become clear and convincing." It was time to begin again—or so they hoped.[41]

Polonsky, Millard Lampell (a member of the original Almanac Singers, later a talented screenwriter, and by 1951 a fellow blacklistee), other blacklisted screenwriters Wilma Shore, Ring Lardner, Jr., Lew Amster, and Lester Cole, blacklisted actor Howard Da Silva, and a group of lesser intellectuals gathered to solicit and edit material. The appearance of younger African-American writers destined for fame, including Paule Marshall, Julian Mayfield, and novelist John Killens, was the journal's other most notable feature. White writers intensified their own efforts to encompass African-American themes, as in "Potiphar's House," a play by Lester Cole and former *Daily Worker* editor Alan Max in the first issue. Polonsky serialized two chapters of *A Season of Fear* there, reprinted a film essay from the *Hollywood Quarterly*, and contributed "A Slight Disturbance," his only published original short story after the commercial yarns of the 1940s.[42]

"A Slight Disturbance," which linked the themes of the "ad game" and the Korean War, stands for the various forbidden topics of the day among liberal or conservative fiction-writers. One Myra Maitland, a good-looking and fast-rising ad writer, is invited by her boss and his wife to meet industry powerhouse Arnold White. White is a philosopher of the times, a man who enjoys having intelligent women in the office to help work out the next year's campaigns and the larger logic behind them. Society has reached the stage, he observes, where institutional advertising has become an important source of public education. Like other sources of "news," the "social invention of the social war" takes place alongside military conflicts. Myra more than agrees: she has thought this through and concluded with the sweeping intellectualism of an Arthur Schlesinger, Jr., that she has no opposition on fiscal or any other grounds to a large, permanent standing army and huge defense budgets:

> Remember what Hemingway did with [bullfighting]. He gave it the shock of death without nastiness. He mentioned the nastiness, but he classified it as unimportant and necessary. They made death pure, the killer and the killed. In the last war, our mood was . . . wait til we get away from all that nastiness

and come home to all this easy, rich fullness. From now on our mood is: let us welcome the nastiness. It's inevitable because we are going ahead and there is a just price to be paid. *Not,* let's get the job done. *But,* let us dedicate ourselves to the job.[43]

The neatness of Myra's logic is undone by the appearance of a soldier, the nephew of Myra's boss. Just returned from a year in a North Korean prison camp, he has been awarded an impressive medal because he had been reported dead. His hand is twisted into a claw, the result of an infection from an enemy soldier's bite in some no-man's land between armies. His story seems to exhaust the listeners quickly, despite their all-American cheerfulness, but he looks as if he wants to escape again, and says resignedly, "America is such a lonely place."[44] For the story's ad-people life will go on, irrespective of society's plunge into a new barbarism, no doubt because other than the occasional soldier everyone in America is shielded from the actual gore and conscience-wrenching realities of running a world empire.

For all its inherent interest, *The Contemporary Reader* was a straw in the wind. While the CIA-backed *Encounter* featured the prestigious and fast-rising intellectuals of the cold-war liberal (and future neoconservative) generation in prestigious universities, *The Contemporary Reader's* back pages were covered with ads from blacklisted and out-of-work intellectuals offering piano and writing lessons.

Polonsky did all he could to sustain the lives and work of his heavily attacked friends. When the witch hunt spread to the radio industry in the middle 1950s, he informally donned his lawyer's hat to coach prospective victims on how to confront their respective congressional committees. According to Madeline Gilford (a character actress in radio from her childhood until the McCarthy era and the wife of blacklisted comedian Jack Gilford), no one could have devoted more energy than Polonsky to the often lost cause, sometimes winning small victories by chipping away at the blacklisters' legitimacy.[45]

In 1956, Khrushchev rocked the Communist world during the Soviet Twentieth Congress with his revelations and admissions of Stalin's massive wrongdoings. When the reputedly reformed regime nevertheless sent tanks to crush the workers' uprising in Hungary, those American intellectuals still remaining in the Communist milieu went into shock. A move to replace the American CP's Russophilic and undemocratic leadership initially looked likely to succeed. Within the greatly diminished organization the reform faction had the numbers, but the hard-liners outlasted them, as the majority of ordinary members simply quit. Still, the up-

heaval prompted an unprecedented openness of dialogue during 1956–
57. As *Masses and Mainstream* floundered, it suddenly welcomed het-
erodoxy in Polonsky's pseudonymous essay on a most revealing subject,
the French left wing's intellectual crisis.[46]

"The Troubled Mandarins," by Timon, took as its formal subject
matter Simone de Beauvoir's novel *The Mandarins*.[47] But Polonsky's
real subject was the Communist intellectuals who had so proudly dis-
tanced themselves from the psychic dilemmas of previous generations,
the "agonies of vacillation"—until the "fresh wind from Moscow"
proved "that despair was everybody's business. And," Polonsky added
pungently, "it was about time. There may be two systems but there is
only one humanity."[48]

Polonsky believed de Beauvoir had marvelously detailed the particu-
lars of the French intellectual Left. The middle-class idealists of the 1940s
knew little about the painful struggles of the Depression and the "difference between the imaginary comprehension of man's fate and the dirty
job of killing." The Occupation gave them purpose; its end deprived
them of that purpose and left them on their own again. Soon, however,
Marxists everywhere would have to answer the questions facing French
intellectuals: could there be a Left independent of communist parties;
were intellectual freedom and commitment compatible; could one act
morally in literature and politics simultaneously; and perhaps most
important to Polonsky at the moment, was "the Western European tradition of humanism basic to socialism or irrelevant to it?"[49]

Even here, amid the most political of musings, the conflict of the sexes
drew Polonsky to de Beauvoir as an important artist of the age. Her
female protagonist (a fictionalized characterization of herself) has an
affair with a Chicago novelist (Nelson Algren), during which she repli-
cates her husband's (Sartre's) dilemma: "She finds it impossible to be possessed or to possess and be independent at the same time." Authentic
happiness, according to de Beauvoir if not to Polonsky, comes not from
the possessing (since we can only possess ourselves) but from "the facing
of death, the ultimate nothing, and the liberation that comes from its
recognition," which is no more than "the state of one's own consciousness . . . hovering over extinction."[50]

Could this be true? Communist intellectuals (and not only intellectuals) had "sacrificed their fortunes, their happiness and their lives" for the
idea of man's "significant social destiny." They had tied their fate to the
belief that the abolition of private property would "liberate the full
potential" of the citizen. If this formulation had fundamental problems,

they had not been and evidently could not be discussed openly, freely, and democratically in Communist circles. Corollary to this philosophical problem was the subordination of the individual conscience, even in the West, to the party's purpose. This subordination had brought a mini-tyranny on the Left mirroring the maximum tyranny from the Right that cold-war liberals heartily supported. The Maltz controversy (savaging the screenwriter, as Polonsky noted, in *New Masses*, "the forerunner of this very magazine") inside the Commuist Party, ending in Maltz's "recantment and personal abasement at the hands of his friends," had foreshadowed McCarthyism's "abasement of left-wing intellectuals by their enemies."[51] Some if not all readers would have heard of Polonsky's vote a decade earlier for the quavering Maltz and against party-imposed discipline. Now he was throwing that same wrong-headed attitude back in the face of the intellectual party faithful.

All of these tyrannies might be attributed to the terrors of world events, beginning with the First World War. But the tyranny on the Left had grown also from a fundamentally mistaken view of the artist that took shape during the Bolshevik movement's struggle to survive under barbarous conditions:

> The role of the artist is not to worry about the political sensitivities of people, but to stimulate them into new areas of experiment and expression. A real work of art is a very great discovery made through a complex process of creation. It is a process in which one kind of reality is transformed into another and so the product always contains more than the artist can conceive. . . . [A] work of art, like a fundamental discovery, is [therefore] not really about those things with which practical politics, tactical lines, etc., [are] concerned. The tendency in social commitment is uniformity, as in the United States and in the Soviet Union. Yet if people are offended because their cherished illusions are shaken or their covering faith is outraged, well, that is the very point of literature, that is the very notion of a truthful life, to be shaken up, to be disturbed, to be awakened, even from the dream of the American or Soviet Paradise . . . [52]

Of course, Polonsky had followed this creed in his own work, at least in regard to his own main subject, American life. But he had learned new lessons in applying it, thanks to his cryptic work as one of television's most important (if also most thoroughly disguised) writers.

4

It came about in a curious way. By 1953, fellow blacklisted scriptwriter Walter Bernstein, destined to be known best for scripting such films as

Fail-Safe (1964), *The Front* (1976), and *The Molly Maguires* (1970), provided Polonsky a way to make a good living and enjoy himself enormously: writing for television under the table.

After attending Dartmouth, writing for the *New Yorker,* and serving as a correspondent for *Stars and Stripes* during the Second World War, Bernstein had a brief film career working with Robert Rossen and others in the late 1940s. Following his six months in Hollywood, all he had to show for his efforts was his script for *Kiss the Blood off My Hands,* a noir that Leonardo Bercovici rewrote for Kirk Douglas. But Bernstein had important New York connections, above all his close friend Martin Ritt, who was directing live television at that time and was about to be blacklisted as an actor but not as a director. Bernstein had also bravely helped organize an ad campaign in the *New York Times* against the blacklist. For a time he even published a newsletter covering the witch hunt in ways that no existing newspaper or magazine dared. For those crimes alone, Bernstein would have been unwelcome in Hollywood for the duration.[53]

Meanwhile, Martin Ritt had gone on from *The Somerset Maugham Theater* (1950–51) to the more enduring *Danger* (1951–55), directed by Yul Brynner. Bernstein went along, writing under his own name and pseudonyms. When Ritt and Brynner returned to the theater, Sidney Lumet and Charles Russell filled their slots on *Danger.* Lumet, a child actor in the Yiddish theater of the 1930s, was more than familiar with the Left and more than a little sympathetic, even if he had remained just distant enough to escape the blacklisters' hands. Russell, a shy man with no political history but a dedicated liberal in his own way, would work still more closely with Bernstein and his comrades through the depth of McCarthyism. In his memoir, *Inside Out,* Bernstein recalls the hair-raisingly hilarious incidents that provided some of the material for *The Front:* executives praising him while insulting his nom de plume; finding and (even harder) keeping fronts, people who would allow him to use their names; and dodging sponsors and advertising agencies who pressed the blacklist on reluctant network executives. Happily, Bernstein experienced this angst for Polonsky, who had the comparatively easy task of doing the work so cleverly that left-wing bias would be undetectable even while he performed the script acrobatics required to drive home political points and create real art—within television's limits—for audiences much bigger and more diverse than had ever seen his films.[54]

A handful of other writers, including Hunter, Robert Lees, Paul Jarrico, Adrian Scott, Ring Lardner, Jr., Frank Tarloff, and Al Levitt (joined by his wife, Helen, formerly an assistant to John Garfield), found their way into television as well. For the most part, they worked behind fronts in sitcoms and family shows until 1960, when the doors began again to open slightly.[55]

Bernstein and Polonsky, who did not know each other before the early 1950s, had a go-between in a mutual Hollywood comrade and pal, Arnold Manoff. The very writer who had turned over the Enterprise Studios prize-fight project to Polonsky when his own movie career skidded to a halt, Manoff came back to New York with a 1950 play, *All You Need Is One Good Break*. During the play's successful road production and while preparing for Broadway, Manoff met and soon married Lee Grant, the young actress who had received an Oscar nomination for her supporting role as an Italian-American teenage shoplifter in *Detective Story* (1950). Otherwise, *One Good Break* was a colossal disappointment, bombed by the Broadway critics and quickly closed. Brilliant and charming, a talented poet who had spent some of the Depression recording children's games for the Works Progress Administration, Manoff also had been blacklisted by this time and was looking for work. He had the inspired vision to suggest Polonsky as the third member of a possible writing team.[56]

Charles Russell willingly took them on for *Danger,* and the three writers quickly became close personal friends—within limits. Polonsky was happily married, devoted to his family, and uninterested in the stag life of prizefights and horse-race handicapping that gave Manoff and Bernstein (sometimes joined by Martin Ritt) a much-needed emotional outlet. Manoff suggested that if anyone found work but needed help with a script, another member would always assist, and if anyone got excess work, he could offer it to the group and whoever needed the assignment most would take it.

For all too obvious reasons, *Danger*'s most familiar theme was betrayal and alienation. Polonsky's script for "Border Incident" (broadcast in April 1952) was a typical treatment of these themes in a story about Americans abroad. Magazine journalist and former war correspondent Hank Jefferson is a Gary Cooper–abroad type. Ruggedly handsome but socially untutored, he prefers mountains and goats to cities and girls (much to the disappointment of an embassy secretary named Renee) and goes off to the Alps for a holiday. There, a stranger slugs him unconscious. The stranger wakes Hank later and questions him about his identity, which he plans to assume. Like Hank, the man is a native Californian stationed in Europe. Wrongly accused of a wartime killing in a barroom brawl, he escaped with his future wife to fight behind the lines with the Partisans rather than returning to his unit and military (in)justice. Now the woman holds a gun on Hank, and her pleas as he disarms her must have been eerily familiar to those who knew the fate of the exiled blacklistees:

> Help us . . . help him. I know he will not be happy anywhere. He thinks of nothing but home . . . to go home. He talks of nothing but mountains . . . and high places there . . . and wooden houses and rivers like giants . . . of cities like the old cities with towers . . . of strange and incredible things that are home . . .

When Hank asks her if he does not blame America for his fate, she answers, "How can you blame that place that is home[?]" Eventually, Hank helps the stranger cross illegally into Italy, but the man ultimately returns Hank's passport by mail, having chosen finally to go back "to face it." Though Hank's reasons are less certain, he seemingly has avoided returning to America in order not to need anyone. Now, he too resolves to go home.[57] Within the limits of a twenty-four-minute drama, Polonsky had offered considerable food for thought by recalling moments that much of cold-war America wanted forgotten.

The writing trio snagged other work here and there, but the real thing landed in their laps in late 1952 when CBS selected Charles Russell (and his boss, William Dozier, who had in earlier years sworn to bar Polonsky from Hollywood forever) for the television version of a recent radio standard, *You Are There*.[58] Using newsmen in modern dress to interview historical personalities in their own environments, with Walter Cronkite as the final commentator, the show had a unique twist, not quite realistic but not quite campy, either.

Resolving not simply to follow the radio show's familiar facts-and-patriotism frame, Bernstein, Manoff, and Polonsky pitched something different. Their key insight and contribution was to incorporate the plot device of conflict, meticulously worked out in twenty-four minutes of air time. By choosing subjects of contemporary interest, they went straight (and, seen in a certain way, almost exclusively) to the great subject of their own experience: the continuing history of free speech (or free artistic expression) and those who sought to suppress it. Polonsky, not only older than the other two writers but possessed of the most stature as an artist, crafted Walter Cronkite's lasting tag line, "What kind of a day was it? A day like all days, filled with those events that alter and illuminate our time . . . and YOU WERE THERE!"

The key phrase was "alter and illuminate." The three clearly had a different notion of altering and illuminating than the network, the sponsors, and very likely most of the public. But the shows themselves, with talented younger stars like Paul Newman, Rod Steiger, Robert Culp, and John Cassavetes—often under Lumet's careful direction—put across the idea of illuminated history in a big way. The first television "docudrama" and in many respects the best (or at least the best written) in the entire history of the genre, *You Are There* initially ran from February 1953 to June 1955, with Russell at the helm and Bernstein, Manoff, and Polonsky providing the master material.[59]

Decades later Polonsky told an interviewer that their scripts were in no sense propaganda but "political interpretation," not an attempt to press a didactic viewpoint of historical events but to create an impression of them through the popular presentation of history scrutinzed for accuracy.[60] Some episodes on specific events, like the flight of the Wright Brothers, the Hatfield-McCoy feud, or the Mallory party's tragic attempt to climb Mount Everest, had no discernible affect. Others, including a distinct majority of the twenty-four that Polonsky penned, amounted unmistakably to what might be called historical revisionism. The mighty often looked like tyrants, the suppressed like heroes.

Polonsky wrote the premier episode, "The Landing of the *Hindenburg*," which aired February 1, 1953, and was directed by Sidney Lumet. Walter Cronkite's narration tellingly begins,

> What kind of day has it been? In Spain, the Civil War continues with its usual ferocity while the great powers jockey in the international arena. Hitler's Germany promises Baldwin's England not to air raid Spanish civilians, while British civilians prepare for the pomp and circumstance of the coronation of George VI. . . . [Meanwhile] in the Third Reich, the sentencing of Catholic priests for so-called immoral practices began today, another step in the campaign of religious persecution in Hitler's Germany.

As Cronkite awaits news of the landing of the *Hindenburg*, the largest lighter-than-air craft in the world, a messenger delivers a news item to him and Cronkite continues, "In Hollywood the motion picture producers again refused to agree to a closed shop and the [writers'] strike continues." The rest of the show is straightforward, with the political sidelight that Germany now threatens to control the world's airways and the conclusion that in the accidental burning of the *Hindenburg* "Adolf Hitler's dream of German domination of the air [has] prophetically crashed and burned to dust." Even if the political side-glances probably went right by the average listener, they remain unmistakable.[61]

Polonsky delivered other politically and artistically memorable lines
for Galileo preparing to face the Inquisition, "These eyes of mine have
seen more than any man since Adam. And there is more to be seen";
Nathan Hale preparing to face the hangman, "I know I'm quite young.
Nevertheless, I am too old to betray what I believe is just"; poet Andrew
Marvell, "I am not like those in the land, who having shared the life of
the republic, would now find safety by being first to cry down their old
companions. . . . He who dies after his principles have died, sir, has died
too late"; John Milton against the Roundheads, "When a king forbids
books and free thought, it is his nature; but when a free government does
so, that teaches men to hate such governments as if they were hating
tyrants"; or even John Scopes of the Scopes trial, "I will oppose this law
in any way I can. Any other action would be in violation of my ideals."[62]

And perhaps most memorable of all are Polonsky's lines for Kubla
Khan, addressing the contradictions of the West in the episode on Marco
Polo's visit to China:

> I tell you I find the Western world inscrutable and incomprehensible. I cannot
> find by what standards they live, nor why they have ignored their own inher-
> itance for a thousand years and returned to [the] state of black ignorance
> worse than those which the great Genghis himself led. . . . Did you hear how
> on their own crusade to save their God from the infidels in Jerusalem, they
> turned and sacked their own holy city of Constantinople and acted there as
> did the Mongol hordes whose actions they all shudder to recall. . . . Mind you
> sir, I do not condemn these actions, for men will do what they must and his-
> tory always happens in the very way we most dislike. But what I find full of
> laughter is their words, the marvelous words of peace and piety with which
> they clothe their wicked acts. The great Khan Genghis when he went to
> destroy said, "I come to destroy." He did not say, "I come to save you" when
> he meant to slay.[63]

Thus the logic and human cost of the West's own empires. But
Polonsky contributed considerably more to the series than thinly disguised and carefully rendered politics. As in his two previous works on
Paris (rehearsed here as an episode entitled "The Liberation of Paris,"
drastically shorter than his intended film and theatrical pieces and without the powerful sexual undercurrent), he reached an artistic level
through exploration of ambiguity, rarely television's forte then or
ever.[64] His Beethoven, growing deaf, is tormented by the need for a continuing public persona (including patronage) as much as the reality of
his advancing debility. "I, who love the distractions of society people,
gaiety, life and the world. I am slowly being doomed like a wild beast
to solitude, to silence, to the prison of despair." This Beethoven finds

within his mind an "ineffable language" of his own past suffering and of the poor's continued misery.[65]

Polonsky's Jelly Roll Morton, in an episode costarring Louis Armstrong, proclaims that African-American suffering has given birth to the blues. A Parisian in the days of Liberation responds, "The war is something thrown on us by the failure of the old. . . . It is the proof that their culture and civilization amount to nothing but one grand zero. So people here, the young, the intellectuals, the artists, they seize upon jazz as a message from the future."[66] Likewise, his Freud has a humane message: "through the study of the sick, the ill, the despised, the condemned, through the study of what people refuse to admit existed . . . we found a clue to the secrets of the human mind in general."[67] Polonsky used this forum to approach other vistas—the borderline miscegenation in "Cortez Conquers Mexico," with the Spanish conqueror's Aztec mistress and guide attempting to demand his loyalty: "What soldier does not have a wife somewhere across some sea?"[68] Or Savonarola burning artworks in the name of an Italian populace that seeks to overturn the elite.[69] Given the opportunity, the scriptwriter could have gone considerably further.

Ironically, as Bernstein later observed, You Are There's writers could take no credit for their work, even (or especially) when many viewers and critics came to respect it as television's first "quality" show. After two and a half successful seasons, CBS decided to move the show's production from New York to Hollywood. Dozier promptly pushed Russell out of the spotlight and imaginatively claimed You Are There as the fruit of his own creative genius. Adding insult to injury, he "informed" the network of the scripting trio's true identities, putting them instantaneously out of work.

The new series for 1955–56 might sarcastically be termed history lite. It returned to the simple-minded patriotic tunes of the radio original and was pulled in June 1957. Perhaps four and a half televised seasons were all the concept could endure. But those first years constituted a marvelous achievement, far greater than the three could have hoped to achieve by conducting "guerilla warfare" in the mainstream while earning their bread.

Looking back from nearly half a century, Lumet summed the experience best. He claimed that he could always tell which scripts Polonsky wrote. They showed a "flow to the dialogue and a beauty in the language that was completely rare in most American scripts," making him "one of the few writers who could write believable European period dialogue without it sounding silly." If he never actually met Polonsky—no doubt due to both sides' discretion—he could still marvel at work that almost directed itself. Good work remained rare in television scripts, Lumet concluded, but a reading of Polonsky revealed even decades later "what we missed when this marvelous writer was caged but also what we gained, and why that time is still referred to as the Golden Age of television."[70] Coming from one of the medium's most serious and talented directors, this was high praise indeed.

About writing for television, Polonsky himself could say, like the title character in the *You Are There* teleplay "The Tragedy of John Milton," "my life is my work, and what I write merely the form that my life takes."[71] His notebooks from these years are filled with closely written (or scribbled) ruminations on the essentially literary question of finding a new language for the visual arts, above all for cinema, even as he had little opportunity to work that venue except under the table and with no creative influence on the outcome.

Bernstein quietly continued to make his way in television, thanks largely to David Susskind, who would produce the earliest of the fighting liberal shows. His *The Defenders* and *East Side/West Side* at the dawn of the sixties presaged *M*A*S*H* and Norman Lear–style "social comedy" and topical TV movies a decade later. What Polonsky might have done in later television had he been available to work on Susskind's theatrical-style projects is a matter of speculation. As it was, he took a smattering of other assignments, including scripts for a Canadian-based show with other blacklistees in its credits and no hope of American viewers, and the very occasional United States television drama that he could write from deep in the closet.

Polonsky meanwhile retained his interest in theater, as his uncredited contribution to the most distinguished film version of *Oedipus Rex* demonstrated. In 1956 a left-leaning lawyer who knew that Polonsky was working under the table approached him about reworking a screenplay of the classic, whose production was about to begin. Polonsky later remembered reading through the Yeats translation and saying, "You're out of your mind! I'm not going to rewrite *this!*" Polonsky was nevertheless prevailed upon to meet the financial backers and the slated director, Irish theatrical impresario Tyrone Guthrie, on the set in Stratford, Ontario, at the start of the annual Shakespeare Festival there. Dressed in their street clothes, the actors performed the play impromptu for Polonsky in an otherwise empty theater. He immediately looked over the costumes and successfully convinced Guthrie that the production had to be in color, notwithstanding the considerably greater expense.

Polonsky shortly discovered that the distinguished Irish director, who knew nothing about film, was letting the cameraman and the editor pick all the shots. This was a catastrophic error, because neither knew much about the play's difficulties or potentials. The producer warned Polonsky that the imperious Guthrie would simply send him away for pointing out the mistake, and he was almost right. Guthrie responded to Polonsky's criticisms by announcing that he would not see the American visitor anymore. Guthrie eventually cooled down, and thanks to his wife's sage judgment, accepted Polonsky's advice. The film benefited enormously. Was Polonsky denied a credit of some kind because of the blacklist? He put it best himself. "A smart friend does not have to be in the credits." Often criticized as "contained" or "restrained," Guthrie's *Oedipus Rex* lacks the modernizing, campy zip of Pier Paolo Pasolini's 1967 version but remains the standard for the classroom.[72]

Meanwhile, Polonsky was working more and more steadily under the table on film projects that interested him or paid well. Certain movies directed by Otto Preminger or Vincent Sherman bear Polonsky's stamp in their Jewish garment district themes, in their treatment of United States history, and even more so in their sympathetic treatment of African-Americans as complete characters, both heroic and unheroic. Polonsky refused to reveal any details, and the writers who served as his fronts are also gone. We do know, however, that at least some of his under-the-table projects involved serious works and that several made lasting contributions to the film of the period. As Bernstein recalled, Polonsky was discovered not by blacklisters but by Harry Belafonte, one of the stars for whom he very likely had written more than once already.[73]

5

Odds Against Tomorrow (1959) is a tense little heist film, pseudonymously written by Polonsky based on a novel by William F. McGivern. Polonsky's front was the left-wing African-American novelist John O. Killens, who had been published previously in *The Contemporary Reader*. Released by Universal, the film was financed and produced by Belafonte as a Harbel Production (contracting *Harry* and *Belafonte*). Its director, Robert Wise, was the reason both for the movie's long-term viability on the art cinema scene and for at least some of the elements that disappointed Polonsky.

Wise was an extremely interesting choice. Even more than his contemporary Robert Aldrich (who directed several important films pseudonymously written by blacklistee Hugo Butler), Wise had been so well acquainted with the 1940s Left that only a combination of caution and luck had saved him from investigation. In a recent interview, Wise indeed described himself as "part of the left" who somehow "didn't belong to enough" proscribed organizations to be tabbed.[74] As Aldrich had served as assistant director for *Body and Soul,* Wise's second directorial assignment (after *Curse of the Cat People*), was *Mademoiselle Fifi* (1944), an antifascist historical vignette about a patriotic proletarian miss during the Franco-Prussian War, written by future blacklistee Josef Mischel. Among later films, Wise's *The Day the Earth Stood Still* (1951) is an antiwar sci-fi classic with aliens who eradicate human superweapons; *Executive Suite* (1954) is a sometimes savage critique of business standards; and *I Want to Live* (1958) is a protest against capital punishment. After *Odds Against Tomorrow, The Sand Pebbles* (1966), according to Wise's own account, offered a statement against the Vietnam War.[75] Among these and the many other films he directed, including *West Side Story, Odds* has remained one of Wise's all-time personal favorites.

One of the last important noirs shot in black and white—and for some critics the fitting climax to an era of classic noirs—*Odds* has Polonsky's 1940s touch in many important respects, while remaining a characteristic late 1950s film in others.[76] *The Defiant Ones* (1958, coscripted by the blacklisted Ned Young) had most recently established the heroism of a black character in a major role, but Martin Ritt's 1957 *Edge of the City* (a teleplay readapted for film) centered on a character similar to Belafonte's in *Odds,* with Sidney Poitier as the blue-collar worker torn between the respectability of his more middle-class life and the tough demands of the street.

The idea for *Odds* came first to Belafonte. At the peak of his fame and determined to seize the moment's political possibilities through film as he had through folk songs about work and struggle, he formed HarBel, he told *Ebony,* "to make films that show Negroes just as we are . . . working, succeeding, failing, loving, hating and dying."[77] Struck by the novel's possibilities, he sought out the perfect craftsman and confirmed his choice in a face-to-face meeting with Polonsky, who showed himself "uncompromising in how he speaks on his life and his beliefs."[78] United Artists had already been trying to skirt the blacklist in various projects, and when Belafonte secretly brought Polonsky together with Wise, the deal was set. Harbel contributed a quarter million dollars to the budget (hardly twenty percent of the usual figure for a film of this kind); Belafonte waived his own acting fee; and Polonsky got a munificent thirty-five thousand dollars. Harbel would get half the net profits, a nest egg for future productions—if *Odds* succeeded at the box office.

Polonsky reworked the novel so thoroughly that little beyond the framework of the original remained. In a recent public exchange, Polonsky asked Belafonte to recall his first words on bringing him the novel. Belafonte instantly replied, "Fix it!"[79] Polonsky at once set himself to purging some of the novel's key negatives, most of all the thinness and weakness of Belafonte's screen character. McGivern, a former police reporter for the *Philadelphia Evening Bulletin* and the writer of twenty some thrillers (including *The Big Heat,* adapted for Fritz Lang's 1953 film), had definitely intended a theme involving American racism. He introduced the future Belafonte character in what must have seemed, in 1957, distinctly sympathetic terms: "a small and slender man in his middle thirties, neatly turned out in a pearl-gray overcoat, glossy black shoes and a light-gray, snap-brim fedora which he wore slanted at a debonair angle across his forehead. There was a dancer's rhythm in his light sure footsteps. . . . Ingram was a negro." But McGivern's Ingram was more caricature than character, for we learn a few lines later that he "seemed merry rather than clever, as if he were dressed for a masquerade party and realized his costume was an outrageous contradiction of his true station in life."[80]

The ostensible realist detective writer McGivern was trying to establish a contrast to another of the tale's characters, the southern racist prototype Earl Slater. Both men are broken by society, but Earl has turned mean and vicious. Beaten down by the system and internalized self-hatred, McGivern's Ingram has no family and no room for development. By contrast, the Belafonte incarnation is a hip and definitely talented blues singer and xylophone player stuck playing in dives. His gambling addiction (as in the novel) has put him in an impossible spot, but he still maintains a strong sense of self rather than merely a sly determination to survive.

Another of Polonsky's revisions makes Ingram resentful enough on race issues to castigate his urbane and sensitive ex-wife for meeting with the mostly white PTA: "those ofays . . . drink enough tea with 'em and stay out of the watermelon patch and our little colored girl might get to be Miss America, is that it?" He loves his young daughter desperately and hopes for a reconciliation with his ex-wife if only he can do the impossible and make a new start. He is no less desperate than McGivern's original but is no clown and much less a simple victim.

The rewrites, fluently realized in Belafonte's sophisticated mix of melancholy and rage, worked especially well in a Central Park scene that Polonsky added. Ingram is shown watching his daughter on the merry-go-round and then realizing in horror that the mobsters are watching her, too. He finally chases them off by talking to a cop. He is a tragic figure who can only go to his doom, but he has so much verve and mature pathos that we never pity him.

The casting of Ed Begley and Robert Ryan as the other two principals was equally inspired. Begley, a quietly progressive actor known for his pro-union views and his portrayals of conscience-torn businessmen in television and films, is the ex-cop Burke. With "thirty years on the force," he is nabbed in a corruption scandal and dumped from a career and expected pension. In the novel, he is just a crooked policeman who got caught; in Polonsky's version he becomes an honest crook, a nonsquealer ("had a session with the State Crime Committee and got a year for contempt . . . because I wouldn't talk") who has paid the price and knows it. Never married, he has only a German shepherd to love, and he treats the animal with a mixture of love and harsh responses to disobeyed orders. Burke lives for the big score that will raise him out of his reduced life.

Ryan, one of the Left's favorite actors, was another leftish liberal who had been too cautious to be caught up in the blacklist but bravely supported the right to free expression. He distinguished himself in *Tender Comrade* (1942), *Crossfire* (1947), *Caught* (1947), *The Boy with Green Hair* (1948), *Act of Violence* (1949), and *God's Little Acre* (1957), all written by left-wingers, under their own names or pseudonyms. In *Odds* Ryan plays Slater, the racist ex-con who is always close to violence and barely hanging on to his live-in girlfriend, Lorry. Played by Shelly Winters—yet another actor often close to the Left in her personal life—Lorry hardly appears in the novel.[81]

Unlike the novel, which is really a crime story with racial overtones, the movie is on one level *always* about race. It opens with Ryan-Slater on the streets of Manhattan, very much like the Ryan of *Act of Violence*, then a revenge-crazed GI about to go after the officer who betrayed him and his buddies to the Germans. But this Ryan is only going back to the apartment that he shares with Lorry. When a group of shouting black and white children run by, he cheerfully picks up a black boy and greets him in "Negro" jargon. In his own mind, Slater is nothing like a vicious racist; evidently a typical lower-class white Southerner, he "knows" African-Americans and even enjoys them—when they are in their proper place.

Slater therefore must be shocked when Burke introduces him to Ingram, the last member of the team for a caper they have in mind. Burke's plan

Polonsky moved his family to France because of the blacklist. Here he is with his children, Hank and Susan, in Cannes, around 1950.

Harry Belafonte and Robert Ryan as the mismatched pair of small-time criminals in *Odds against Tomorrow* (1959).

Conferring with Robert Redford
during the filming of *Tell Them
Willie Boy Is Here* (1969).

Rehearsing *Romance of a Horsethief* with
Lainie Kazan and Yul Brynner in 1971.

Discussing a scene with Eli Wallach on
the set of *Romance of a Horsethief*.

Going over the script with Yul Brynner
during the production of *Romance of a
Horsethief*.

Polonsky in the 1970s.

With his wife, Sylvia.

calls for someone to look like a delivery "boy" at the side door of a bank, but for Slater a black man's place is not in a life-or-death situation. Slater does not so much dislike Ingram as distrust him. As the singer asserts himself, however, the two impulses become one. Even when Ingram proposes helpful details (a package of coffee and donuts so large that the chain on the bank's side door will have to be removed and the door opened wide), Slater sniffs disapproval of the lesser creature's suggestions.

Race divisions mark their common doom. Driving up the Hudson River Valley to the fictional town of Melton (actually Hudson, New York, filmed on site) for a trial run, the group surveys an industrial village very much like Polonsky's Tarrytown. It is plain, hardly picturesque even at its waterside edges, yet sufficiently rural that while waiting for the caper with gun in hand, Slater spots a rabbit and almost blows it apart before deciding not to shoot. Melton is also so homogeneous that when Ingram crosses the street at the time of a traffic accident, a cop immediately spots him and asks for information and identification. The unsuspecting bank is nevertheless badly guarded even after the train comes in town with its fat weekly payroll bags, which are transferred to the bank by armored car. Nothing can go wrong.

But of course everything goes wrong for the doomed trio, almost from the beginning. Their car nearly runs out of gas, and the souped-up engine's modifications startle the service-station attendant, who is checking the oil. Ingram barely manages to convince the cop that he brought no identification with him; Slater nearly picks a fight with Ingram, warning that at some later point they will inevitably have it out. "You're just another black spot to me," he tells Ingram, whose comeback is, "You're NOT just another white spot to me." In the trial run, Burke pulls them back together, but Slater gets a concession: Ingram will not hold the car keys during the holdup.

This proves critical when an unforeseen delay puts Ingram and Slater in great jeopardy. Burke, sensing trouble, is coming in from the car with the keys in hand when the police spot him, and they trade shots with him. Wounded and hopelessly trapped, Burke puts a gun to his head. Only a quick run to the car by Ingram could conceivably get him and Slater away from the scene, but without the keys they are left on foot with no means of escape. Ingram and Slater are thus like fellow blacklistee Ned Young's cinematic "defiant ones," but without the relative safety of the swamp or the learned empathy that makes possible the earlier film's racial détente. Instead, facing certain capture or death as they run through an old refinery, they seek to take revenge upon each other.

Novelist McGivern gave Ingram a parting soliloquy, mouthing brotherly closing phrases. Polonsky threw out those lines to reveal the two "engulfed in the immensity of their hatred," then engulfed in an explosion when an exchange of gunfire sets off the giant natural gas storage tanks around them. The two men have been burned virtually beyond recognition. A hospital attendant asks the police chief which body is which (that is, which is white and which is black). The chief answers with a shrug, "Take your pick." Thanks to their mutual betrayal they are alike in death after all.[82]

Polonsky originally planned a "simple death," not unlike what Rossen wanted for *Body and Soul;* after all, these petty criminals were no heroes, whatever our sympathies for Belafonte's character. Wise, looking for something more spectacular (and hoping, Polonsky said, for a major film award), determined to put Ingram and Slater in a miniholocaust that would eviscerate their racial identification. To Polonsky's way of thinking, the metaphor was too grand for such small potatoes. Belafonte, however, wanted to do whatever Wise said, and Polonsky reluctantly caved in. He was not on the set in any case and his name would not be on the film.[83] By now he was inured to the wounds of writers who do not direct the films that they script. Too, he admired his collaborators and generally approved of the film, even if he did not agree on this point.

Whatever the ending, several subtler elements made *Odds Against Tomorrow* memorable for all concerned, even more so for film buffs and scholars. Cinematographer Joseph Brun's cityscapes and his ability to visually depict in them the characters' psychological states place the film's aesthetic noir "look" alongside *Force of Evil*'s. Brun not only had done the work for Ritt's *Edge of the City,* but was nominated for an Oscar as the cinematographer of *Martin Luther* (1953), a Lutheran-church-funded, German-made biopic by director Irving Pichel. (Pichel had been among the initial Hollywood Nineteen but apparently evaded the blacklist by working abroad and then dying in 1953.) In later years, Brun expressed gratitude for the opportunity to abandon conventional visualization in *Odds* and strive for an aesthetic sense of menace and impending catastrophe. It offered him an extraordinary freedom and gave neo-noir filmmakers another model of the dark city.

Odds Against Tomorrow's music also was unique. John Lewis, founder of the Modern Jazz Quartet and a formulator of 1950s cool jazz, was one of the very first jazz artists to personally prepare a film score (as opposed to contributing one piece or another). An important set piece features Quartet star Milt Jackson's solo on vibes, dubbed for an enraged

Belafonte, who turns his nightclub act into an expression of fury at the state of the world and his place in it.[84]

Critics at the time did not appreciate nearly enough of this, giving *Odds Against Tomorrow* mixed reviews at best. *Newsweek*'s description, "one part message, three parts mayhem," defined the general tone. The *Nation*, which might have been expected to respond the most sympathetically, concluded that "the appeal to vicarious sadism and the call to social decency are so far apart that the spectator becomes emotionally befuddled." Bosley Crowther complained in his *New York Times* review that Belafonte's heroism against Ryan's racism "cannot be too helpful to the cause of race relations as a whole," then nearly reversed himself nine days later, suggesting that among assorted high-minded films currently playing, "the values are right" in *Odds* and "the melodrama is generally absorbing." Even the hostile reviews managed to applaud the location shooting, the crisp camera work, and the direction. None of the reviewers, however, noted what Polonsky scholar John Schultheiss observed decades later: the most classically noir scene was not in the novel at all. Using diagonal framing and shaded lighting, the scene shows Ed Begley, "the brains," explaining the plan from an occluded hotel room across from the bank. Entirely Polonsky's invention, it supplied one of those famed referencing scenes destined to become common in noirs of the 1970s–90s.[85]

The full importance of Polonsky's writing for Belafonte has become clear only in retrospect. The film roles that made Sidney Poitier a star during the 1950s (the almost-forgotten early version of *Cry, the Beloved Country*, *The Defiant Ones*, and *Edge of the City*, the first two cowritten by blacklistees and the third directed by one) depicted the suffering, deeply Christian figure that whites wanted in black protagonists. His characters were not creatures of and for themselves. Belafonte, already a star of magnum proportions with the first platinum record in history and almost a James Dean–level icon with his "cool" trademark turtleneck sweater and shades, was by contrast the diffident character who had little luck with pushing his roles in films like *Island in the Sun* (1957) to their potential. "I had tried to do things in Hollywood, but every idea was rejected," Belafonte commented later. "I always had to be reliant upon some white hero." *Odds* was designed "to change the way America was doing business . . . and in that climate Abe and I then saw the opportunity to put a point of view on the screen." Indeed they did. In Belafonte's own account, his film personality differed from earlier black characters simply by being who he was. "He walked in and demanded his dignity *by just his presence*. . . . No black guy ever talked to white guys that way in films." Ingram gives no quarter, not only because he is tough but because he is intellectually superior. In contrast to Sidney Poitier's roles as what his friend Belafonte called "the good and patient fellow who finally wins the understanding of his white brothers," Belafonte's Ingram was fully human, fully realized.[86] It might have been a winning, and lasting, combination.

Polonsky had expected to continue with Belafonte and Poitier, then the foremost black actor in Hollywood (in terms of pay scale, very likely in the whole world). The three of them hatched a plan to produce a series of films about African-American life, for which Polonsky would be the principal screenwriter. A progressive circle would supply the finances. According to African-American film documentarian (and later close friend of Polonsky's) Carlton Moss, the whole idea was commercially unrealistic. Thirteen years later critics thrilled to *Sounder,* directed by Martin Ritt (and starring Cicely Tyson), in which the lush southern scenery and the sheer goodness of black families avoided difficult questions on all sides. But in 1959, blacklisted actor-director John Berry's slave drama *Tamango* almost ruined his career. Even a decade later, critics hooted at the dramatic black rebellion in *Slaves* (directed and produced by another blacklistee, Herbert Biberman).[87] America was not ready to deal adequately with the racial divides in artistic or any other terms.

But Belafonte and Polonsky had left some real cinema in their wake. At a crucial moment awaiting the imminent caper, Ingram looks down at the edge of a rotting dock and sees old boards, rags, ropes, and a doll with what may be a red dress. In that dross of the everyday, he experiences a vision. Polonsky later commented that he had been trying to show "possibilities for profound communication" in the most evidently mundane of objects. Because "the aesthetics of a work of art plays the same role as the mathematics which are basic to the scientific description of the nature of events," it pushes aside the irrelevant while bringing to light apparently unimportant details and giving them meaning. "This," Polonsky insisted, "is what poets do. That's why they write poetry instead of equations."[88] It was as well what a working film aesthetician did.

Despite the disappointments, Polonsky had retained throughout the 1950s a large underground reputation among Hollywood's older radicals and those younger intellectuals who knew about his work. The volatile 1960s and their aftermath would give him one last chance to prove his combined political and artistic abilities, if only the necessary elements could be marshaled.

5

TRIUMPH AND RETROSPECT

IN RETIREMENT, POLONSKY GREW FOND of quoting one of Proust's characters, who says he discovered, late in life, that he was married to the wrong woman. Deeply romantic in the old-fashioned way about his own late wife, Polonsky meant, of course, the wrong industry: movies. The Marxist who repeatedly defended working in commercial films as the only possibility for full artistic expression, Polonsky nevertheless expressed serious qualms. He could shrug off the normal disappointments of the immediate postwar years because he appeared still to have plenty of time, as well as a track record of some stunning early successes. Television memoirist Charles Russell (Polonsky's boss on *You Are There*) wrote that the blacklist offered the "best of times in the worst of times," when remarkable things could be done, even if not necessarily in films, to combat the national hysteria.[1] As the cold war eased, Polonsky had the scripts and (he thought) the right collaborators for a monumental comeback.

Polonsky's return certainly worked out partway. *Madigan,* his first credited script after the blacklist era, appeared at least a half-decade too late to achieve its full potential, but it unquestionably etched lasting celluloid images of the neo-noir. *Tell Them Willie Boy Is Here,* though overshadowed by the star power of *Butch Cassidy and the Sundance Kid* and never a box-office smash, was a remarkable film, which its bitter attackers realized perhaps more clearly than its devotees. Finally, despite serious editing errors and certain weaknesses in the cast, *Romance of a Horsethief* offered Polonsky a directorial romp as well as a return to the

Jewish themes of his literary efforts. After *Romance,* his heart would be too weak for the rigors of directing.

Now Polonsky was back to the powerless world of writing scripts with no creative control, the world that so often renders good writing and socially minded plots into bad writing and triviality. The future would confirm his forebodings, if not entirely. At sixty he should have had another ten years of writing and, perhaps, editing; instead, he moved into an early, though intermittently active, retirement as a classroom aesthetician who wrote when it suited him. He experienced further high points, near misses, and modest satisfactions. He could not expect too much from ventures in which he merely improved adaptations. Other disappointments drove home a similar message, the same one heard by most serious Hollywood writers, especially the older ones. After *Force of Evil,* he could not help feeling that, like so many talented Hollywood figures of the 1940s and by no means all of them blacklistees, he had missed his best chances.

Polonsky's best efforts and very occasional good luck should be measured against those of his real contemporaries, the other blacklistees who did not succumb prematurely to heart attacks, strokes, or cancer during their stressful political exile and somehow made the right connections for a comeback. Inevitably mixed, their stories offer a cautionary tale for popular culture's committed and cerebral artists.

Among the blacklisted directors, Jules Dassin and Joseph Losey thrived abroad, and Jack Berry made a little-acknowledged handful of outstanding films. Otherwise the moment had virtually ended for directors. Nor did briefly successful producers like Adrian Scott ever find their way back. Only Martin Ritt, neither a writer nor a director before the blacklist but an actor, and also younger than the great majority of other blacklistees, directed admired films and Hollywood hits and kept directing them for close to twenty years. Ritt's best writer arguably was none other than Walter Bernstein, Polonsky's old pal from *You Are There,* and by a large margin the most prolific of the ex-blacklistees. Unlike Polonsky, Bernstein successfully worked a considerable number of genres, from political thriller to comedy to the 1997 Emmy-winning telefilm *Miss Evers' Boys.* As the century closed, Bernstein was the blacklist's only victim still working.[2]

A large handful of other former blacklisted writers made their way back, sometimes grandly, albeit with less adaptability or persistence than the redoubtable Bernstein. Dalton Trumbo, Marguerite Roberts, Lillian Hellman, Carl Foreman, Ring Lardner, Jr., and Waldo Salt all had bigger names, or at least longer track records, than Polonsky before the black-list. For those reasons, perhaps, they returned as successfully as conditions in Hollywood and their individual health allowed. Roberts and Lardner even won Oscars. The other most successful writers by a long stretch were Salt, widely admired for *Midnight Cowboy* and *Serpico*, and Michael Wilson, who recovered his major credits only after his death (*Planet of the Apes* credited but *Lawrence of Arabia* and the *Bridge on the River Kwai* unrecognized.)

The great bulk of the blacklisted writers, including once-huge names like Donald Ogden Stewart, Albert Maltz, and Sidney Buchman, remained among the virtual missing, fortunate if they managed an additional film or two before illness or other problems forced them into retirement. This silenced generation could not resume creating their semi-collective oeuvre. Nor could their work be passed on easily to generations of screenwriters who had been deprived of mentorship, to say nothing of comradeship. The American "art film" in imitation of European styles, like *The Balcony* (1961), written by blacklistee-turned-cooperator Ben Maddow, was a typically lethal combination of Hollywood and Rome or Paris. The "political" films that emerged during the 1970s had, for the most part, different roots.

In the long run, Polonsky was vindicated in many other ways. He found himself cheerfully acknowledged as a major personal influence by Robert Aldrich, who had worked under him at Enterprise and remained a close friend into the 1960s. Aldrich's remarkable, very quirky films (some of them almost certainly rewritten in parts by an unadmitting Polonsky) ranged from the neo-noir classic *Kiss Me Deadly* (1955) to the heavily political *Twilight's Last Gleaming* (1977, partly scripted by another ex-blacklistee, Edward Huebsch). Cinema giant of the last quarter century Martin Scorsese likewise acknowledged the noir master's imprint on the crime film and the noir mood, his own *Raging Bull* and *Goodfellas* being prime cases in point. Even Steven Spielberg has expressed a reverence bordering upon awe for Polonsky, from whom he got no more than an initial studio boost.

The continuing influence of Polonsky and his milieu on filmmaking is a more complex and more interesting question. But if Hollywood has been able to turn out films like the *Godfather* epics, *Silkwood, Tin Men, Dog Day Afternoon, I'm Not Rappaport, Wag the Dog,* and *Bulworth,* and if figures like Sidney Lumet (Polonsky's television director), Sidney Pollack, William Goldman, and among the younger crowd Barry Levinson and Tim Burton, all weigh in heavily, it is because they have had a little-

acknowledged tradition on which to build. At the cerebral center of that
quietly sustained left-wing tradition will remain the Polonsky of Hollywood's Golden Age, just as long as writers, directors, and actors continue to
study the canon of Hollywood movies in the process of learning their art.

1

To begin with Polonsky's enduring disappointments, "Sweetland,"
whose final version dates to 1960, is not only an unmade *Sounder* but
arguably an unmade *Roots* as well. Its field of vision is large: the history
and weight of slavery not only as a highly profitable social system but
also as a supremely sexual arrangement. Subsequent historians of
women's lives in the antebellum South have dwelt with good reason on
the complications of powerful white men and presumably powerless
black women, with the plantation master's betrayed and enraged wives
as witnesses and agents of revenge, mostly upon the injured parties.
Polonsky reimagined the distinctly divided black-and-white South of Sir
Walter Scott–style cavalier fantasies and *Gone with the Wind* Hollywood nostalgia as a violently dysfunctional interracial family on the
verge of ripping apart a nation. On occasion accused of creating characters to fit a part, in "Sweetland" Polonsky managed to create extraordinarily full characters who also fill their historical roles superbly.

The conversation of the slave-owning class provides a crucial background for the real action, which centers on the slaves. A plantation
owner, Colonel Colby, has raised himself from the relative poverty of a
small farm and a few slaves inherited from an aunt to prosperity. In the
process, however, he has exhausted his passion for life. He had been
deeply in love with one of his slaves, and when she died in childbirth, he
kept the baby, Mingo, with him as a slave. Although Colby's wife,
Harriet, is aware of the real relation, their own son, Frank, is not. The
interracial saga continues through the generations. Frank has been slated
all his life to marry Marion, a kindly if naive white woman, but for years
he has been having an affair with a beautiful slave named Daidy. As the
first southern states secede, able-bodied men face the looming reality of
battlefield gore. While Colonel Colby sees only gloom and Frank faces
the situation stoically, the nouveau riche planter Larry is eager for glory.
Deeply in love with Marion, Larry also hates his social superior's lack of
southern patriotism.

At the bedrock of the drama we find Sarrey, an extraordinarily able
and politically minded older slave woman, and her nephew, Mingo,

whose mother was Colby's lover. Sarrey directs the runaway slave traffic (via a sympathetic white boatman who has taken many risks to assist runaways) and knows what must be done for the escapees. Daidy, desperate for some of the privileges of the white world if only at its fringes, is helpless to resist the temptations around her. It is Mingo who must choose between revenge and strategy for black liberation, but along with a desire to live free, his ambiguous status makes him hate himself.

In what could be seen as a more black-centered, earlier situated, violent version of Lillian Hellman's classic *The Little Foxes,* history closes in. For the luckier members of plantation society, the springing trap recalls the world of their ancestors, fighting the Revolution or the Indian Wars and building the cotton trade in a fleeting moment of glory. For the slaves, the trap's reality is the accumulated power of the system (emphatically including its repressive apparatus of armed patrols and the daily brutal beatings) and the seasoned adaptation of blacks and whites alike to its continuity.

The catch-spring of the plot snaps when Mingo delays assisting a runaway because Daidy has begged him to peek with her into the Big House at a gala event. At that moment, as Frank asks Marion to wed, she explores her own emotions, knowing that his love and passion lie somewhere else but willingly accepting the lesser relation of prospective wife and mother. As the colonel announces the engagement, Larry discovers Mingo and Daidy watching the excitement, and he slaps Mingo carelessly, indifferently, cutting his lip.

Making excuses, Mingo hurries too late to the scene of attempted escape. The patrol has caught and tortured the runaway, further humiliating Mingo because he is dressed better than the poor whites who do this work. Stunned by the horror and by his own failure, Mingo returns to the Big House after the others have gone. He finds Daidy alone there, wearing a harlequin mask, fantasizing life as a mistress in New Orleans, uttering French verses, and talking about escaping "this jungle, this sadness, this horror."

On this of all nights, Harriet sees Frank about to leave the house and head for Daidy's; unable to stand the duplicity, she pours out her rage and hysteria about her loveless marriage and—for the first time—tells her son the family secret. She later states her case clearly:

> Tell me what's my honor or the honor of any woman of the South when we know that our husbands and sons are fathering bastards on their slaves, when we know that the embraces, the kisses, the tenderness we crave is squandered elsewhere? What's love . . . you tell me . . . what's honor? Horror, I call it the

horror of Southern men. . . . And . . . all the time, the general silence. Silence.
Yes, the silence and the horror.[3]

A maddened Frank finds Mingo with Daidy and mercilessly beats him
nearly to death. With remarkable self-control, Mingo attempts to block
the blows rather than returning them. Only the appearance of the
colonel prevents a murder.

As the drama nears its climax, Polonsky halts the movement to place
a visiting businessman (actually, a Yankee spy) with the colonel. The
pairing enables him to draw the parallels between the evils of bound slavery and those of wage slavery. Goaded by talk about the hated auction
block, the colonel brags, "Uncle Tom's Cabin is no worse than an Irish
shanty in Boston or a cotton spinner's shack in Lancashire." When the
colonel jibes, "Remember the Mexican dead?" the visitor responds,
"That was war!" And when the colonel presses, "The Indian corpses?
The land we stole from them?" the astonished visitor asks, "Are you
equating slavery with national progress?" The colonel states outright,
"I'm equating progress with war, injustice and economic advantage.
Naturally, you've got to have a stomach for it . . . down here we have the
stomach for slavery."[4]

Mingo survives in body, albeit horribly scarred, but his spirit has
turned wild with a Fanonesque desire for violence as a purgative, psychological release. (He calls it "better than freedom.") The colonel offers
him manumission in Canada, but Mingo refuses because in some strange
way, although he hates the thought, he nevertheless accepts himself as
one of the Colbys and their madness. Frank, home on leave to be married and scheming to send Daidy to New Orleans, realizes just as surely
that he can prevent neither his love for a black woman nor its destructive
consequences. At the close, Mingo abandons his chance for easy freedom, and Daidy hers for easy slavery. They head off together as the
whites stiffen themselves to live with the pain at hand for their South.

Harry Belafonte wanted badly to make this film. Among its other
potential investors (and actors), Paul Newman became deeply interested.
Newman, like his wife, Joanne Woodward, had been quietly close to left-
wing circles for years. He had worked in Martin Ritt's major southern
dramatic film *The Long, Hot Summer* (1958) and was just going to work
in *Paris Blues* (1961), written by Walter Bernstein. According to
Polonsky, Newman judged the risk too great, not only financially but
professionally, as he was then still a new star. The interracial love affairs,
the violence, and the guerilla-war-like conclusion were, as Polonsky said

in retrospect, "*intended* to cause a need for more historical explanation—and that always causes fear." Had Newman been able to put it across, American films treating race might have leaped forward from *The Defiant Ones* rather than slipping backward toward the maudlin and the almost nonexistent. Just as possibly, to judge from the reception of *The Chase* (1966) or *Black Like Me* (1964), contemporary interracial southern dramas produced a few crucial years later and written by returned blacklistees, "Sweetland" might also have gone down to hostile critics and a mediocre box office.[5]

Polonsky regretfully abandoned the idea of an African-American series. Belafonte paid him advances for one more major script, to be called "Calypso," not a melodrama this time but a musical comedy along the techno-madness lines of *Doctor Strangelove*. They intended to use music, dance, and farce rather than straight political satire, shifting the sardonic, surreal quality of *Strangelove* into an unwinding spiral of the entire human experience that culminated in the face of threatened nuclear self-annihilation.

The two even had lined up a cast: Belafonte himself as Donny, a West Indian entertainer and man of the world; Zero Mostel as Dr. Zero, the brilliant huckster; and Polonsky's old pal Danny Kaye as Rear Admiral B. B. ("Buzzer") Bohen, the genius engineer and organizer of space projects both military and explorational.

At the outset, Bohen meets a Japanese lieutenant general, and the two of them head for a music hall in Tokyo where the very Belafonte-like Donny is doing his signature number, "Matilda." (This is perhaps too close to life: Belafonte's cover of the well-known Caribbean tune, "Matilda," had been a giant hit only a few years earlier, and it remained his signature piece for decades.)[6] The woman in the act is, however, a real Matilda, a beautiful creature who has spent years entertaining sailors— we can only imagine how. The mysterious Dr. Zero has recently taken her under his protection.

Zero is a third-rate magician and fake hypnotist who survives by leading, pimp-like, a troupe of girls to sailors' dives around the Mediterranean and Pacific. He is also a multilingual freelance intelligence agent who picks up information and sells it to any convenient bidder. Recruited by Buzzer to serve American interests, Zero signs on as sound engineer of Donny's troupe, which gains a new star when Donny buys Matilda's contract for $250 "plus three quarts of whiskey." Though a commercial entertainer, Donny loves and understands folk music and forms from around the world—again, close to the real Belafonte—and

he seeks an escape from commercial venues into the world's older, indigenous and surviving cultures. Soon, he and Matilda leave the whole scene,
en route to some unknown destination.

Among the musical numbers, which range from a Japanese monks'
chorus to nightclub girlie shows, and the assorted confusion, some of the
oddest characters in all of Polonsky's considerable menagerie turn up.
When Buzzer contracts a fever, his nurse looks strangely like Matilda but
is scarred terribly, a symbolic and actual survivor of the Hiroshima A-
bomb attack. Matilda herself temporarily loses her charm and becomes
a "treacherous slut from the dockside of Honolulu," a Salome of the sea,
luring divers into life-threatening risks for her own pleasures.

Donny and Matilda enter a Polynesian island that they first think is an
untouched paradise but turns out to be a United States satellite tracking
station, "patiently testing space for destruction and doom." The bull-
dozed roads, the radios playing jazz and commercials, are certain to
destroy the fragile native culture, and the island's indigenous inhabitants
know it. From the viewpoint of the international military-scientific elite
entrusted with keeping secrets, however, all is well: working for Buzzer,
Matilda has now positioned herself to kidnap Dr. Zero, take him back to
the United States, and force him to reveal the source of his dangerous
knowledge and his ultimate purposes. To make this possible, Buzzer levels with Donny, revealing to him "a world without morality or feeling"
where each powerful nation is prevented from destroying the others only
by a mutual terror.

Odd sidelights meanwhile find Donny and his troupe in Calcutta,
where a demonstration and jail scenes resemble those of the civil rights
movement during the 1950s and early 1960s in the American South.
Intellectuals discuss threats to peace. Students sing songs from various
parts of India and invite Donny to sing along, revealing through music
"the obstinacy and determination of life" amid the growing peril. Then
the scene suddenly switches to an Israeli kibbutz. Buzzer, secretly on
hand, sees this location as offering his best opportunity to kidnap Zero
with the help of an Israeli intelligence counterpart, as Donny sings
among a Bedouin tribe at a famed archaeological dig.

An archaeologist-philosopher interprets Donny's song as having
passed from civilization to civilization and now surviving among the
remnants of assorted peoples who once ruled great stretches of the
known world. In the song, all the powerful pass away, and nothing
remains "but the eternity of God." Even "Man himself will pass away,
perhaps the sooner the better." Scrolls reveal texts earlier than the Bible,

uncovering God's message about the miracle of nature and its desecration by those who use knowledge to destroy each other.

His conscience pricked, Donny is finished with power politics: he cannot commit an immoral act even for a moral end. Threatening to reveal dangerous secrets if any further attempt to kidnap Zero is made, he takes off to newly independent Dongoland for his African concert. There, he becomes the African-American returned to Mother Africa in triumph, eliciting "a carnival of welcome . . . a new stage in Dongolese history, a people reborn," with Zero and his girls of the world gloriously on hand. Donny is seated upon a golden throne, holding broken gold chains in his hands while a "thrusting ballet of people" surges around him. Buzzer, however, has laid a plan to trap Zero in the mining zone, the new country's central economic resource, which is under United Nations control until various management details can be ironed out.

Here, the penultimate act unfolds. The mine "lies in a region so gruesome and tormented that it seems as if nature wanted to warn men not to enter," volcanic caves long considered an entrance to the underworld. Suitably, the area had became a virtual slave labor camp under colonialism. Donny now realizes that he, too, has been betrayed. Pursuing his enemies through the bowels of the earth, he successively becomes Orpheus, Ulysses, Theseus, "everyman in the underworld of treachery and anxiety, amongst shapes and sights unholy."

Then we abruptly find the sometime lovers Donny and Matilda on the remote West Indies island where Donny was born. After another night of dancing and revelry—"the opposite of the underworld, of the darkness"—the crucial, final events unfold. Following still more adventures including a *Strangelove*-like "delirium tremens of science" in the space laboratories secreted there, Zero reveals his and Matilda's real secret. They are extraterrestrial creatures. En route to survey the earth, they collided with a satellite and polarized into the bodies of the rascal Zero and the libidinous Matilda. After close study, Zero has concluded that human consciousness is "a misfit in the universe," mankind "a disease in the galactic systems," a threat to superior forms of consciousness outside the Milky Way. Matilda (whose human form has fallen in love with Donny) requests one last survey. Zero allows a final stay of execution—the length of their human comrades' lifetimes—for the changes to be made. As Dr. Zero scoffs at the humans' petty schemes, Matilda marvels at their capacity for the love she has experienced. Two tiny incandescent suns of unearthly bodies then shimmer and vanish. Donny stands alone musing, and Buzzer mulls the folly of *Homo sapiens*, convinced that he has personally "looked into the ultimate of the universe only to find that once again he has merely scratched the surface of the infinite."

"Calypso" was never made. Like "Mario and the Magician," perhaps no one except the high-rollers in the Hollywood of the 1960s could have produced it, and they clearly had other priorities. Working abroad, writing under the table for an unnamed producer-director, Polonsky vented his exasperation in a remarkable 1962 essay printed in the French journal *Présence du Cinéma*. The resulting manifesto was the closest Polonsky ever would come to stating his own theory of film and is worth quoting at considerable length, without break.

> Experienced screenwriters know that the film script is not a play script. The play, while it does not direct the actors' acting or the director's overall interpretation, generates them both because a play is only a set of dialogues which either by implication or specific reference originate the entire work. Stage actors and directors are, so to speak, virtuosos of interpretation and performance. This is exactly what a film director is not. And no writer, producer, actor or businessman can force him into this role without destroying the film. The set of images in film is, together with the set of dialogues, the actual motion picture. The dialogues of the play occur in real time on the stage. The set of dialogues in the film occur in the psychological time of the set of images which themselves [also] happen to occur in real time. Inexperienced writers may confuse these different sets of dialogues because both call on common literary sources and happen, on occasion, to be interchangeable in a limited way.
>
> The writer's instinctive impulse . . . to create an individual work of art forces him to become a director of his work when he can, or to burden his script with technological ineptitudes which the understanding director ignores. This being the case, theoretically speaking, the serious writer who cannot direct should stop writing for film.
>
> I suggest, however, that there is a solution to his problem. It moves in a direction away from technology, away from exhaustive analysis and description of the shots. It is toward compression, density, structure, elegance, metaphor, synthesis, magnitude and variety, all held within a unified verbal structure. I am, of course, speaking of poetry, and the literary form I have in mind of the screenplay is the poem.
>
> I am using the terms *poetry* and *poem* to characterize a screenplay which instead of conventional camera angles would guide the attention through concrete images (as in metaphor); which instead of stage directing the action would express it; which instead of summarizing character and motive would actually present them as data; which instead of dialogue that carries meaning where the film image fails, would be the meaning that completes the film image. Much of the modern invention in the novel and poetry are direct literary sources for this suggested technique, and certainly the old religious and national epics are vivid precursors.
>
> I expressly eliminate that collage of history, psychological, journalistic dialogue, gnomic wisdom and ruminative story telling which is called the tradi-

tional novel. The set of images in this screenplay would not exhaust the set of images in the film but be the literary paradigm for the work of the director just as, for example, the set of dialogues are the generating source of the actor's enormous technical and human contribution.

The strategy of the film would exist as a set of images continuing the very action, characterization and flow over which the brooding genius of the director could hover, assimilating such inventions as were about and generating in him others the writer never imagined. Of course, the director would have to learn how to read, and writers would have to be poets. In the end, we might have in direct tension with the motion picture a literature of the film whose existence would confront the work of the director with the opportunity he had fulfilled, surpassed or failed. In the end we might escape from the paralysis of naturalism which has for so long distorted the reality of our condition on the screen.[7]

These propositions were avowedly utopian. When Polonsky presented the manuscript to Frank Rosenberg, the hard-working director-producer's response was, "C'mon Abe, stop kidding around!"[8] Which is to say, get back to work at script-doctoring; this speculation is not for (perhaps not even from) the real world.

But the thought distills, even overdistills, what Polonsky had explained already to film-writing classes and public audiences over the years and would continue to explain more often in the decades ahead. Film scripts are not play scripts or novels; they are entirely different, as film is a genuinely new art form, perhaps (until television) the only really new major art form in centuries. Others—dance, song, theater, even sport considered in this way—continually revive and revise ancient practices. Movies, to the ruminative Polonsky, are more like that storytelling around the fire that was the setting of *Homo sapiens'* first sustained fictional narratives.

Movies are, then, "magic" in the anthropological sense. The thought was not original but Polonsky gave it fresh meaning, albeit far more in practice than in theory. *Force of Evil* had transcended the "paralysis of naturalism" by realizing naturalism completely—in the framework of a B "meller." But it could have been made only under the best of conditions, and certainly not during the blacklist era or the following periods of imitation art films and overblown spectaculars. No one work of art, unless it be Dante's *Inferno,* has proved capable of seizing the vernacular and making it the new language of the poetry and common street patois to follow.

Polonsky's spare paragraphs might have inspired a new generation of radical film artists and critics—but they did not, not even among the culture-minded New Left Marxists who turned overwhelmingly toward

Parisian philosopher Louis Althusser, toward structuralism, and finally to poststructuralism and its postmodern variants without ever confronting that original paralysis of naturalism. Instead, like his earlier essay on de Beauvoir and the crisis of Marxist intellectuals, Polonsky's theoretical musings, like 1940s Left film, disappeared within a quiet monument to lost utopian hopes, noticed only by those who were looking very hard to find them.

2

Like so many of his career moves, Polonsky's return to studio life was curious. Working under the table for more than a decade but seeing others come back into the open, he wrote a script for the pilot of a television series on his old school tie, the OSS. The pilot never aired and the series was abandoned. Even the script vanished. When the series' would-be producer, Frank Rosenberg, was offered another film prospect, however, he chose Polonsky for the job after French screenwriter Henri Simoun took an unpromising first stab at it. Making enough money to live comfortably, Polonsky hesitated at first. But the offer promised a means to get off the blacklist honorably, and finally he could not refuse.

After fifteen years' absence, the Polonskys returned to California and the utterly transformed world of the modern studio. By then, Twentieth Century–Fox lacked nearly all the lavish atmosphere and accouterments of Hollywood tradition. In contrast to the grand and almost factory-like exploitative kingdom of old, it had come to resemble a rental space. Most of all, Polonsky missed the moguls like Harry Cohn who could personally decide to produce a film the director wanted to make—if the director would first make a film the mogul wanted to produce. Now, millionaire stars and their investors rolled the dice, and despite the relative sexual and political freedom, getting an interesting, individualistic movie made was far harder than during the 1940s. Rallying camaraderie among the writers was also next to impossible. By now they often hardly knew each other, and they got younger by the decade, pushing veterans either into television or into career oblivion.

The atmosphere nevertheless had a certain openness that Polonsky liked, despite all the unpleasant changes. A very young, would-be director named Steven Spielberg, for instance, looked promising to Polonsky. With his personal reputation for observing talent, the veteran could use Spielberg for a few incidental scenes and recommend that the studio execs "give the kid a chance." Would Spielberg have made it anyhow? Un-

Hollywoodishly, Polonsky refused all credit—but admitted that the later big *makher* of modern film remained respectful almost to a fault. Perhaps Spielberg's reverence has a simpler explanation: like Scorsese, Spielberg knows talent and integrity, and recognizes their role in film history.

At any rate, the grizzled left-wing filmmaker got his assignment, revealing that he still had the talent but also that he had paid for his return to the mainstream. When *Madigan* was released in 1968, its tone and handling of the subject matter were already visibly dated. The film was based on Richard Dougherty's *The Commissioner*, a novel cued in many critical ways to the ambiance of the Kennedy years. With the civil rights, antiwar, and student movements challenging American internationalism and the nation polarized between law-and-order visions of hero cops and left-wing visions of "pigs," the big-city police department was an impossibly anachronistic stage for moral arguments. The director was Don Siegel, whose 1972 success, *Dirty Harry*, developed themes clearly inspired by *Madigan* but tilted to the right. But not even Siegel's action skills could rescue *Madigan* from a 1950s snap-brim breeziness, a weakness continuously compounded by Don Costa's inappropriate, game-show-sounding score. Indeed, given television's cultural lapse during the late 1960s, the film script (or novel) naturally might have been adapted for that medium first, possibly with more success. Yet something about the moral uncertainties remained useful, and Polonsky's characters and dialogue overcome to a surprising degree the narrative structure's basic weakness.

Even in novel form, *The Commissioner* had offered a police procedural drama curiously void of the procedures that define law enforcement. *Madigan*'s plot comes to life when a pair of workaday Manhattan detectives, played by Richard Widmark and Harry Guardino, head for Brooklyn on their own initiative to question a gun-sales suspect whom they sent to prison years earlier.[9] In the film as in the novel, they get him out of bed with a girlfriend, intending only to take him in for questioning. But Widmark is momentarily distracted when the naked woman walks to the closet. Suspect Michael Dunn grabs a gun, compels the cops to turn over their weapons, and escapes. Two days later, following a major embarrassment and a great deal of revelation about the protagonist's milieu, the cops track him down and recover their weapons, but only after a shoot-out in which several innocents are killed. The plot is so spare that Polonsky invented a third action sequence in the middle of the film to remind the audience that the bad guy was worth chasing.

Nonetheless *Madigan* was, to some degree, an artistic success. That it inspired a season-long series of television films suggests its strengths. But very much like the novel, the film was merely the kind of journalism that brightens realism by outfitting it with authentic if not necessarily important details. Novelist Richard Dougherty had come up through the reporting ranks of the old *New York Tribune* in the 1950s and actually served as a deputy police commissioner of New York City during the same decade. Those experiences gave him a firsthand knowledge guaranteed to provide new grist for fans of the entirely naturalistic detective genre. Dougherty could describe, for example, a nearly complete list of clubs and associations for cops of every rank and ethnicity, estimate the membership size of each, and calibrate its role in the bureaucracy's equilibrium. (One of the regrettable if understandable disappearances from book to film was Dougherty's careful delineation of Irish-American, Roman Catholic tradition in sustaining police camaraderie and minimizing job competition, especially at the upper levels.)[10] Dougherty, a Columbia graduate, was also shooting for something more than eye-level reporting, and Polonsky's script goes a long way toward representing Dougherty's real but unelaborated concerns about the ambiguities of corruption and the inhumanity of command.

The transition from book to film censored some hard-to-explain psycho-sexual material (like Madigan's Roman Catholic wife's being nearly bedded down with another police officer, changing her mind at the last moment, shouting, "Keep your Jew hands off me!" and then immediately apologizing for her double lapse of judgment).[11] Polonsky's script also shifted the weight of the protagonist from the commissioner to the detective. Perfectly cast with Henry Fonda, the commissioner's character survives in reduced form as the lonely-at-the-top bureaucrat of the day. True to the novel, he is something of a prig, the one cop who years earlier returned a Christmas turkey from a meat wholesaler, knowing full well that every other cop ate or shared with relatives his private, off-the-truck seasonal reward. The film omits an abundance of other biographical details, but the point comes across perfectly.

The commissioner is the essence of the bloodless intellectual-bureaucrat, cold and aloof and full of judgments about how cops should remain free of any trace of corruption or favoritism. Incapable of friendship, he worries about the "moral collective" of the police department. The novel (not the film) reveals that his reading of "radical Marxian socialists" in younger years liberated, or at least alienated, him from Roman Catholic dogma—likely a judgment of Dougherty himself. But while the commissioner never hesitates to judge the character of everyone around him, he engages in an adulterous affair without compunction.[12] (The film softens this lapse by killing off his repressed and fussy wife before the narrative starts, so that only his mistress is married.)

The commissioner meets his moment of truth, as harshly in the film as in the novel, when his chief inspector falls in a hole after a lifetime of loyal service. The chief inspector is played brilliantly by James Whitmore, who was already a veteran of half a dozen films written by left-wingers, most recently the then-controversial *Black Like Me*. The son of a police commander who ushered forward the future commissioner, the chief inspector has averted his eyes from a gambling violation. We soon learn that he has done so only because his policeman son and financially reckless daughter-in-law are into the same pocket for shylocked debts. The inspector's sin surely is forgivable, but he asks no undue favors. Confronting the damning evidence, he reprises mobster Lloyd Gough's line from *Body and Soul*, "There it is in black and white, everything else is conversation." Luckily for the chief inspector, the commissioner's mistress prevails upon him to let his heart rule his head.[13] And luckily for the blacklisted and once highly sought after actor Gough, Polonsky deemed that the inspector needed an assistant inspector. In writing the part, he provided de facto rehabilitation for the highly talented actor's last few years of film work.

Madigan, the detective who occupies far more territory in the film than in the novel, has all the flaws of the street-wise cop. A former college basketball star, he could have risen further but stayed with the job that he took during the Depression. Moreover, he stayed on the street. He lives by maintaining a network of informers within the New York demimonde; a bedraggled bunch, they in turn are fiercely loyal to him, as much for friendship as for money. He also takes advantage of the bribes and small favors of businessmen who rely on the cops for protection, referring sarcastically to his "police discount," and he uses that margin to maintain the flow of his own payments to the street informers. As the chief inspector observes, "Madigan's always lived a little on the arm, but on the other hand, he's never really been on the take." All this remains far, far beyond the grasp of his wife, played by Inger Stevens, who (uncharacteristically for Polonsky) lacks room to grow or even to display the complexities revealed in the novel, which provides a nuanced exploration of her wifely frustrations.

Madigan was, after all, Siegel's picture, and the book's climactic scene and artistic coda become more an epilogue to the action of the film. In *The Commissioner,* Madigan has to die—surely an inventive fate for the hero of an action-thriller. Alone and naked, his mistress hears the bad news on the radio; his wife meanwhile blames his death on the commissioner, whose inordinately high standards for "moral" behavior drive detectives to take senselessly heroic risks in order to win approval. The juxtapositions are already set by the contrast between the mistress's copies of *The New Yorker, Ulysses, Tropic of Cancer,* and *Introduction to Zen* and the still working-class world where informers cry and where magic Manhattan looks old, part of an earlier twentieth century slipping away in an emerging reality of newer buildings and less certain values.[14]

The film's message is different and more unambiguous than the novel's. The commissioner of the novel would not be so abstract or so judgmental if only he were more human, more capable of understanding that at least the more forgivable aspects of what outsiders see as corruption are the ordinary traffic of human beings relying on each other to get by. The movie, however, does not allow him to drift toward any such understanding. The action-drama of the film also leaves many thematic possibilities simply hanging. What if, for instance, Madigan's wife had learned of his continuing affair with singer and sophisticate Sheree North, another potential Polonskyan heroine who never grows to her dramatic capacities? (In the film he merely drops over to sleep in her apartment and North tends to his other needs.) Wife and mistress might have altered their views of corruption and its costs and grown in the process. Or perhaps not. We never find out.

In the end, *The Commissioner* is little more than a Smollet-like plea for society's leaders to understand the creases and tears in the papyrus of ordinary humanity's book of life, a kind of twentieth-century *Humphrey Clinker* without the humor. But it is not difficult to see how such a work might have affected Kennedy-era readers looking for signs of the reemergence of social criticism. The comprehensive repression of the 1950s, with its *Dragnet*-style conception of law 'n' order, was finally lifting. *Madigan* builds on that, as much as the times would allow. If the novel or film seems merely pro-cop or appears to be an argument for the indulgence of minor payoffs, whether financial or psychological, it was by the standards of the late 1950s or early 1960s about as critical of the police as a novelist, producer, or director with an eye for the main chance could be, particularly in depicting the much more systematic corruption of officials higher up than Madigan. Still, the *New York Times* reviewer who described the film version as a "rather routine man-hunt" was, lamentably, not far wrong.[15]

Dougherty noted later that one critic said *The Commissioner* was "good for the Fire Department"; that is, an embarrassment for their perennial rivals, the cops. A decade after its publication, the fifty-year-old Dougherty quit his day job as a journalist, gave up his pension, and joined George McGovern's presidential campaign as press secretary. He eventually wrote a book about the experience, *Goodbye, Mr. Christian*. For all its limitations, the McGovern campaign was the closest thing to a major party crusade leftward since FDR's 1936 reelection bid, and Dougherty, who stepped back into obscurity, can surely be appreciated as an idealist.

It is tempting to read into *Madigan* the emergence of Polonsky's concern with the bureaucratic "moral collective" that he and his friends had abandoned in the wake of their 1956 disillusionment with Russia. Although he took up that concern more explicitly a few years later in *Monsignor*, *Madigan* follows Dougherty's narrative so carefully that Polonsky's primary concern must have been his frustration with "Hollywood naturalism." In fact that was his own memory of the script and the film production.

As limiting as Polonsky may have found the script, it nevertheless affected the detective genre in several ways. Siegel, the action specialist, seized the theme of the moralistic police commissioner and politicized it by turning him into an archetypal flabby liberal who succumbs all too easily to pressures from socialites at the expense of justice and the ordinary guy—the cop. Although *Dirty Harry* (1972), starring Clint Eastwood in his swaggering "Make my day!" persona, was somewhat accurately seen as a semifascist response to the demands for law and order during the tumultuous 1960s, it is less accurately viewed as director Siegel's sequel to *Madigan*.[16] The real sequel, the made-for-television *Madigan* films, showcased Widmark as Widmark, tough, existential, subtly romantic, perhaps still looking for the kind of parts that left-wing film writers had given him during the late 1940s and early 1950s rather than either the avenging angel or psycho of his type-casting. Polonsky's *Madigan* is more psycho than avenging angel; the writer looked upon the trope of American individualism as entertainment, the same old gunfight ethos reworked through the crime genre. At any rate, the film had been worthwhile for Polonsky because it made him "legit" and opened the door to his most elaborate and straightforward antiracist project, *Tell Them Willie Boy Is Here*, which would star Robert Redford and Robert Blake.

3

In the summer of 1969, Polonsky's first directorial effort in twenty years was released to critical praise and condemnation alike. Anyone looking for a moderation of his views, a gesture of accommodation to his critics or to the larger society, would find no such compromises in *Tell Them Willie Boy Is Here*, his only western and arguably his most vividly political film. Indeed, the artist-theorist who had returned to the director's chair at the age of fifty-eight was still at the peak of his powers. For more than a few older moviegoers, close-ups of Robert Blake were strikingly reminiscent of the young John Garfield; it must have been tempting to regard *Willie Boy* as in some sense a continuation of the themes in *Force of Evil* and to imagine that Polonsky had simply resumed his work where he had left off. Except that both films lie squarely within the traditions of their genres, that notion was not widely held and Polonsky certainly did not share it. "*Force of Evil* dealt with what they used to call Angst," he said. *Willie Boy* "ignores that. This film starts long after we're used to Angst."[17]

This was a prophetic observation. For the rest of his career, Polonsky's defenders were just as likely as his critics to mischaracterize and misunderstand his work. The one thing that admirers and detractors have in common has been their reflexive liberalism; conservatives seem to have ignored Polonsky after destroying his early career. The most famous liberal critics savaged *Willie Boy* immediately upon its release. *New Yorker* staffer Pauline Kael, who started her career on the Bay Area pacifist-left Pacifica radio station KPFA and has been paying penance ever since, correctly saw in *Willie Boy* something larger than the critique of daily life in Polonsky's B films like *Body and Soul* and *Force of Evil*. She was horrified to see this full-blown Polonsky A production, complete with a marketing budget, lay out the entire American empire for autopsy. Her capsule review of the film ran for months in the *New Yorker*. The longer version charged wildly that the film represents "schematic Marxism and Freudianism and New Left guerilla Existentialism and late-60s American self-hatred," with a sheriff "named Coop so that his actions will symbolize the ultimate cowardice and failure of the Gary Cooper hero figures." Kael also objected to the "woman doctor (Susan Clark)," who, as superintendent of the reservation, "is a patronizing-to-Indians liberal . . . ashamed of her sexuality (like all liberals)."[18]

Other reviewers were far more respectful. The *New York Times* heartily welcomed Polonsky back to films; *Nation* reviewer Robert

Hatch cheered "the best Western I've seen in years" and "a personal victory" for its director. Stanley Kauffman reflected more appreciatively in the *New Republic*, "Polonsky has done superbly," while *Time* and *Newsweek* offered more so-so reviews.[19] *Variety*, with its journalistic ears close to Hollywood ground zero, was perhaps most favorable of all, calling it "the most complex and original American film since 'Bonnie and Clyde,'" a movie that mainstream critics rejected out of hand as too rebellious and dangerous only to reverse themselves when its impact upon the youth market became evident. It was indeed a "deeply personal and radical vision of the past and future of this country," but it lacked the backing to survive the censorial attack.[20]

The excess of Kael's review is partly explainable by her long-standing if occasionally inconsistent revulsion at the blacklistees' work. (She had cursed the warm treatment of women and Chicanos in *Salt of the Earth* as "communist propaganda.") But the times were more to blame. The war in Vietnam raged on with no apparent hope of resolution; the black revolt was at its peak in the wake of the assassination of Dr. Martin Luther King, Jr., and hope for a radical reordering of American institutions was emerging among white youth. So, aside from her flippant reference to existentialism, Kael got it about right: *Tell Them Willie Boy Is Here* was a historical piece that Polonsky intended to examine the neocolonial system and transcend his earlier films' questions about the domestic price of capitalism. Not least, the movie constituted Polonsky's testament, as he called it, to the New Left.

The writer-director gave a flood of interviews after the success of *Willie Boy*, including a *Johnny Carson Show* appearance in 1970.[21] One of the earliest, frankest, and most spontaneous was with Eric Sherman and Martin Rubin in 1969. It included Polonsky's extended remarks about his political purpose in making the film:

> It had to do with most of the young people I knew today, living in a transitional period and being driven by circumstances and values they couldn't control. . . . I thought I could play around with this romantic investment we have in the past, along with a lack of comprehension for the realities of the present, and show these two things pushing one way and another. . . . This picture is intended for young people not yet committed to the disasters of history. If I had one specific intention in my mind, it was to tell my feelings about this to your generation. Not to mine. . . . I have a particular feeling about this general problem. Not just because they're Indians, but because this is a general human situation. It's fundamental to human history—this terrible thing that we do. Civilization is the process of despoiling, of spoliation of people, which in the past we considered a victory, but we now suspect is a moral defeat for

all. My feeling about this film, in making it, was to address it to your generation and say, "This is what I think about this. This is the way I see it. This is what this experience is—and you should know it."[22]

The story of Willie Boy first came to Polonsky's attention when it was proposed that he write a television "long form" (broadcast-film-length) script based on a western buff's book. Published by a small press in 1960, the book was essentially journalism using fictional devices to tell the story. Polonsky first turned down the assignment because, he said, he had "no particular interest in the Old West or in the New West, or the Old East or the New East, or anything like that." Then he caught the story's scent of a generation on the run.[23]

In brief, the tale of Willie Boy concerns an Anglo-led pursuit of a Chemehuevi Indian laborer. Willie had killed another Chemehuevi man in 1909 and then ran off with his victim's daughter. Although the story is based on a real incident, there is little agreement on what actually happened or on the individual motives of his pursuers. Regional-color author Harry Lawton, who wrote the novel about the incident, saw a saga about the twilight of the Old West; earlier writers had seen a tale of Indian perfidy; two scholarly historians writing since the film appear to have seen in the film the perfidy of Hollywood.[24]

At its heart, Polonsky's film is a story about four people who find themselves on the American empire's fault line at the moment of its consolidation. They include a western white man and an eastern white woman, the latter a self-described "bluestocking" who lived on the remote colonial edge of the American purpose, and another couple, Willie and Lola, who live next door, but on the Indian side of that considerable arroyo. Although the Anglo couple are indisputably dominant over Willie and Lola, they can also express respect, as when Coop, the white man, tells a greenhorn in a bar that he would be dead if Willie Boy had intended to kill him. They can also desire intimacy, so long as the Indians accept it obediently, as when Dr. Elizabeth Arnold, the white woman, first shouts at and then embraces Lola in the marketplace after the girl has laughed inappropriately at the mayhem caused by a horse.

Equally important is the gender axis in the two couples' relationships. Within those couples, each individual tries to impose on the other a life that he or she cannot live. Lola cannot accept Willie Boy's demand that she live as a traditional Indian wife in the desert, and he cannot accept her desire for him to become a farmer in Nevada. Similarly, Coop cannot imagine living in New England at the side of a Brahmin, and Dr. Arnold cannot accept the notion that she will languish in the wilderness at the side of a man whose notion of lovemaking is primordial at best. Polonsky emphasized the importance of these four characters' intimate lives to the larger story by relentlessly cutting back and forth between scenes of the two couples' lovemaking. He explained, "I treat both love affairs as a single affair, being acted out by different people at different times."

The movie's central concern is the impositions of empire on the four protagonists' ordinary humanity. That was not so easy to see at the time of its release in 1969. During the age of Che Guevara on American campuses, the picture resonated as the story of one man in armed revolt. Of course, that has always been an important part of Willie Boy's appeal in fact and legend. For others, the story's appeal is more the reprise of the ancient theme of the fading West played out in *The Wild Bunch* (1969) and in so many other movies, and perhaps most memorably for the young in the nonwestern *Bonnie and Clyde* (1967). For the fans of the western in particular, *Willie Boy* remains much as Lawton saw its basic story, with Willie the very last of the (western) Mohicans. But acute moviegoers then, as now, realized something much more provocative must be going on when a genuine crusader like Dr. Elizabeth Arnold disrobes, weeping with disgust at her own desire, and drives from her bedroom the apotheosis of the Old West, Gary Cooper. (Kael was correct in this comparison.)

Interesting as the contrast of historical types was at the time—if only to expose the guilt of a Boston liberal at the height of a war launched and guided by the Ivy League's "best and brightest"—the scene retains its strength for deeper historical reasons. The supervisory class's ongoing sexual distortions, for example, which are expressed with wan wisdom in Dr. Arnold's amazing, ostrich-feathered Edwardian bonnet, become abundantly apparent moments later when she cannot take responsibility for her own orgasm.

Doubtless it was scenes like these that earned Polonsky the "existentialist" sobriquet both from liberal enemies like Kael and from friendly commentators like Scorsese. Polonsky, however, wonderingly laughed off that label in several interviews and explicitly rejected it in his writing. American film critics and historians may simply be more comfortable using the term *existentialist* than the more accurate but discomfiting *Marxist*.

In any case, *Willie Boy* seems to invite descriptions like Kael's "Marxism and Freudianism and New Left guerilla Existentialism" both as praise and as disapproval. If nothing else, such descriptions express the idea that this is an intellectually ambitious film that cannot be reduced to the usual expectations of the western or, for that matter, to the notion of the moving picture as entertainment. *Tell Them Willie Boy Is Here* is a fully developed work of art that leaves the conventions of the novel behind, using conscious innovations in music and cinematography to integrate its themes at a higher narrative level.

Dave Grusin's music was an intentional departure for that period. Though its devices now seem familiar because they have been copied for more than three decades, they were stunning at the time. Rejecting the usual hymns and marches that earlier composers and music directors had used to evoke the Old West, Grusin introduced a series of "organic" sounds that suggested something very remote from the daily life of the Anglo audience. A marimba frames the running scenes with a ten- or twelve-note figure. A bass flute (often in a tape loop to provide an echo) illustrates the protagonists' isolation during moments of rest from the chase. Additional instruments include a soprano flute, tuned drums in ascending tattoos, wood blocks with rattles, and heavy chords of chimes underscored with pronounced bass notes.

The effect is deliberately nonorchestral and percussive, perhaps for the nondesert dweller evoking the foreign qualities of desert life forms. The only recognizably European notes are struck in the scenes between Coop and Dr. Arnold, when an ascending line in Arnold Schoenberg's serial style underlines their alienated sexuality. The film's influence on Hollywood's musical style is evident in Grusin's having gone on to compose the music for *The Electric Horseman* (1978) and *Reds* (1981). He won an Academy Award in 1988 for *The Milagro Beanfield War*.

Polonsky asked *Willie Boy*'s cinematographer, Conrad Hall, to desaturate the film's color, lending the sky and sand a shadowless, silvery cast. The studio was unhappy with the technique because of the additional expense of treating the film stock and because they were afraid the movie would look washed out on television and thereby lose air play (and considerable profits). But Polonsky got what he wanted. Again, the result was worlds apart from the 1940s noir films, in which single-source lighting created heavy shadows and the negative presence of things unseen and unseeable by the camera. Or was it so different from noir, after all? Polonsky's comments on the point are provocative but elusive:

> I probably have a natural tendency which is impossible to escape. I present the contrary in every case, and that lends an air of suspicion to everything I do. In *Willie Boy*, unlike *Force of Evil*—it's not deliberate. *Force of Evil* is bathed

in ambiguity; in *Willie Boy,* the whole thing is bathed in clarity in order to trap you in the ambiguities; it's a different technique, but it's only technical, the difference, I would say.[25]

In *Willie Boy* Polonsky consummated his art of cutting from "meaning to meaning" rather than from scene to scene; that is, from the heart of one scene to the next without bridges of extraneous dialogue. Toward the end, this most gifted of dialogue writers began to abandon language altogether. As Coop chases Willie up Ruby Mountain in the closing scenes, the script becomes almost entirely an abstraction, little more than written direction with scraps of dialogue. Yet even within this silent conversation between the hunter and his prey, the rocks and the sky, Polonsky's hand is unmistakable. He once referred obliquely to these scenes as "the non-dialogue I have in *Willie Boy.*" They are, in part, the realization of the ideal he described in "Manifesto for a Utopian Cinema."

4

Polonsky's last contribution as a director was, at first glance, a most unusual choice. Less than two years after *Tell Them Willie Boy Is Here* and three years after *Madigan,* he shot a film about a world as far removed from Willie Boy's sierras as from his old favorite, Manhattan. Based loosely on short stories by the noted Yiddish novelist Joseph Opatoshu, *Romance of a Horsethief* (1971) was scripted mainly by the novelist's son David Opatoshu, a youthful actor on the Yiddish stage, later a film and television actor and a longtime friend of the Hollywood progressives. The film's central tale, "Roman fun a Ferd-Gonef" (Story of a Horse Thief), was published in the premier Yiddish literary series, *Shriftn,* in 1912, five years after the elder Opatoshu migrated to New York from Poland.[26] "Roman fun a Ferd-Gonef" has never been translated into English, but its significance in Yiddish letters was firmly established almost immediately. As one scholar of Yiddish literature observes, the story shockingly introduced to Yiddish readers the Jewish underworld with its joys and dangers, its tremendous vitality, its hot passions, and its not altogether respectable moral values.[27]

Opatoshu's full-blooded rascals, smugglers, and drunkards were a world away from Sholem Aleichem's generally frail, impractical, heaven-gazing shtetl dwellers. Indeed, just as the short story would inevitably be compared to the fable-like literary standard of the day, its film dramatization should be seen as a counterpoint to *Fiddler on the Roof* (1971), which was readapted from Arnold Perl's stage adaptation, "The World of Sholem Aleichem."[28] As Polonsky has slyly suggested, his film is the revolutionary version of *Fiddler*.

Romance of a Horsethief follows Eli Wallach and Oliver Tobias as a pair of high-spirited turn-of-the-century Jewish-Polish horse rustlers who fence with the Czar's local proconsul over military conscription during the early days of the Russo-Japanese War. While mixing business and pleasure, the antiheroes end up promoting generalized subversion of the Czar's authority. The proconsul, played by that old friend of the Left Yul Brynner, has been let down by life simply by being posted to such a distant and backward region; like Brynner's character in *The King and I* (1956), the proconsul loves the symbols of authority (especially fancy clothes) but does not care to notice the events taking place under his nose. The politically subversive element and the foppish proconsul were scarcely present in the original. Polonsky had not read "Roman fun a Ferd-Gonef" but worked instead on the existing script, tightening a weak story line and restructuring the plot to dramatize a political ending.

At the onset of the film, the rascals Wallach and Tobias manage to make their living a bit easier (but obviously with more risks) than the other impoverished Jews around them, who struggle to earn their bread through honest village toil. The two have especially mastered making bigger and more respectable gentile crooks think they are putting across a brilliant deal. Actress Lainie Kazan plays the town madam and Wallach's lover; she finds him hilarious, domineering but also sexy and lovable. Tobias, irresistible and always romancing someone, is suddenly and overwhelmingly drawn to Jane Birkin, playing a wealthy gentile who has returned from a radicalizing Paris education complete with a nerdy French fiancé. She soon finds herself both protecting and being protected by Tobias. He seduces her physically, but as a well-meaning revolutionary intellectual, she also seduces him into a sort of political understanding. He finally wins her heart as well as her body when he manages to distribute antidraft leaflets at a meeting the proconsul has arranged to announce conscription for the soon-to-be disastrous Russo-Japanese War.

Because all the horses of the district are to be conscripted along with the men, Wallach and Tobias will soon be out of business—unless they can somehow steal the animals back. They accomplish this by posing as visiting high officers whom the Czar has sent to halt the spread of horse disease by burning infected documents and taking away the horses, apparently to be slaughtered. The garrisoned soldiers also willingly surrender their "infected" breeches, which the scoundrels burn before their ruse is discovered. Hopelessly and hilariously, on foot and in their underwear, the soldiers finally give chase to the rascals and the horses. Amidst all this confusion, Brynner grows more weary than angry. At the film's close, seeing the horse thieves across the border with their booty, Brynner officially declares them all carriers of disease. In driving them from his domain, he has thus heroically protected the Czar's own.

In a sense everyone wins, or at least escapes history's judgments, when, during the usual run of things, the authorities violently crush those who are out of line, becoming themselves the worst of criminals. The most sympathetic critics credited Polonsky's contribution to the concept of the collective hero, a shift from the lone protagonist to the revolutionary mass comparable, for instance, to George Lamming's contemporary West Indian historical novels. Of course, Polonsky's comedy had another point: Opatoshu's leading character could not stand the weight of becoming a swashbuckling hero any more than the naive Birkin could be a Joan of Arc or the sympathetic Brynner a monster in Czar's clothing. By moving the script further toward interrelated destinies, as Eric Sherman put it,

> everything changes, whether we want it or not. This universal principle is profoundly applied by Polonsky to occurrences in the film that would ordinarily be taken by liberals to be political givens. A "cell" meeting turns into a romantic picnic; an impossible impersonation leads to the escape of everyone who wants to escape; a horse being led through the halls of a whore house goes unnoticed by the villain Brynner; a young horse thief risks all just to ride a beautiful white horse. In fact, this last scene is one of the most lyrical in film memory, evoking the transient quality of "real" time and space . . .

Thus, in *Romance* thieves don't really steal; commandants don't really command; revolutionaries don't really revolutionize; emigrants don't really emigrate. The picture's last image—an ensemble of the leading characters blending with the woods that have provided their camouflage—is perhaps the most succinct statement of Polonsky's overriding ethic: the determination apparent in all dogmas about social behavior narrows the range of human interaction. The complete story requires an examination of how people become something other than what they start out to be.[29]

This world of muscular, hard-drinking, sex-loving, and sometimes revolutionary Yiddish-speaking Jews gave Polonsky a context as comfortable as any of those he enjoyed in the popular American film genres.

In one of his most dramatic and personal essays on his own films, Polonsky wrote that the images in *Romance of a Horsethief* "signify something beyond, because they come by way of the tales my grandmother told me, worked through the stories of the Opatoshus, father and son. It is her voice I hear all through the movie and it was her voice and her face which toured the locations." More than that, doing the film brought to mind "the antic continuously imaginary world" he enjoyed as a child, movies "irrevocably and richly rooted in kitsch, in childhood, in story telling, in the rubbish of paperbacks and sitting under the streetlights while off in the zoo across the lots flowering with burdock, lions roared out their fantasy of freedom."[30] Critics, deprived of Polonsky's cut, seemed nevertheless to appreciate that he had rescued a film from a problematic script with actors who seemed almost randomly cast from an international troupe. If arguably not the best possible director for such a fanciful project, the *Times* reviewer noted, he was "endlessly intelligent, resourceful and tactical enough to appreciate the conventions of the form."[31]

Romance was Polonsky's fantasy of freedom from the weight of history, and he enjoyed it thoroughly. He freely admitted that it was "a great pleasure to make a movie again," meaning to direct a movie as he had done shortly before with *Willie Boy*, after so much waiting. Returning at once to his other lifelong fantasy, he further commented, "Nothing is better; perhaps revolution, but there you have to succeed and be right, dangers which never attach themselves to making movies, and dreaming."[32] Perhaps no more strongly surrealist statement has been written about film except by the surrealists themselves.

This does not quite resolve Polonsky's stance on Jewish topics. While eloquent and precise about his work's political content, he begged off discussing such themes. Like other Jewish artists and intellectuals of his generation, he was preoccupied with the universal issues that go to the heart of Western culture and history, of capitalism and revolution, of loyalties and betrayals that have less to do with ethnic identities than with the rise and fall of cultures and states.

Nevertheless, before the 1950s Polonsky may have regarded the Jewish element in his work as incidental, the details necessarily collected by any story line that grows out of personal experience. But at the very least he came to regard it as what he understood best. Central characters in all of his novels after *The World Above* are Jewish, and had his health permitted him to continue directing, there are good reasons to think he would have addressed the paradoxes of Jewish life that he expressed so well in *Zenia's Way*. There, the "rags and leftovers, the refuse of life . . . become the objects of new artists," reinventing them for museums by refashioning perhaps the very same objects "thrown out of the museum's door and now repurchased through the front door by foundations made from the wealth of the industries that made the objects in the first place."[33] To foreground the Jewish role in business contorts the Jewish role in popular as well as high art. Upward mobility and artistic striving are interrelated but never amiably, save perhaps through the artist's self-deception or the businessman's successful rise to patron status. The relation between art and business is fruitful but never comfortable.

When Polonsky left the project in Yugoslavia, his task was finished, as far as he knew. After his departure, however, *Romance of a Horsethief* was edited disastrously. Scenes were cut or mangled, and a confused soundtrack was thrown in, purportedly to attract a wider American audience. The film's real weaknesses, like Birkin's improbably starched English accent, were made worse, and the intermittently chaotic action came rather closer to narrative confusion than the Jewish surrealism that Polonsky (or either of the Opatoshus) had intended.

Still, Polonsky saved the film from being a total disaster. It is as fascinating as many another loosely plotted admixture of drama and comedy. For all its faults, it may very well be the most revolutionary *Jewish* film ever made, in stark contrast to those numerous movies about victimized European Jews whose fate depends on outside aid from gentiles, as well as in contrast to the naive and overly precious world of Sholem Aleichem's Tevye, the good-hearted milkman. (Polonsky insisted repeatedly that *Romance of a Horsethief* was not a Holocaust film, even if the world of the Jewish shtetl had to be physically recreated for the film because the Holocaust had eliminated the Jews in those very districts.)

In any case, after Polonsky returned to Hollywood, his doctor called Sylvia into the office and pronounced the director's heart too weak for any further such efforts.

What had he missed? Unquestionably great films were made during the last era of his career, and however indirectly, many bore his stamp. He was always happy enough to consult with his favorite younger people. Aldrich, whose fondness for his mentor remained great, repeatedly asked in his last days to see Polonsky and delivered his friend's principal eulogy at the Directors' Guild.[34]

In the broader view, Polonsky's former comrades, working always picture by picture, managed to express a great many of the moods that had seemed to him valid and cinematically possible. *The Front* (1976), scripted by Walter Bernstein—and made possible by Woody Allen's participation—comes to mind, of course, as does *Guilty by Suspicion*. So do Ritt's *No Down Payment* (1957), a beautifully claustrophobic drama about suburban materialism and madness (not forgetting racism); his iconoclastic and revealing *The Spy Who Came in from the Cold* (1965); his antiracist western, *Hombre* (1967); his class-struggle-themed *The Molly Maguires* (1970) and *Norma Rae* (1979); his deeply feminist *Cross Creek* (1983) and *Nuts* (1987). To be sure, Ritt (like his frequent scriptwriter Bernstein) was a far more straightforward storyteller than Polonsky, but with their similarly radical Jewish personalities and political passions Ritt clearly was completing his part of the project begun earlier on smaller budgets, while the Film Code hung suspended over the artists' heads.[35]

Would Polonsky have wanted to script other works of blacklistees writing for fronts or returning on various films like *The Defiant Ones* (1957), *Lawrence of Arabia* (1962), *Hud* (1963), *Sands of the Kalahari* (1965), *The Group* (1966), *Two Mules for Sister Sarah* (1970), *M*A*S*H* (1970), *A Doll's House* (1973), *Julia* (1977), *Roads to the South* (1978), or B choices and star exploitation extravaganzas like *Cleopatra* (1963), *Gold for the Caesars* (1965), *Fall of the Roman Empire* (1963), and *Horror Express* (1972)? He characteristically demurred from the question: he was not asked; the writers involved made their own deals, and their work interested him even when he could not admire it artistically.[36]

He admitted to a particular fondness for Waldo Salt, an affinity that makes sense. Salt was a phenomenally bright midwestern boy who graduated from Stanford at sixteen and moved through the network of young lefties into thirties film writing. He won accolades for strictly mainstream work (with a few touches of antiwar sentiment) in *Shopworn Angel* (1938). He regained his place among American screenwriters with *Taras Bulba* (1962), an early recovery film from the blacklist, and also with staggeringly wonderful scripts for *Midnight Cowboy* (1969, for which he won an Academy Award), *Serpico* (1973, for which he was nominated), *Day of the Locust* (1975), and *Coming Home* (1978, for which he shared an Oscar). Not really experimentally inclined but willing to try (as in the surreal passages of *Locust*), Salt had a genius for the realism of the social margins and an unstoppable political commitment. Luckier than Polonsky, he also was better suited to Hollywood as it existed before the blacklist and as it became afterward.

It is easier to see the personal connections among other blacklistees on the Hollywood television production scene—Adrian Scott, Alfred and Helen Levitt, or veterans of the old left-wing radio crowd like comedy-writer Frank Tarloff. Despite television viewers' continuing fascination with detectives, noir-style technical experimentation had been absent from television generally, apart from a very occasional episode of *M*A*S*H* (1972–83) in black and white or sans sound. Apart from *You Are There,* television's production conditions rarely suited Polonsky.[37] Only decades later, with the stylings of *Miami Vice* (1984–89) and, more so, the short-lived but brilliant *Crime Story* (1986–88), did noir carve a network niche. Barry Levinson's brainchild *Homicide* (1993–99), with its angled camera-work, cinematic treatment of odd characters, and depiction of the daily injustice in blue-collar Baltimore, finally reached beyond the strict law-and-order premises of rather experimental cop shows to a new level of existential observation. It achieved some commercial success but not enough to survive several seasons of mediocre ratings. Nonetheless, *Homicide*'s often brilliant dialogue could not approach the stylized prose of *Force of Evil;* no network audience was likely for that sort of fully realized art form in sustained doses, although the worlds of cable and the Internet perhaps offered still untouched artistic and political possibilities.

5

His directing career finished, Polonsky still had notions of scripts he would pursue if only their prospects of production seemed serious. The notebooks in his collected papers are filled with ideas never fleshed out. But several of his scripts did get produced, at least one with awful results.

Fascinated by a genre in which the little he had done met no success— the unproduced script for "Out of This World" is a vivid case in point— Polonsky turned to a science fiction classic that he had long admired. Arthur C. Clarke had become a monumental figure in film when *2001: A Space Odyssey* reached the screen in 1968 (never mind that *2010,* made in 1984, was an artistic disappointment and a near-bomb at the box office). But Clarke's literary masterwork, and arguably his most political novel, was *Childhood's End* (1953), which reflected the widespread sense that the arms race would probably destroy the planet unless something dramatic halted humanity's rush to self-immolation. Director Robert Wise's *The Day the Earth Stood Still* (1952) had depicted a semi-divine version of intervention, with austere aliens banning weapons and pronouncing world government. *Childhood's End*, like Clarke himself, was more mystical and philosophical.

Clarke's plot, too, has aliens suddenly at the helm of earth's fate, impervious to the weapons the earthlings throw against them. But the aliens' ultimate purpose remains unknown. The aliens prevent wars and accelerate technological development to make possible a sort of libertarian socialism where people will work only as much as they want—or they can continue on the path to self-destruction, or they may possibly unite with the mystically cosmic Overmind, leaving corporal existence behind. But they insist that only in fifty years will the meaning of it all become clear.[38]

Polonsky's script made decisive changes in personnel and plot. The introduction of a revolutionary woman with "fantastic, radiating youth, energy, a startling beautiful . . . stray streak of violent red hair, green eyes ready to escape like wild things, and a smile" is typically Polonskyan. She reappears several times and, as an elderly figure, watches over the apocalyptic conclusion. Clarke's work ends with the alien Karellan traveling away in space and turning his back "upon the dwindling Sun."[39] In Polonsky's version, the sun becomes one among other stars, no longer surrounded by planets, and at last only the spaceship's viewing screen "is visible, playing its alphabet of color, mysterious and nameless as the universe itself."[40]

This is certainly a curious apocalypse, better than nuclear war, but also apparently far outside the humanist realm of Polonsky's other work. Had he written it to keep his hand in, or simply to make money? No, he insisted, the idea of an adaptation of *Childhood's End* had interested him for decades; this was his shot at getting one produced.

By lamentable contrast, *Avalanche Express* (1979) was a straight job ordered by Polonsky's old friend Mark Robson, and Polonsky was glad enough to accept the six-figure contract as part of his retirement expenses. The cold-war plot had possibilities. CIA agent Lee Marvin utilizes a Soviet defector, Robert Shaw, to lure scientist Maximilian Schell onto a trans-European train. Shaw and Schell are not old-fashioned grateful East Bloc refugees but intellectuals who have come to see the two sides as about the same. They likewise see themselves trapped between contending forces and consider Marvin something of a combined political cynic and madman. Linda Evans, playing an old company hand still in love with Marvin, is the romantic interest, and the ludicrously extended cast even includes football quarterback Joe Namath making several appearances in cowboy boots!

The film's quality was doomed even before the deaths of both Robson and Shaw, whose dialogue was rather clumsily dubbed. Moreover, studio determination to achieve action-thriller status with the film suspended the dialogue between endless shots of the train hurtling through snow into the mountains, a botched sabotage attempt, and hand-to-hand combat. It might as well have been based on a comic book as on Colin Forbes's novel. Polonsky could hardly bear to talk about it.[41]

At the beginning of the 1980s, Polonsky attempted one more political script, "Assassination on Embassy Row."[42] Arguably, it was his most thoroughly (or didactically) political effort. A producer in CBS's theatrical division had contracted him to write "Assassination," and he responded warmly to the idea of analyzing the Chilean military's CIA-connected 1973 conspiracy to eliminate Orlando Letelier, the deposed left-wing government's former ambassador to the United States. Polonsky went directly to John Dinges and Saul Landau's account, likewise named *Assassination on Embassy Row*. Dinges was a respected investigative journalist, Landau a seasoned Latin Americanist with a past distinctly simpatico to Polonsky's. A noted campus left-winger during the later 1950s and a founder of Fair Play for Cuba, Landau briefly served as C. Wright Mills's secretary while *Listen, Yankee!* was being written. He went on to become a documentary filmmaker and high-level associate at the beltline leftish think tank, the Institute for Policy Studies.[43]

Dinges and Landau's *Assassination on Embassy Row* was a tour de force revelation of international conspiracy and the complicity of United States intelligence. Letelier was the leading opponent of Chilean dictator General Augusto Pinochet. A week before a bomb killed Letelier, his widely-read article in the *Nation* magazine exposed the connections between the squeeze placed upon ordinary Chileans by Pinochet and his terrorist security agency, DINA, and the "Chicago School" economics that was to become the model of Reagan think-tankers. A few days before his murder, Letelier delivered a major address in Madison Square Garden, bringing together prominent political refugees and their American supporters.

Agent Michael Townley of the Central Intelligence Agency originally outlined the murder, and right-wing Cuban exiles set it in motion. Arguably this amounted to the most stunning piece of United States government wrongdoing since the Vietnam War. Despite guilty verdicts for Townley, the Cuban exiles, and their DINA contacts, the 1979 trial ended in an anticlimax. Prosecution and defense had worked together to wall off any evidence of Pinochet's guilt, portraying the accused as rogue elements of assorted intelligence agencies. Townley himself spent less than two years in prison before being fitted with a new identity and, presumably, a fat life under the Chilean dictatorship. The repression in Chile worsened and environmental destruction accompanied vast new theft of what had been regarded historically as Indian lands. Yet, after a brief chill, the United States' official and unofficial relationships with Pinochet warmed again and glowing reports of Chile's economic recovery appeared regularly in the business pages of the American press. As in many other instances, Reaganism was already in full sway before Jimmy Carter left office.[44]

The film script, in a fine documentary note, opens with a real-life television report of Henry Kissinger literally embracing the new dictator, Pinochet. Although the secretary of state obviously knew of and almost certainly had a hand in the coup, as did the action arms of the AFL-CIO and the American religious Right, Kissinger denies the allegations: "The cause of human dignity is not served by those who hypocritically manipulate concerns with rights to further their political preferences." Further, Kissinger would not have been ignorant about the subsequent assassination, as subsequent revelations made clear.

The film script shows Letelier speaking in Madison Square Garden as American FBI agent Frederic Dalton uses binoculars to spot a cast of very real characters, including Isabel Letelier, Ronni Moffitt with her husband, Letelier confidant Carol Stone, and their left-wing intellectual comrade, none other than Saul Landau. Meanwhile, CIA agent Townley discusses the planned assassination's details with the DINA agents and Cuban exiles.

In a somewhat fictionalized scene months earlier Dalton steps in on a social afternoon with the Leteliers and warns them of their danger. When they prove unwilling to act "appropriately," he resigns himself to the fact that their lives are at risk. His FBI bosses, uninformed by their intelligence community colleagues and obviously at cross purposes with them, have concluded that Pinochet would not be foolish enough to stage an assassination in Washington, even if it might eliminate his most important Chilean foe.

Polonsky shows the bomb's preparation and detonation in considerable detail, in part to treat the bombers' personalities and the victims' circumstances. On the morning of the car bombing, Michael Moffitt insists on sitting in the back seat while his wife Ronni sits in front with Letelier, who will drive; thus Michael survives and Ronni dies with Letelier. After the violence, the barely fictionalized Landau tells reporters that the

Chilean government has ordered the terrorism. Chilean officials answer that the charge is a "propaganda campaign of the Soviet Union against us," while the Washington papers and their official government sources propose the alternative theory that left-wing extremists assassinated Letelier to "create a martyr" who embarrasses the Chileans. Dalton insistently assures Landau that the Bureau will bring in the real killers.[45]

A cat-and-mouse game follows, with Dalton tracking down the killers, aided by Stone, who reverses her skepticism about the conspiracy after a knife-wielding Cuban exile threatens her. As in reality, another Cuban exile picked up for casual criminal activities spills his guts to Dalton, who quickly finds himself set to track down the assassins. Dalton's boss warns him, "You're over your head. It's politics now. It's Frisbee time in the corridors of power." As newsreel shots of Jimmy Carter and Pinochet shaking hands come onto the television, Pinochet once again insists that he is completely innocent, "a Christian, not an assassin."

Townley, the CIA's point man in Chile, realizes the circle is closing but remains convinced that with the Chilean government's gratitude and help he can personally escape judgment. When Dalton tracks him down, Townley tells him, "In Chile the laws of Chile come before the United States." Dalton answers simply, "There are no laws in Chile. . . . You spent the best years of your life making sure there'd be none."

In the climactic court scene, the extradited Townley testifies only as far as he wishes, and the court rules that all questions relating to DINA and Pinochet are out of order. The consenting judge nevertheless admits that he has never "presided over a trial of murder as monstrous as this." He sentences the Cubans heavily and gives Townley ten years minus time served. After the climax comes the good-bye. Dalton now finds himself with his boss, trying to reason out what the government really knows. With the monuments of Washington visible through the bureau windows, his boss assures him, "Fred, we're working for the same government." Fred demurs, "We're not." As a coda, Polonsky finally added a scene that the book mentions only in passing, a folk concert in honor of Letelier, with Isabel Letelier as its star.

Again and again the drama returns emphatically to the banality of evil. Polonsky's Dalton calls Townley "just an American boy scout type with merit badges in electronics and assassination, the whole thing tied together with a nickel's worth of anti-communism." Make that the banality of imperial evil, American evil, exactly the evil that Polonsky's adversaries, including cold-war liberals, had repeatedly insisted did not and could not happen at the hands of government agencies in free America.

The production of *Assassination on Embassy Row* was put on hold due to the writers' strike of 1982 and then quietly abandoned. By now the Reagan era had begun, taking semiofficial pride in backing pro-American dictators rather than apologizing for their bloodbaths. Without the influential backers and big stars of another political film like *Missing,* so politically presumptive an artwork was guaranteed to fail. Decades would pass before Oliver Stone's *Nixon* could vigorously portray Henry Kissinger (to take a single case). Even then, the characterization was hardly an offensive portrait of the world's best-known war criminal (along with Pol Pot, who came to power with Kissinger's indirect assistance). When government perpetrates the scandals, Hollywood generally has trouble keeping up, although the later 1990s would see both *Wag the Dog* (which Polonsky surely would have loved to direct) and the British government's temporary internment of Kissinger favorite Pinochet, who was under indictment in Spain as a brutal torturer and murderer.

6

Polonsky's still vociferously radical view of America could only be realized in the self-reflective novel that he had worked on for more than a quarter-century, *Zenia's Way* (1980). In many ways, *Zenia's Way* is two books: one is Polonsky's childhood recollections (before his family left the Bronx), overlaid with a political drama and a boy's emotionally impassioned relation with his dynamic aunt; the other is a late-life and late-century commentary, drawn entirely from Polonsky's fertile imagination, on two radical outcasts of twentieth-century history meeting in Israel, a land of countless outcasts and innumerable contradictions. The volume holds some irony but great sadness at the weight of history and not a little philosophy. Compared to *The World Above,* it is incomplete, but incomplete in the way that any life, especially the life of a rebel, is incomplete as it approaches old age. Compared to *A Season of Fear,* it is also morally ambiguous. The real enemies (capitalists, fascists, and Stalinists) remain off camera; the FBI man who interrogates the family at the time of the Palmer Raids is as morally uncertain as the Palestinians who seize a school and threaten to kill all of its inhabitants, including the trapped protagonist and his Aunt Zenia. We cannot see these assorted armed men who serve the state or the would-be state as evil; they represent, instead, the compulsions of order and identity, both personal and collective, in a world of armed authority.

As the novel proper begins, the police raid has established the political theme, and title character Zenia (almost certainly from the Greek *xenes*, a foreigner or wanderer) is a medical student who turns her free days into moments of adventure with Ram. She answers the boy's innocent questions with pearls of wisdom about life that seem to come more from Polonsky's long and frequently contradictory experience than from the mouth of a young enthusiast. To decide to live a real life, a revolutionary life, she seems to be telling him, is no simple matter:

> It takes courage to live in the future. It takes the courage of forgetting everything you once loved. After all, you can be sure of this: the future will have the same sorrows as the past. And when you look back, old sorrows will show up as a kind of happiness and you'll start living each day wondering what might have been if you had never tried this future.[46]

Ram watches meanwhile as suitor after suitor pursues Zenia for marriage. Some offer the simple virtues of working-class experience; Harry, the most reflective (and the kindest to Ram), offers a philosophy to explain his own brother's death in Oklahoma's antidraft "green corn rebellion" uprising during the First World War.[47] Not only immigrants are isolated in America, something that Ram will understand more clearly as he grows. Zenia's eventual decision to return to Russia and all its perils seems as natural as the pursuit of money and upward mobility by many who remain in the New Land.

Within a few months' span, Zenia repeatedly urges Ram to see life without illusion and also seeks to comprehend for herself the meaning of moral or political commitment. Both aims are realized, although at a steep price: they will spend most of their lives apart and, thus, with part of themselves missing. Having known his real aunt very little in life, Polonsky attributes to her the qualities that crystallize Ram's moral-intellectual education within the family circle, complementing the warmth and relative egalitarianism that allowed the child to feel part of a serious and reflective world without abandoning his world of play.

The novel picks up a half-century after Zenia's departure. Ram is going back to the farm in upstate New York that Harry bought in hopes of luring Zenia, and where Harry lived intermittently the rest of his life. Ram recalls the 1940s in the OSS and lives through a heart attack that must certainly have mirrored Polonsky's own: heavy pain, survival against the medical odds, morphine to which he will become temporarily addicted, and a miraculous operation at Stanford, with one remaining downside. His vocal cord severed (again, as in the author's real life), Ram cannot speak for months until the cord grows back and his voice reemerges like "a salamander with a new tail."[48]

Ram survives for good narrative purpose. As the action resumes, Zenia is eighty-one years old, her nephew sixty-seven. The narrative voice has shifted to the third person without explanation, but the point of view clearly remains Ram's. Both figures have obviously led full lives as radicals. As a victim of Stalinism Zenia has spent time in Russian prisons on more than one occasion and, further, lost a husband and son to the Germans; as a civil rights lawyer (drawn obviously on Polonsky's friend Leonard Boudin) and sometime party member (drawn on Polonsky himself and other friends), Ram has suffered many political defeats. Quite remarkably given their experiences, neither of them is embittered by disillusionment or defeated by life. Through the courses of the Russian and American centuries, the two lives complete each other, both psychologically and (for this had grown more important in Polonsky's work) in Jewish experience. Perhaps Polonsky, who never knew his real aunt, intended them to make one another whole in the sense of Yiddish literary giant I. L. Peretz, who was known as the "*gantzer Yid*," the complete or fully realized Jew.[49]

At the novel's end, Ram is visiting Zenia in Israel, where she has resettled. Trapped together in a hostage situation at an Israeli school, they seek to befriend the Palestinian kidnappers, who indeed recognize them as leftists, but also as supporters of the Jewish state. The Israeli government lies about continuing negotiations in order to storm the schoolhouse. In the melee the Israeli force kills all but one of the captors and causes three schoolgirls' needless deaths. Now Zenia and Ram must grapple with a final, existential act. When they spot the surviving guerilla hiding in a ditch, he seems to be waving to them. He is actually hurling a grenade, however, thus giving away his position and being gunned down for his folly.

> She said, "I thought he wanted to thank me and wave good-bye. I wanted him to live, but he had other plans." Here, among the trampled asphodel she called out to history. "It's always that way.
>
> "But truly," Zenia said, "What we've just survived today and yesterday and the day before, what we've lived, was and is exactly the way it has been again and again. Yes exactly. Well," she added in her ever reasonable and questioning way, "a little different each time, after all.
>
> "Anyway," she said, "the defeated are not always the most defeated."[50]

That is the true Polonskyan note and, at age seventy, certainly a statement about his own life. Friendly reviewers took the message as it was meant. A commentator in the *Wilson Library Bulletin* called it "a statement of faith and an affirmation of the possibility of love." In the novel's first half, a *Village Voice* reviewer argued, Polonsky had indeed reconciled the historic alienation of Jews. In the second half, he neither dogmatically rejected the Israeli episode in Jewish history nor hailed Zionism as a practical and moral solution to the Jews' uncertain status in the world. Thus, though he did not resolve the issue, he had stated his theme on Israel brilliantly. If the novel has a flaw, Larry Ceplair identified it in the *Nation*. One of Polonsky's (and the left film colony's) best interviewers, Ceplair pointed out that Zenia is too finished and philosophical a figure (rather than becoming one, over the course of the narrative) and expresses her sentiments too articulately (less kind reviewers would say in too many platitudes). Polonsky might have replied, however, that he intended her to be the voice of history, the "old Mole" of Marxist observation. He *needed* her clear voice for this final novel.[51]

Notwithstanding *Publisher's Weekly*'s prediction that sales could compare to Chaim Potok's Jewish bestseller, *The Chosen*—given a suitable advertising campaign—the novel's greatest weakness lay in corporate shifts beyond the author's control. As the book went to press, its publisher, J. B. Lippincott, was snapped up and the new management ignored most of the house's existing titles. After laboring so hard over his spiritual autobiography, Polonsky was disappointed once again.

7

At the opening of *Monsignor*, which bore Polonsky's final screen credit, *Newsweek* jibed, "The Borgias Would Blanch."[52] As with the disastrous *Avalanche Express*, a friend (this time Twentieth Century–Fox director Frank Perry) had asked Polonsky, as a favor, to fix an adaptation that had proven beyond the initial screenwriter's abilities. Years earlier Perry's directing had elicited praise (including Jean Renoir's) for that famous little movie *David and Lisa*, remembered best in the blacklist community for returnee Howard Da Silva's major supporting role. Just as with *Avalanche Express*, a final writer would alter this script beyond Polonsky's control and against many of his predilections.[53] Although well intentioned, the casting also proved unfortunate. Christopher Reeve had already demonstrated his bona fides as a progressive pop icon in

Superman and had a built-in following. By the same token, however, he could not escape a certain typecasting. Nor could he handle the complexities of Polonskyan dialogue.[54]

In ways that *New York Times* reviewer Janet Maslin pointed out, the film was plainly impossible to get right. It was based on Jack Alain Leger's iconoclastic novel of the same name about papal plots and Father John Flaherty, a fictional protagonist who is so complex that the screen could not easily—perhaps could not possibly—capture his essence. Fatally innocent-eyed as Flaherty, Reeve misses by a thousand miles. Yet Maslin admitted that she had enjoyed the "most extravagant piece of Hollywood junk since 'Mommie Dearest,'" produced and directed by the same showmen, respectively (if not so respectably) Frank Yablans and Perry.[55] Few other reviewers were so kind, although the most intelligent granted *Monsignor* kinship to the classic junk movie made in the late fifties, the golden era of such films. *Monsignor* could not be made "small." But if only it had been played as pure camp, the more playful critics suggested, its faults might still have disappeared; the occasional line of serious dialogue or gesture of serious acting (by costar Geneviève Bujold, especially) spoiled the effect.

Was *Monsignor* meant to be made in that way or any in other particular way? Polonsky's script offers ample clues that a cheesy novel could have been made into a Second-World-War-vintage pic, with stark and complex human drama behind the antifascist struggle. Like other such films made during the 1960s and 1970s by ex-blacklistees and their friends (notably, *Yanks* [1979], written by Walter Bernstein; *The Guns of Navarone* [1961], by Carl Foreman; *The Heroes of Telemark* [1965], by Ben Barzman; and *The Bridge on the River Kwai* [1957], by Michael Wilson; and the film it most resembled, *The Cardinal* [1963], with civil rights scenes scripted by Gore Vidal and Ring Lardner, Jr.), it vindicates the forces of (antifascist) order through the process of stripping off layer after layer of their pretensions.

Either in homage to old Cagney films or simply borrowing from them, *Monsignor* begins with two youngsters about to steal dollar bills pinned to notes on an altar table in an Irish midtown church. Discovered, one escapes, the other is caught. The same good guy/bad guy priest-and-hoodlum motif set up the plot for *Angels with Dirty Faces* (1938). But this time it is the Irish boy who has an attack of conscience. Unlike his Italian pal, he only wanted to get God's attention. With the help of good Father Killarly, the youth resolves to become a priest. Polonsky insisted that his touch here was to authenticate the

Church's political machine–like character, despite its claims to be above the sins of the world.

Break to 1942. Now-Bishop Killarly guides Reeve, the monsignor, into the war effort "to comfort the wounded and the martyrs of this just war!" Before departing New York, Reeve oversees his childhood pal Lodo's (Joe Cortese) wedding amid Lindy hops. Reeve next turns up in a foxhole, endangering himself to give final rites to a dying soldier and then to his own surprise taking over the machine gun and saving the day for the Allies. In his own mind he has sinned, even if in a good cause, and now the plot is in high gear. Savvy Americans in the Vatican see him as just the bright, brilliantly charismatic figure they need at this moment when papist economics are taking a big hit and the global church is being reorganized. Pressed to save the papacy from ruin, Reeve turns to his pal Lodo, now a higher-up in the American-military end of the booming black market.[56]

One form of corruption leads to another as Reeve, acting out his role in the disguise of an American civilian, schemes to keep the church financially solvent. The privilege to enjoy a warm bath, a glass of champagne, and eventually a love affair with a postulant transforms him into a man with a real double life. In a genuine Polonsky film, the most powerful character would have been Reeve's lover, played by Bujold. Throughout most of her role, however, Bujold is merely a damaged and complex woman who has decided to become a nun after a series of disastrous love affairs. Not suspecting her newest lover's real identity, she throws herself into another emotional disaster.

The emotional treachery is outdone by real treachery. The church official who suspects and pursues the monsignor is pinpointed as (in a phrase that only Polonsky could have written) "a spy and a stool pigeon."[57] Toward the film's end, Reeve raises church finances several notches from black marketeering to the business of war surplus, real estate, stocks, bonds, and currency trading. Finally, Bujold spots him in a religious ceremony and then has the chance to quip face-to-face with her cassocked lover, "So you were married after all!"[58]

The pulpy plot winds itself up as a Sicilian mobster saves Reeve from himself, placing a cross around his neck after a drunken orgy. Lodo, who absconded with $40 million after speculating unsuccessfully with church resources, puts Reeve in such moral danger that only the blessing of the pope himself can save his soul and self-respect. (Actor Adolfo Celi plays the pope, looking, as one reviewer put it, almost exactly like E. T.) It was the Vatican that put Reeve to work in the dirty business, and now he will save the day with more successful manipulations. Morally tortured, he wants to resign from his church duties; instead, he is assigned ever higher levels of responsibility.

A reading of the script reveals just how important Polonsky meant his precisely stylized and theatrical phrases to be to the work's overall effect. This is particularly evident when the phrasings misfire, as with Reeve's persistent departures from the text, apparently due to his discomfort with "stilted" language. Time and again the progressive actor successfully made the phrasing more colloquial, more familiar to the American ear, or at least closer to the style of ordinary American realism; in so doing, however, he ruined the poetic effects of Polonsky's language. The film faded badly about halfway through for other reasons, too, one of them being that, given the novel, Polonsky could neither practice his skill with genre plots nor rework everything into something wholly new, as he had done with *Tuckers' People* (the novel on which he based *Force of Evil*) or *I Can Get It for You Wholesale*. Still, the careful observer can see that when a more skilled actor remained loyal to the script, as did Bujold, the dialogue holds together and gives the movie a modicum of dramatic propulsion that it otherwise so notably lacks.

The wisest critics noted that the protagonist maintained his integrity by being sincerely crooked, the very lesson that Irish Catholic (and not a few Italian Catholic) audiences have enjoyed learning all along. A real-life Detective Madigan would have appreciated and perhaps openly applauded the point. That is not much of a consolation for the monsignor's betrayed lover, and not much of a moral for a Polonsky film. Such were the disappointments that left Polonsky bitter (if the term is not too strong) and indifferent to later script writing offers, even one for a cool million bucks. At his age he did not need the money and could not stand the hackishness of it all.

One last disappointment awaited Polonsky in the 1990s. Called in to write a serious film about blacklist Hollywood for French master Bertrand Tavernier, he scripted something close to his own milieu: the rats versus the Reds, with the friendly witnesses (some of them FBI informers) and their families caught in between. Polonsky's script for *Guilty by Suspicion* is a revealing self-portrait of the blacklistee on the run in France, working through his demons, and finally coming home to face some pretty grotesque music. As shot, the film is starkly different, even if genuinely evocative fragments of the original remain. The result more closely resembled *The Front* than Polonsky could have imagined or desired. The protagonist, played by Robert De Niro, is an innocent fellow-traveler, and a gentile at that, who might have turned informer but did not, at great personal risk. Moreover, his adventures approach the bitterly comic, despite frequent bows to real-life traumas such as working blue-collar jobs, being fired after FBI visits, losing family and friends to fear and stress, and above all seeing dear ones fall apart and die.

For a rare moment in the early post-cold-war days, the *New York Times* took up the aesthetic question directly or, more properly, asked *Nation* editor Victor Navasky to do so. Polonsky sparked a controversy over the film with his complaint that "I wanted it to be about Communists because that's the way it actually happened. . . . They didn't need another story about a man who was falsely accused."

Polonsky's script begins with the protagonist testifying before HUAC, an opening that director Tavernier (still in the picture for the moment) and then-producer Irwin Winkler considered too climactic. Loose ends might have been tied up through a modest script alteration, but with Tavernier busy on another project, Winkler decided to direct his first film. Through his agent, Polonsky learned that Winkler had also rewritten the script.[59]

The change could not have been a happy one for Polonsky, whose personal story now was effectively cut out of the picture even though Winkler very much wanted to retain the veteran's screen writing credit, however nominally, with his own. Even if Winkler seriously wanted Polonsky's assent, he nevertheless could not bring himself to make a film that "would be perceived as a defense of Communism," not even of the Hollywood Communists, he told Victor Navasky. Winkler quoted a friend of his, a high Reagan appointee, as saying that HUAC had given anticommunism a bad name "and made the fight against [communism] more difficult." This was liberal cold-war talk, and Winkler concluded, "someone else can make a movie about a Communist." Navasky attributed the intellectual and political differences separating the two men to a generational chasm, "an appropriate metaphor not only for just how far Hollywood has come . . . but also for how far it and political culture at large still have to go" before coming to grips with the real past.[60]

Despite everything, the earlier parts of the film, up to De Niro's leaving Hollywood for New York, sound a Polonskyan note. As the film begins, the fictional director walks off a plane from France and joins a party of merrymakers who are not so merry, all of them fellow intellectuals and stars and starlets on the Left who are desperately trying not to think about the impending hearings. The Hollywood Ten are already in jail, and everyone else expects the ax to fall at any moment. De Niro is supposed to meet producer Darryl Zanuck the next day but learns that he must "clear" himself in order to work. What does that mean? Sam Wanamaker, blacklisted in real life, plays a lawyer—a counterpart to the historical Martin Gang—who puts together the potential blacklistees and HUAC operatives. De Niro learns what he has to do: name a handful of people, one of them being his childhood friend Bunny Baxter.

In a subplot, De Niro is separated from his wife, played winningly by Annette Bening, because of his addiction to work at the studio. He shares her ardent love for their son but finds himself unable to make the commitment to raise a family. He has already failed, in an important sense, and if blacklisting is too severe a punishment, he faces that possibility ready to learn some seemingly apolitical lesson.

The side-glances are better by far. Actress Patricia Wettig stands in for the real-life Dorothy Comingore, burdened with a friendly witness husband (fictional stand-in for Richard Collins, Comingore's husband and a former collaborator with several of the best-known left-wing Hollywood writers) who has her declared an unfit mother and takes away her child. In real life, Comingore drank herself slowly to death; in the film, Wettig takes a suicidal drive over a cliff. Martin Scorsese plays the only admitted Communist in the film—"I was a Communist twenty years ago and I'm a Communist now." Scorsese's shortly-to-be-blacklisted director is about to dodge a subpoena by fleeing to Europe. He could easily be either Jules Dassin or Joseph Losey, since we learn nothing about his films. But the scene, from Polonsky's script version, is true to life.

Too much of the remaining film is simply good blacklist boilerplate. De Niro learns the tough way that the FBI is a mean and ruthless bunch, determined to wear down those who will not cooperate through steady pursuit and blacklisting them from any kind of employment. Even an old girlfriend in New York throws De Niro out, too scared to let him crash. This material would have been welcome in any treatment of McCarthyism, most especially (but rarely used) in films about the civil rights and labor movements facing purges and shutdowns of their progressive edges. Finally coerced to face the committee, De Niro heroically refuses to buckle, knowing the consequences. Like Howard Koch, he is an honest liberal in an era of dishonest liberalism. Perhaps the defensive Winkler did better than he knew or even intended.

Unlike most critics who bypassed the HBO feature with limited comment, Roger Ebert earnestly described it as historically accurate and morally powerful, praising Winkler as the hardworking producer/collaborator of the *Rocky* films and of several Scorsese pictures.[61] But

Ebert, sincere to a fault in his effort to remind audiences of the blacklist saga, could not have appreciated what the film lost when Winkler pushed Polonsky's work aside. Polonsky demanded his name's complete removal from the screenplay—thus depriving himself of a hefty fee—and Winkler reluctantly agreed.

8

In the last half of *Zenia's Way,* Polonsky makes, if sometimes obliquely, the kinds of judgments about the close of life that another writer surely would have saved for a memoir. Of course, Aunt Zenia gets most of the best lines, giving the literary Polonsky a final opportunity to deploy his woman-as-philosopher character. But sometimes Ram plays a considerable role as well.

Take Ram's lawyerly part in a cold-war tale. He is asked to defend a scientist who was accused during the McCarthy era of being a spy for the Russians. The scientist fled and now has turned up in London, seeking to go home. The American authorities, however, do not want him back unless he actually was a spy and has intelligence information to reveal, such as the names of fellow spies who have not been caught. Contrariwise, Ram is willing to take the case only if he knows that the scientist was *not* a spy and merely wants to go home. The two figures thus have a strange, cryptic conversation.

Polonsky has Ram tell a true tale about a fellow OSS agent whose cover was as an army colonel. The Germans captured him during the Battle of the Bulge. He had no information to reveal, however, and they tortured him to no avail before sending him to Dachau. Finally saved by the Americans, he survives to revel in his adventures, all the more because they were so horrible. This man is a real-life metaphor for Ram's fictional client, who first fled the United States to East Germany. He was arrested there under suspicion of spying for the Americans, sent to Russia, and put to work in general theory and mathematics. Meanwhile, the KGB spread a rumor that he had made major breakthroughs in biological warfare. He married happily but made innocent revelations to his wife (who worked for Russian intelligence) about a fellow American scientist who was (unbeknownst to him) a Russian agent. Then he found himself under arrest again, finally to be released and vindicated years later as having been innocent of spying for anyone, ever.

His hope for a free life in the United States depends upon the competing intelligence services' both accepting his story. But military and intelligence authorities are the last ones willing to recognize that Russian and American scientists regularly publish their discoveries precisely to establish their personal authority and that, in crucial matters, meaningful secrets no longer exist.

The story ends years later. Convinced that he could have discovered the double helix, the exile vengefully tracks down and shoots the former colleague whose false accusations sent him into hiding. He then takes his own life, leaving behind a note that says simply, "He cheated me. He prevented me from winning the Nobel Prize." That is all. No larger meaning exists, just the cold war's bizarre, unpleasant, and above all unnecessary toll on personal lives.

Polonsky quickly encapsulates all this in a story about his hospitalization for a heart attack:

> It was then, at his weakest, when he lay wondering after the operation just what he was trying to live for, how absolutely evil it was that men used the same intense care to kill and maim each other and all the other creatures of the earth and how it made no sense unless you believed that in life that very thing that made it a magical existence contained the evil which destroyed it. It was the same in medicine as it was in politics, even in what Zenia had called "the age of socialism." Things were better for more people in many places, and that might be a real good. But then, nothing evil had disappeared and the evil was there in every hiding place of what men thought of as being good. It flowed along as part of life itself. It was, in fact, life itself. It was as much life in its way as anything else, and it was a kind of poetic license to call it evil.[62]

This is a remarkably existential statement, as Polonsky might have been willing to admit. He qualifies it in the novel both personally and politically with humane reassurances for those on the side of the angels and with some wry commentary about those on the other side, the powerful figures of government and business.

Probably reflecting on Thomas Mann's *Magic Mountain* even while describing closely his own medical experiences, Polonsky elucidates the moral consequences of his dissected aorta. Ram survives a life-saving operation that is performed only because of a mistaken diagnosis. If one price is a severed vocal cord (the metaphoric impossibility of communicating), the accompanying addiction to a painkiller might be described as an ideological dependence in his old comrades who could not accept the finality of communism's collapse.

According to Zenia, this is all part of evolution: "Just what happens the way it must happen is exactly what evolution is. Evolution is a grand way of describing a universe of chance and change, whether among the living or the non-living."[63] Or to personalize: Zenia is supposed to have said to her current lover across the dinner table, "Never mind the grain of sand. Give me the human body divine and I'll tell you the secret of the universe." And when her lover asked, "what's the secret?" she threw herself (or at least her arms) across the table and shouted, vibrantly, tempestuously, "Here I am!" Polonsky called this the "ultimate answer to the only mystery"—if, he might have added, there is an answer at all.[64]

A believer in art and revolt rather than scientific socialism (and yet, since childhood, still a believer in science), Polonsky could be accused of never believing in the certainties that many of his generation took for granted—the New Deal, Russian Communism, the war against fascism. Or perhaps he believed in them differently, more as great and hopeful events within a chaotic stream than as building blocks to paradise. The elderly Zenia asks the aging Ram, "what great things have you done that I haven't heard about?" He replies, "Whatever you read in the press," to which she responds, "Who can help it? You accumulate a life. It's a working solution in spite of everything."[65] No doubt speaking for Polonsky about the world and not just Stalinist Russia, she says that suddenly after all she had been through she found herself "free to go anywhere, as if all the while I had only been a tourist in history." She thus comes to terms with the past, including "everything [that] I would never accept."[66] So we can say for Polonsky.

Conclusion

Asked how this book might find an ending, Polonsky had a ready answer. In his mind, the final scene was properly one that he did not write himself. On her deathbed, Sylvia first made him promise not to try to balance the checkbook. That done, she vowed to be reunited with him in the years to come. "But we'll be stardust somewhere in the galaxy," he objected. "How will we locate each other?" Her dying words were these: "Haven't I always been able to find you?"

This is a bit too neat as a scene, sidestepping the realities that Jewish atheists hold dear. But it is not so far, after all, from the radical utopianism of *Romance of a Horsethief,* a dream that marvelously came true despite all the weight of history and molecular movement against it. In the end, the romantic in Polonsky wins out over everything else.

So soon after the distinctly anti-utopian twentieth century, the full measure of Abraham Polonsky's work probably cannot be taken. His high standing in and considerable influence among the rest of the left-of-

center film community remain as they have for decades, overshadowed
by the larger issues of the blacklist. So much more has been spoken about
him than written that his fame since the 1940s remained confined to a
small circle of critics and peers—at least until the middle 1990s, when
Martin Scorsese spoke out on his behalf.

In a 1996 *New York Times* feature, Caryn James reviewed a minifes-
tival celebrating the documentary *A Personal Journey with Martin
Scorsese* and the films that Scorsese had returned to prominence, beginning with *Force of Evil*. The festival highlighted what James called "the
work of obscure directors like Abraham Polonsky."[67] (The *Times*'s art
department did better: dominating the newspaper page, a large and
lovely still from *Force of Evil* showed Garfield climbing over a fence,
down to the water beneath the Brooklyn Bridge.) In a more casual comment, *New Yorker* film critic Anthony Lane hailed George Clooney's
film *Out of Sight,* adding that if the production did novelist Elmore
Leonard proud, "just think of what a director like Abraham Polonsky,
blacklisted into oblivion, would have made of this stuff."[68] At the end of
the century, Polonsky had not quite been "blacklisted into oblivion."
Indeed, he seemed to be returning from it.

Movie and television viewers might fancifully envision how we would
have valued Polonsky's screenplays for Yiddishist artistic soul mates like
actors Mandy Patinkin or Richard Dreyfuss, his direction of writers like
the Coen Brothers (of *Barton Fink* fame), his consultation with directors
like Mike Nichols and Oliver Stone and with writer-directors like Tim
Burton and Sidney Pollack, among others. Or we might wonder how
well Polonsky might have placed himself in any of a hundred socially
critical films from *Quiz Show* (1994) to *Wag the Dog* (1998), neither
written nor directed by his old crowd.

Scorsese's kudos for Polonsky's influential films were all the more welcome for being unexpected. Far from being pals, the two never shared a
room. What they did share, they shared vicariously, no more than any
other young artist studying a master. *Mean Streets* (1973), shot on a tiny
budget with film equipment borrowed from New York University, made
Scorsese's further trajectory possible, and he makes clear how much its
conception owed to the talk and style of *Force of Evil*. Watching and
rewatching *Force of Evil*, Scorsese saw the possibility of making such a
film about daily mob life, especially in Manhattan. *Raging Bull* (1980)
owes at least as much to *Body and Soul,* not because protagonist Jack La
Motta is a sympathetic Garfield type (far from it), but because Polonsky
captured "the game" without clichés. La Motta even reads from *On the*

Waterfront (1952) to prepare himself for his role, a phony learning to become a better phony, with Robert De Niro a perverse version of John Garfield.

After retiring to teach aesthetics to film students and enjoy his later years with his wife and grown children, Polonsky must have wondered more often than he cared to admit what Hollywood might have done with his talents rather than without them. At the dusk of a long life, the stream of memory brought together more and more of his created selves. In *Zenia's Way,* Ram tells a cab driver, "In the 'fifties I discovered friendship. In the 'thirties I discovered myself."[69] Each moment had its purpose.

The former screenwriter and director continued to discover himself in old age, mainly in witty and telling remarks to interviewers, students, and interested film watchers of all types. After former CBS president Frank Stanton was awarded a First Amendment award in April 1999, a *New York Times* contributor had the perspicacity to note that Stanton had overseen the network's blacklist during the early fifties. Polonsky was given the last word: "They're not rewriting history. . . . they can't rewrite the facts, but they can rewrite what we think about those facts." Polonsky quipped that he was chosen to offer that last word because he was the only one of his generation and politics in Hollywood still alive.[70]

The Los Angeles Film Critics' Lifetime Award in January 1999 put Polonsky in his perfect element, the final speaker in a night of speakers, reportedly holding in the palm of his hand an audience that stretched from Warren Beatty and Annette Bening to the hardworking journalists who had never stopped admiring his character and his work. After Steven Spielberg's touching personal tribute to Polonsky, the crowd rose to its feet and the applause went on and on.

But Polonsky was not only a raconteur and a past filmmaker. Even at an extremely advanced age, he still enjoyed being a puzzler. Twenty-one months earlier, in October 1997, he had risen to speak at the Hollywood talent guilds' dramatic fiftieth anniversary blacklist event. He offered only one line, and that in Greek! To the audience's shouts for a translation, he noted that it was one of Santayana's favorite quotations from Aristotle: "The good is decided through action!" If Polonsky perfected his role as an historical icon—the blacklist-generation survivor who lived to tell the story—he also determined to leave a last political message to those who followed. Good thoughts are not enough; if you sincerely want to redeem the world from its deplorable condition, you must act upon your ideals. No doubt Polonsky had heard the line from Aristotle in Moses Raphael Cohen's classroom at City College well over a half-century earlier. Classicist to the end, he had pressed the point once more. To be an artist committed to his art and to a cause—that was enough for a life.

Abraham Polonsky died October 26, 1999, in his Beverly Hills apartment. A cook who was coming in to make Polonsky's supper found him dressed in a bathrobe and sitting in a comfortable chair with the *Los Angeles Times* on his lap. For someone who had stirred so much excitement and found so many new admirers at the end of his life yet had remained an acerbic and often hilarious critic of the efforts to vindicate the now equally aged friendly witnesses, he had passed quietly. A not unfriendly *New York Times* obituary called him "an early master of Hollywood film noir . . . who worked under many disguises after being blacklisted."[71] The *Washington Post,* the *Los Angeles Times,* and a few other papers weighed in, and several Los Angeles area newspapers covered the December 14 memorial service at the Writers' Guild auditorium.

That event brought together the old crowd, perhaps for one last time. Director John Berry, originally expected to be one of the featured speakers, had died in Paris a few weeks earlier while editing his latest directorial effort, an adaptation of an Athol Fugard play. Frank Tarloff, the most successful television writer among the blacklistees, had passed in June, and blacklistee-turned-"friendly" director Edward Dmytryk in July. Fellow writers Edward Eliscu, Millard Lampell, and Paul Jarrico had died within the previous few years. Firsthand recollections of the 1940s milieu and the blacklist experience were disappearing fast.

Still, survivors showed themselves in Polonsky's memory and obviously soldiered on as best they could, some still working on their memoirs, others like John Randolph and Jeff Corey occasionally acting, and still others (notably Ring Lardner, Jr., and Abbott-and-Costello scripter Robert Lees) firmly retired but morally undaunted. Of the blacklisted writers, only Walter Bernstein, Polonsky's collaborator on *You Are There,* continued to write for screen and television. Film and video clips from Polonsky interviews and his films drove home a simple message that the outside world had scarce opportunity to grasp and had no conceptual means to comprehend: Abraham Lincoln Polonsky was the deep thinker, the aesthetician of a destroyed generation, a destroyed opportunity for American film and culture to leap forward. But perhaps that lesson would not be lost if viewers of his film and television work saw for themselves what had been possible, what is still possible, for popular art.[72]

APPENDIX

The following telephone conversation, taped by the FBI, took place between ABE POLONSKY in Los Angeles and IRA WOLFERT in New York on March 20, 1948. Wolfert was the author of *Tucker's People,* the novel upon which *Force of Evil* was based.

POLONSKY: New York City. Person to Person. Trafalgar 4-3094.

GIRL: Hello.

OPERATOR: Hello. Mr. IRA WOLFERT, please. Los Angeles is calling.

GIRL: What? Los Angeles? Well, OK.

WOLFERT: Hello.

OPERATOR: IRA WOLFERT?

POLONSKY: Hello, Ira?

WOLFERT: Abe?

P: How are you?

W: Pretty good. How are you?

P: Oh, I'm tired, brother.

W: I'll bet. What has been going on?

P: Mighty.

W: Really?

P: Yes, but it looks like we're winning.

W: Who are we winning against?

P: We're winning against the studios. They are trying to get control of our content and our cutting. And it has been very tough, let me tell you.

w: I'll bet. Is the deal set?

p: Well, it looks like it is going to be set on Monday. Keep this under your hat. Don't tell GARFIELD (JOHN) if he calls. There will be two of you.

w: (Laughs)

p: Of course, it may be delayed another few days again. And that guy hasn't got any sense about these things.

w: Yes. Who are you setting it with?

p: We are setting it with a major studio but we are going in completely as an independent. And if that is the case I will be in New York Wednesday or Thursday.

w: Oh, boy. That's wonderful.

p: And I wanted you to find out a few things so we wouldn't have to waste any time with that. I want to tell you some of the reactions to the script.

w: Yes.

p: Now, in one of the places we had a bad reaction to the script on the grounds that "What are you trying to do—overturn the system?" So we dropped them like a hot potato. But other places do not say anything about the real content. It makes it look good for us. They are going to try to—. Either they are sensitive to it and they will try to kill it while we are making it. But that's a normal flight, as they say. That's what you call ordinary combat.

w: Yes.

p: Or else they just don't understand it that way.

w: Yes.

p: As one guy says, "I consider this the sheerest melodrama."

(Both laugh.)

w: Don't enlighten them.

(Both laugh.)

p: No.

(Laughter.)

p: We have the following problem—as I see it. For ourselves, you know, to work out. We have the problem of DORIS and ED to get, for one thing, you see. And I think that we will stick back that scene now. It looks like they won't object to it. The scene where they are paying off the numbers. You see.

w: Yes.

p: And then there are a few other inferior dramatic points that keep coming up, you know—about reactions—that I want to discuss with you. But I don't want you to worry about it now. We will talk about it then.

w: Yes.

p: There is one very serious thing—which is a question of exposition. And you have got to find out or think about some way so we can make it clear. And that is the question of policy itself. Nobody understands it, you see, except those people who lived in New York and played it. The other people just can't make head nor tail about it. They just have got some kind of feeling about it. And that has been a constant beef. So I think that we will have to do something about it.

w: You'll have to take a number up from the playing of it to the odds.

p: That's right. And we will also have to explain the distribution of the odds and that kind of stuff—without making an exposition. How we do that I don't know yet.

w: Yes.

p: What I want you to do now until we get there is to go down and find out— I don't know—You've researched it before. Now try it again. You know what I mean?

w: Yes.

p: Just exactly how the whole racket plays out at every single point. Suppose you had to write an article on it. About this big fix—You know what I mean?—to explain it to someone in Azusa, California—taking nothing for granted. And try to write it out in a series of say sixteen or twenty steps— whatever it is—IRA, and then we will find and select from among them and just build it right in. You see?

w: How the fix is put in?

p: There are two things. One, how the whole system of it works.

w: Yes.

p: You see, and secondly, precisely how the fix was put in, if you can find it out.

w: Yes.

p: But in real detail. And, secondly, what the numbers look like in the paper. And know what I mean?

w: Yes.

p: And how they read off their three numbers as of that period. Now, another thing I think we have to do is fix the story some time. Say around in the middle thirties. We will have to stay it some place.

w: Why do we have to do that?

p: Because—In order to explain part of the motivation for BAUER. That jobs were hard to find. Because people say why the hell don't he just leave, you know? Or why did he ever work there. That kind of stuff.

w: Yes.

p: It is very trivial stuff. But as long as they are talking about these points, we make a big fuss about these points.

w: Take their minds off other things.

p: And we take their minds off the real point of the story, which is the big game I have been playing here—and it is wearing me down—(both laugh)— really wearing me down.

(Both laugh.)

w: You say you will be here towards the end of next week? Week or something —you know—so that the contract is in but there is something to be decided.

P: [Deleted in original]

W: Yes.

P: Then if it gets really tough—BOB hasn't been insisting—if it gets really tough then you'll have to give in and just trust to the three of us, you know.

W: Yes.

P: And we will have to do the best we can. Because it looks like we will be able to keep it—at the place we are going, I don't think we will have any trouble.

W: Yes. You don't want to mention the name of the place?

P: No, I don't yet.

W: Is your phone tapped?

P: Yep.

(Laughter.)

P: By the FBI—not by the studio.

(Both laugh.)

P: You know, we're not living in a police state, you understand that.

W: Oh, no, no.

P: We're living in a free democracy.

W: We're in a convict state.

P: I read in the newspapers that the United States sold out Palestine.

W: Yeah. That's bad.

P: That bastard.

W: That's certainly a crime.

P: That's really a shame.—Because that's going to make some bloodshed there.

NOTES

Introduction

1. Roger Greenspun, "Screen: *Willie Boy Is Here* Opens," *New York Times,* Dec. 19, 1969. Greenspun added, "the intervening 20 years [since Polonsky's blacklisting] . . . have invested Polonsky with considerable exemplary glamour and saddled him with a reputation no director of a second film should have to justify."

2. *Martin Scorsese Presents Force of Evil* (1996).

3. See "Abraham Polonsky," in Robert Siegel, ed., *The NPR Interviews* (Boston: Houghton Mifflin, 1994), 62–67; and Stephen Holden, "An Actor's Portrait, in Noir and White," *New York Times,* Aug. 9, 1996, about Polonsky's lecture on his own films during a Garfield film festival at Lincoln Center. Polonsky also appeared at the Lincoln Center for the showing of several *You Are There* television episodes and again for the showing of *Odds Against Tomorrow.* He continued to appear at regional film festivals until his death.

4. "Voters Pick the 100 Best American Movies," *New York Times,* June 17, 1998. Lyricist E. Y. Harburg arguably restyled *The Wizard of Oz* and established its plot for production, making six of the first thirteen; adding *On the Waterfront,* already in conceptualization when Elia Kazan appeared before the committee, would indeed make a majority of the first thirteen. Likewise, including Charles Chaplin as an escapee who only managed to evade the blacklist would raise the number (excluding Kazan) to sixteen of the first hundred. Those sixteen are: *Casablanca* (#2, coscript by Howard Koch), *Lawrence of Arabia* (#5, script by Michael Wilson), *The Wizard of Oz* (#6, lyrics by E. Y. Harburg), *It's a Wonderful Life* (#11, script contribution Dalton Trumbo), *Bridge on the River Kwai* (#13, script by Michael Wilson), *Maltese Falcon* (#23, based on a novel by Dashiell Hammett), *Mr. Smith Goes to Washington* (#29, coscript by Sidney Buchman), *High Noon* (#33, script by Carl Foreman), *Midnight Cowboy* (#36, script by Waldo Salt), *The Philadelphia Story* (#51, script by Donald Ogden Stewart), *All Quiet on the Western Front* (#54, script contribution by Gordon

Kahn), *Gold Rush* (#74, script and direction, Charles Chaplin), *City Lights* (#76, script and direction, Charles Chaplin), *Modern Times* (#81, script and direction, Charles Chaplin), *Frankenstein* (#87, coscript by Francis Faragoh), and *A Place in the Sun* (#92, script by Michael Wilson).

5. Victor S. Navasky's *Naming Names* (New York: Viking, 1980) remains the definitive treatment of the blacklisting process and its complications. Polonsky is cited frequently as a sage voice in complex matters.

6. Michael Denning, *The Cultural Front: The Laboring of American Culture in the Twentieth Century* (London: Verso, 1996). In several sections of this fine volume, Denning casually mentions many other details of film, but he nowhere offers a sustained critique of the industry or its left-wing artists.

7. Larry Ceplair and Steven Englund, *The Inquisition in Hollywood* (New York: Anchor Press, 1980), 426–29.

8. Patrick McGilligan and Paul Buhle, *Tender Comrades: A Backstory of the Hollywood Blacklist* (New York: St. Martin's, 1997).

9. Dorothy B. Jones, "Communism and the Movies: A Study of Film Comment," in *Report on Blacklisting*, vol. 1, ed. John Cogley (Washington: The Fund for the Republic, Inc., 1956), 197.

10. See Peter Biskind, *Easy Riders, Raging Bulls: How the Sex-Drugs-and-Rock'n'Roll Generation Saved Hollywood* (New York: Simon & Schuster, 1998), which despite its title is a study in disillusionment, with ungrounded personalities unable to sustain their early promise.

11. Daniel Patrick Moynihan, who insists in *Secrecy: The American Experience* (New Haven: Yale University Press, 1998) that Communist spies were rife, makes the point that their passage of low-level scientific data to the Soviet Union could have had little effect on the course of the cold war. Perhaps it should be added that even at the height of the wild charges, no one ever suggested any particular Hollywood radical was directly involved in espionage. They were guilty, at most, of belonging to a proscribed political organization and holding unpopular views. See Kenneth Lloyd Billingsley, *Hollywood Party: The Untold Story of How Communism Seduced the American Film Industry in the Thirties and Forties* (Rocklin, Calif.: Prima Publishing, 1998); Billingsley's is the latest and in some ways the most sophisticated version of this charge, although he scrupulously avoids serious analysis of the artistic content of films either written or directed by Communists and makes a large and unintentionally hilarious series of factual errors along the way.

12. The rest of the antidiscrimination committee included Howard Koch, who coscripted *Casablanca;* Professor Franklin Fearing from UCLA; and master animationist Chuck Jones, creator of the Road Runner. A most dangerous crowd!

13. FBI Document #100–138754–0297. See chapter three for details. A microfilm collection of these documents, Communist Activity in the Entertainment Industry: FBI Surveillance Files on Hollywood, 1942–1958, is now housed at Brandeis University. The guide to the collection, under the same title, was prepared by Daniel J. Leab (Bethesda: University Publications of America, 1991).

14. FBI Document #100–138754–469; a section of this is reprinted in the appendix.

15. Roger Ebert, "Guilty by Suspicion," *Roger Ebert's Video Companion,* 14th ed. (Kansas City: Andrews and McMeel, 1996), 297.

Chapter 1

1. Abraham Polonsky, *Zenia's Way* (New York: Lippencott and Crowell, 1980), 10, 12. Here and elsewhere in the book, incidents in Polonsky's life not footnoted refer to the numerous interviews we conducted with him. These will be available to the researcher at the Oral History of the American Left, Tamiment Library, New York University.

2. Polonsky, *Zenia's Way*, 3.

3. Unpublished and untitled novelette, 1940, Polonsky Collection, State Historical Society of Wisconsin (WSHS).

4. Polonsky, *Zenia's Way*, 27.

5. Polonsky, *Zenia's Way*, 52.

6. Polonsky, *Zenia's Way*, 14.

7. Polonsky, *Zenia's Way*, 6–23.

8. Polonsky, *Zenia's Way*, 14.

9. Polonsky, *Zenia's Way*, 14.

10. Abraham Polonsky Collection, WSHS. Unfortunately, most of the notebooks Polonsky deposited with the historical society are fragments of unrealized projects and the handwriting is virtually indecipherable.

11. Polonsky said that the images in his late film *Romance of a Horsethief* "signify something beyond, because they come by way of the tales my grandmother told me. . . . It is her voice I hear all through the movie, and it was her voice and her face which toured the locations. . . ." (Abraham Polonsky, interview by Dave Wagner and Paul Buhle, 1996).

12. Aaron Lansky, "Artistic Voice and Implicit Social Theory in the Early Yiddish Fiction of Mendele Mokher Sforim" (master's thesis, McGill University, 1980), 29–30. Many thanks to Lansky for insights delivered long ago, before he became the famed founder and director of the National Yiddish Book Center.

13. Sholem Asch, "What I Believe" (1941), quoted in Joseph L. Baron, ed., *A Treasury of Jewish Quotations* (New York: Crown, 1956), 463.

14. Avram Kampf, "The Quest for a Jewish Style in the Era of the Russian Revolution," chap. 1 in *Jewish Experience in the Art of the Twentieth Century* (S. Hadley: Bergin & Harvey, 1984), especially 15–43; for Polonsky and his milieu, it was no accident that the most profound experimentation took place in Russia, both shortly before and for some years after the Bolshevik Revolution.

15. So much of this is captured fictionally in *Zenia's Way* (103–07) that one wonders whether memory has not merged with imaginative re-creation. See also Abraham Polonsky, "Abraham Polonsky, the Most Dangerous Man in America," interview by Mark Burman, in *Projections 8: Film-makers on Film-making*, ed. John Boorman and Walter Donohue (London: Faber and Faber, 1998), 233.

16. See Floyd Dell, *Intellectual Vagabondage: An Apology for the Intelligentsia* (New York: George H. Doran, 1926), 165.

17. There is an interesting parallel here with C. L. R. James, born a decade earlier, who learned to become a novelist by talking with the kept women of the "barracks" slums of his native Port of Spain, Trinidad. See Paul Buhle, "Trinidad Home Boy," chap. 1 in *C. L. R. James: The Artist as Revolutionary* (London: Verso, 1989), and James's semiautobiographical novel, *Minty Alley*, 3rd ed. (Jackson: University of Mississippi Press, 1998).

18. Polonsky, "The Most Dangerous Man in America," 238.

19. Elizabeth K. Helsinger, *Ruskin and the Art of the Beholder* (Cambridge: Harvard University Press, 1982), 206.

20. Meyer Libin, "CCNY: A Memoir," *Commentary* 40 (Sept. 1965): 64–70.

21. Untitled, undated manuscript (1939?), Polonsky Collection, WSHS.

22. Untitled, undated manuscript (1940?), Polonsky Collection, WSHS.

23. "Last Clear Chance," undated manuscript, Polonsky Collection, WSHS.

24. Nor is it an accident—to continue the comparison—that C. L. R. James's Trinidadian Creole milieu, which published the first literary magazines in the English-speaking Caribbean of the late 1920s and early 1930s, was largely gay.

25. Abraham Polonsky, "The Lovestory of Peter Snark," *Lavender,* March 1932.

26. Philip Furia, *Ira Gershwin: The Art of the Lyricist* (New York: Oxford University Press, 1996), 10.

27. Abraham Polonsky, "Gargoyles," *Campus,* Mar. 15, 1932.

28. Abraham Polonsky, "Gargoyles," *Campus,* Nov. 25, 1931.

29. A. Polonsky, "Gargoyles," *Campus,* Dec. 7, 1931.

30. Abraham Polonsky, "Gargoyles," *Campus,* Mar. 20, 1931.

31. Abraham Polonsky, "The Dancers," undated manuscript, Polonsky Collection, WSHS.

32. Alan Wald, *The Revolutionary Imagination* (Chapel Hill: University of North Carolina Press, 1983), 35.

33. This observation is drawn from a reading across the left-wing press of the time. In the Yiddish literary world especially, that the social democratic *Jewish Daily Forward* or the Poale Zionist *Yiddishe Kempfer,* among others, could, after an early sympathetic period, scorn the American Communists and Russia as totalitarian yet cling to a realism not far from contemporary Communist literary ideals provides the surest evidence.

34. Harvey Teres, *Renewing the Left: Politics, Imagination and the New York Intellectuals* (New York: Oxford University Press, 1996), 51–52.

35. Raymond Williams, *Marxism and Literature* (Oxford: Oxford University Press, 1977), 53.

36. See Edna Nahshon, *Yiddish Proletarian Theater: The Art and Politics of the ARTEF, 1925–1940* (Westport: Greenwood Press, 1998).

37. See Joel Saxe, "Workers Laboratory Theater/Theater of Action," in *Encyclopedia of the American Left,* 2nd ed., ed. Mari Jo Buhle et al. (New York: Oxford University Press, 1998), 899–900.

38. See Michael Denning, "The Left and American Culture," pt. 1 of *The Cultural Front: The Laboring of American Culture in the Twentieth Century* (London: Verso, 1996), 1–50.

39. Polonsky, "The Most Dangerous Man in America," 214.

40. This story has been recounted many times, but Alan Wald tells it best in *The New York Intellectuals: The Rise and Decline of the Anti-Stalinist Left from the 1930s to the 1980s* (Chapel Hill: University of North Carolina Press, 1987), 46–74.

41. Morris U. Schappes, "Philip S. Foner at City College: Victim of the Rapp-Coudert Committee," in *Culture, Gender, Race and Working Class History,* ed. Ronald C. Kent et al. (Westport: Greenwood Press, 1993), 180.

42. *The New Masses* also published, especially in its peak years between 1935 and 1939, a great deal of intelligent literary commentary in addition to some politically connected ax-grinding. The *Partisan Review* (before its shift out of the Communist orbit) and the journal *Science & Society* carried some Popular Front literary interpretation, but none was interesting enough to impel Polonsky to join in.

43. See Harold Meyerson and Ernie Harburg, *Who Put the Rainbow in the Wizard of Oz? Yip Harburg, Lyricist* (Ann Arbor: University of Michigan, 1993);

and Edward Eliscu, interview by Patrick McGilligan and David Eliscu, in Patrick McGilligan and Paul Buhle, *Tender Comrades* (New York: St. Martins, 1997), 225–49. Eliscu went from theatrical success to write songs for more than a dozen film musicals and to script or coscript a handful of others.

44. Syracuse University Library's Special Collections has been kind enough to provide sample episodes from 1936; here we draw on Episode #81–83, "A Means to an End," broadcast May 4, 1936 (Gertrude Berg Collection). See Polonsky's account of this episode in Polonsky, "The Most Dangerous Man in America," 235–36.

45. The film's original title was *The Goldbergs*. It was a low-budget film whose supporting actors included, fascinatingly, David Opatoshu, Polonsky's collaborator on his last directorial film, *Romance of a Horsethief* (see chapter 5).

46. Abraham Polonsky, interview by Paul Buhle and Dave Wagner, 1998.

47. Orson Welles's radio work is perhaps the most ignored aspect of his career, but see Michael Denning's illuminating chapter on Welles in *The Cultural Front*, 362–402. See also Anne Froelick, interview by Paul Buhle, in *Tender Comrades*, 250–59. An interview of William Alland by Paul Buhle is still waiting publication.

48. Abraham Polonsky, interview by Barbara Zheutlin and David Talbot, in *Creative Differences: Profiles of Hollywood Dissidents*, ed. Barbara Zheutlin and David Talbot (Boston: South End Press, 1978), 58–59.

49. See Steven J. Ross, *Working-Class Hollywood: Silent Film and the Shaping of Class in America* (Princeton: Princeton University Press, 1998).

50. Abraham Polonsky, interview by Paul Buhle and Dave Wagner, in *Tender Comrades: A Backstory of the Blacklist*, 492–93.

51. Denning, *The Cultural Front*, 86.

52. "Reminiscences of Dorothy Parker," interview by Robert and Joan Franklin, Columbia University Oral History Project, 1959, transcript at Columbia University archives, 1–2.

53. The leftish magazine *New Theatre* had considerable influence in the world of 1930s entertainers. It had become *New Theatre and Film* in 1936, just when the Communists determined to abandon their political isolation and dropped their support of the project. It died a premature—and unnecessary—death in 1937. See Herbert Kline, "The Beginning of the End of *New Theater*," in *New Theater and Film* (New York: Harcourt Brace, 1985), 363–68. As will become painfully significant, it was John Howard Lawson, under pressure from cultural functionary V. J. Jerome, who dropped the dime on Kline's participation and, in essence, on the publication as well.

54. "Reminiscences of Carl Foreman," interview by Robert and Joan Franklin, Columbia University Oral History Project, 1959, transcript at Columbia University archives, 18.

55. Abraham Polonsky, "The Discoverers," manuscript copy in possession of the authors and in the Polonsky Collection.

56. Polonsky, "The Discoverers," 82.

57. Polonsky, "The Discoverers," 58.

58. Polonsky, "The Discoverers," 71.

59. Polonsky, "The Discoverers," 341.

60. Polonsky, "The Most Dangerous Man in America," 233.

61. See Schappes, "Philip S. Foner," 177–80. Schappes himself, later editor of *Jewish Currents*, was one the victims.

Chapter 2

1. "Out of This World," unpublished play script, Polonsky Collection, WSHS, unpaged.

2. Emmett Hogarth [Abraham Polonsky and Mitchell Wilson], *The Goose Is Cooked* (New York: Simon and Schuster, 1942), 66.

3. Hogarth, *The Goose Is Cooked*, 6.

4. Hogarth, *The Goose Is Cooked*, 30.

5. Hogarth, *The Goose Is Cooked*, 143.

6. Hogarth, *The Goose Is Cooked*, 222.

7. Near the end of the novel, the hero realizes that "he had never really seen the crew, and at the beginning of the journey, all the way back in Galveston, he remembered not having considered the crew. The crew made the ship run. It was like an extension of the engines and the hull. But this surge of voices broke through the skin of conventional habit. These were living, human men, waiting below, unable to rise" in more senses than one (Abraham Polonsky, *The Enemy Sea* [Boston: Little, Brown, 1943], 235).

8. Evelyn Sager, "Aboard an Oil Tanker," *New York Times*, June 13, 1943.

9. Polonsky, *The Enemy Sea*, 10.

10. Polonsky, *The Enemy Sea*, 15–16.

11. Polonsky, *The Enemy Sea*, 6.

12. Polonsky, *The Enemy Sea*, 48.

13. Polonsky, *The Enemy Sea*, 199.

14. Polonsky, *The Enemy Sea*, 160–61.

15. Polonsky, *The Enemy Sea*, 148.

16. Polonsky, *The Enemy Sea*, 129.

17. Polonsky, *The Enemy Sea*, 258.

18. Polonsky, *The Enemy Sea*, 276.

19. This might be compared to the seaman Arnold who has sold out to the Nazis but nevertheless despises Denhim as a "windbag" and explains to M'Cloud, "I'm a perfect capitalist. I sold out to the highest bidder in the open market. Uncle Sam offered me a petty officer's treatment and a good starvation salary. I took the ten grand" payoff for delivering the oil to German subs (*The Enemy Sea*, 223).

20. Polonsky, *The Enemy Sea*, 288.

21. Polonsky, *The Enemy Sea*, 268.

22. Polonsky, *The Enemy Sea*, 154.

23. Polonsky verified this as his intent.

24. See Philip Dunne, *Take Two: A Life in Movies and Politics* (New York: McGraw-Hill, 1980), 110–14.

25. In fact, Dubinsky's agent in this matter was Jay Lovestone, former Communist Party factional leader, soon to become point man for the America Federation of Labor's international, CIA-funded programs. See Paul Buhle, *Taking Care of Business: Samuel Gompers, George Meany, Lane Kirkland and the Tragedy of American Labor* (New York: Monthly Review Press, 1999), a close study of business unionism with some emphasis upon Dubinsky and Lovestone; and Ted Morgan's hagiographic but still interesting study, *A Covert Life: Jay Lovestone, Communist, Anti-Communist and Spymaster* (New York: Random House, 1999).

26. See Roger Keeran, *The Communist Party and the Auto Workers Unions* (Bloomington: Indiana University Press, 1980), for the account most sympathetic to the Communists. Nelson Lichtenstein, *The Most Dangerous Man in Detroit*

(New York: Basic Books, 1991), offers the most recent and best (but not uncritical) treatment from the Reuther brothers' own standpoint.

27. Capsule histories of nearly all these assorted Left unions can be found in Mari Jo Buhle et al., eds., *Encyclopedia of American Left,* 2nd ed. (New York: Oxford University Press, 1998).

28. See Paul Buhle, "Meany Takes Command," chap. 3 in *Taking Care of Business.*

29. Sefton Delmar, *Black Boomerang* (New York: Viking Press, 1962), 253–54. Delmar never seemed to have connected the "writer of film scripts named Polonski" was the noir master and blacklistee.

30. Delmar, *Black Boomerang,* 254–55.

31. The best account of Polonsky's international activities is in Polonsky, "The Most Dangerous Man in America," 241–45. U.S. Congress, House Committee Hearings, 82nd Congress, Senate Library, Vol. 1348, 1951, 399–400, 402; also see chapter 4.

32. Sam Moore, "Introductory Note," *Hollywood Quarterly* 1 (Jan. 1946): 186.

33. Abraham Polonsky, "'The Case of David Smith,'" *Hollywood Quarterly,* 1 (Jan. 1946): 185–95. Other writers for the series included Polonsky's comrades Sam Moore, Carlton Moss, Lou Solomon, Harold Buchman, Janet and Philip Stevenson, and future friendly witnesses Pauline and Leo Townsend and Silvia Richards.

34. Franklin Fearing, "Commentary," *Hollywood Quarterly* 1 (Jan. 1946): 195. This comment was followed by a highly interesting, somewhat technical several pages of director's notes by Cal Kuhl, a nonpolitical radio producer-director.

35. Polonsky also wrote a bit of low-grade radio drama, including a ghost story, "Florry and the Country Green" (1946?), manuscript in the Polonsky Collection, WSHS.

36. Hearing quoted in Polonsky's HCUA appearance: U.S. Congress, House Committee Hearings, 82nd Congress, Senate Library, 1951, 398–99. Regarding Communists' being allowed to speak, Polonsky told the commission, "If it is a public controversy in which the subject affects the interests of all the people who could listen to our station and they want to hear the various sides of the issue and the Communist side was one of the sides to it, then I think so long as the Communist Party is legal in the United States, they should have the right to present their side of the case."

37. Abraham Polonsky, "A Little Fire," *Collier's,* Aug. 3, 1946, 18, 50–51.

38. Abraham Polonsky, "The Marvelous Boy," *American Mercury,* Nov. 1946, 550–62. It was followed immediately by the literary warning of Ruth Fischer, former leader of the German Communist Party, against "Stalin's Secret Agents." The cold war was on.

39. Abraham Polonsky, "No Neutral Ground," *America Magazine,* June 1946, 163.

40. Bernard F. Dick, *The Star-Spangled Screen: The American World War II Film* (Lexington: University Press of Kentucky, 1985), offers the closest look at left-wing film shortly before and during the war, but only in the directly political or military genres and only in part (although carefully considered) concerning the future blacklistees.

41. John Weber, interview by Paul Buhle, in McGilligan and Buhle, *Tender Comrades,* 685–86.

42. Alfred Lewis Levitt, interview by Larry Ceplair; and Robert Lees, inter-

view by Paul Buhle and Dave Wagner, both in McGilligan and Buhle, *Tender Comrades*, 416–69. We wish also to acknowledge a very useful conversation between the late Carlton Moss and Paul Buhle in 1991.

43. Nancy Lynn Schwartz, *The Hollywood Writers' Wars* (New York: Knopf, 1982), 86–87.

44. Dick, *The Star-Spangled Screen*, 220–21. Dick regrettably does not treat the "frivolous" films like musicals and slapstick, but otherwise his judgments are thorough and serious, if often also highly personal matters of taste.

45. The best single treatment of this era is Brian Neve, "Post-War Hollywood" and "Post-War: New Directors and Structures," chaps. 4 and 5 in *Film and Politics in America: A Social Tradition* (London: Routledge, 1992), 84–144. Bernard F. Dick's *Radical Innocence: A Critical Study of the Hollywood Ten* (Lexington: University Press of Kentucky, 1989) has considerably more detailed coverage, but only of the films written or directed by the Hollywood Ten. One of the best sources is the film-by-film analysis in Alain Silver and Elizabeth Ward, eds., *Film Noir: An Encyclopedia Reference to the American Style*, 3rd ed. (Woodstock: Overlook Press, 1992).

46. None of the existing accounts of the Maltz episode deal sufficiently with the context, although Victor Navasky's *Naming Names* is the most dispassionate and thorough investigation ([New York: Viking, 1980], 287–302). See also the assorted oral history accounts in *Tender Comrades*, which help to raise new questions. Albert Maltz's own papers at the State Historical Society of Wisconsin continue to be a fascinating source for further interpretation.

47. See *Writers' Congress; The Proceedings of the Conference Held in October 1943 under the Sponsorship of the Hollywood Writers' Mobilization and the University of California* (Berkeley and Los Angeles: University of California Press, 1944). *The Hollywood Quarterly*, reorganized and renamed *The Quarterly of Film, Radio, and Television* in 1951, struggled on and during the 1960s regained its avant-garde status as the *Film Quarterly*, though in a very different political context. See Brian Henderson, introduction to *Film Quarterly: Forty Years—A Selection* (Berkeley and Los Angeles, 1999), 1–8.

48. We gratefully acknowledge the assistance of Robert Hethmon, a prospective Lawson biographer, in making available to us parts of an unpublished memoir by Lawson, archived at Southern Illinois University.

49. See Schwartz, *The Hollywood Writers' Wars*, 235–37.

50. So large did this meeting loom that future friendly witnesses creatively rearranged its contents to suit their rationalizations. Thus Leopold Atlas (who suffered two heart attacks before testifying and died a few years afterward) recalled that he had been "enormously pleased" with Maltz's initial article and horrified by the consequences. Atlas also recalled incorrectly that the Maltz meeting in Hollywood had taken place at Polonsky's house and that Atlas's intimate friend Leonardo Bercovici had bravely defended Maltz. Bercovici later observed that Atlas was "the only stoolpigeon who broke my heart" and that Atlas's memory was "atoning for naming me" (Leonardo Bercovici, interview by Paul Buhle, in McGilligan and Buhle, *Tender Comrades*, 38; and Thursday, Mar. 12, 1953, *U.S. Congress, House Committee on Un-American Activities in the Los Angeles Area*, 83rd Congress, part 5 [Washington D.C.: U.S. Government Printing Office, 1953], 935).

51. Recent accounts coincide with Polonsky's memories. See especially John Weber, interview by Paul Buhle, in McGilligan and Buhle, *Tender Comrades*, 683–97.

52. Bernard J. Stern to Albert Maltz, Apr. 19, 1946, Maltz Papers, State

Historical Society of Wisconsin. This odd New York sequel to the usual Hollywood side of the Maltz controversy seems to have escaped nearly all other
commentators.

53. Schwartz, *The Hollywood Writers' Wars,* 237.

54. Jeff Lawson, "An Ordinary Life," in *Red Diapers: Growing Up in the
Communist Left,* ed. Judy Kaplan and Linn Shapiro (Urbana: University of Illinois, 1998), 58–59. See also "John Howard Lawson: Hollywood Commissar,"
in Dick, *Radical Innocence,* 45–69. This substantial chapter deals with Lawson's
stage, screen, and theoretical work and assorted reflections on his relation to the
Hollywood Left.

55. Jean Rouveral Butler's oral history recollection of a conversation with
Foreman after the shooting of *Champion* supplied the key here. Hugo Butler, on
the verge of such experimentation himself, was driven from Hollywood,
although he later worked with Luis Buñuel in the same direction. Jean Rouveral
Butler, interview by Paul Buhle, in McGilligan and Buhle, *Tender Comrades,*
155–76.

56. Special thanks to John Weber and Robert Lees for sharing this notion
with the authors.

57. Abraham Polonsky, "Paris Story," undated, unpaged manuscript, Polonsky Collection, WSHS.

58. A. H. Weiler, "Report," *New York Times,* Nov. 16, 1947.

59. Polonsky, "The Most Dangerous Man in America," 244.

60. Abraham Polonsky, "The Wayfarers," Polonsky Collection, WSHS.

61. Weiler, "Report."

62. "The Gypsy in Marlene," *Newsweek,* Nov. 3, 1947, 88; "Cinema: The
New Pictures," *Time,* Dec. 15, 1947, 103; and "The Screen," *New York Times,*
Dec. 4, 1947.

Chapter 3

1. Ian Hamilton, *Writers in Hollywood, 1915–1951* (New York: Carroll &
Graf, 1990), 299.

2. William Wyler, in "Hollywood Fights Back," radio script, 1947, Albert
Maltz Papers, WSHS.

3. For most of the 1940s, critic David Platt ran the *Daily Worker*'s movie section. Several decades later he would be the editor of the English-language pages
of the Yiddish *Morgn Freiheit* in its (and his) last years. In that capacity, he had
occasion to talk with Buhle about the earlier *Daily Worker* treatment of movies.
Belonging to a circle of early 1930s documentarists and devotees of Russian
film, Platt never transcended socialist realism and its liberal cousins, although he
was capable of bending on Jewish themes.

4. This is only a slight exaggeration: top writers like Albert Maltz and John
Howard Lawson were identified with their films during wartime and afterward,
perhaps because of their political purposes as much as their screenwriting. From
the middle 1930s, the *New Masses* carried somewhat more film coverage but
rarely ventured from single-film reviews to wider exploration. The party's theoretical organ, *The Communist,* renamed *Political Affairs,* was even worse. Since
its origins in the 1920s, its main functions had been to justify the recurrent dras-
tic shifts of political line and to curse deviationists, especially the followers of
Leon Trotsky. Other than for political purposes, films did not exist here.

5. *Writers' Congress: The Proceedings of the Conference Held in October*

1943 under the Sponsorship of the Hollywood Writers' Mobilization and the University of California (Berkeley: University of California Press, 1944). Of special interest are Francis Edward Faragoh's preface, ix–xii; Robert Rossen, "An Approach to Character," 61–67; John Howard Lawson, "Cultural Changes in America," 470–73; and "An American Writer's Credo," 611–16.

6. John Houseman, *Front and Center* (New York: Simon & Schuster, 1979), 157.

7. Sylvia Jarrico, interview by Paul Buhle, May 1992, Pacoima, California.

8. Lawrence S. Kubie, "Psychiatry and the Films," *Hollywood Quarterly* 2 (Jan. 1947): 113–17; John Houseman, "Violence, 1947: Three Specimens," *Hollywood Quarterly* 2 (Jan. 1947): 63–65; Dorothy B. Jones, "The Hollywood War Film," *Hollywood Quarterly* 1 (Oct. 1945): 1–19; Chuck Jones, "Music and the Animated Cartoon," *Hollywood Quarterly* 2 (Jan. 1947), 365–69.

9. Kenneth MacGowan, "Make Mine Disney: A Review," *Hollywood Quarterly* 3 (Sept. 1947): 378.

10. Abraham Polonsky, "*The Best Years of Our Lives*: A Review," *Hollywood Quarterly* 2 (Apr. 1947): 257–60.

11. Polonsky, "*The Best Years*," 257.

12. Polonsky, "*The Best Years*," 258.

13. Polonsky, "*The Best Years*," 260.

14. Abraham Polonsky, "*Odd Man Out* and *Monsieur Verdoux*," *Hollywood Quarterly* 2 (July 1947): 401–07.

15. Polonsky, "*Odd Man Out*," 401.

16. Polonsky, "*Odd Man Out*," 402.

17. Polonsky, "*Odd Man Out*," 406.

18. William Appleman Williams, *The Great Evasion: An Essay on the Contemporary Relevance of Karl Marx and on the Wisdom of Admitting the Heretic into the Dialogue about America's Future* (Chicago: Quadrangle Books, 1964). See Paul Buhle and Edward Rice Maximin, "Trouble, Foreign and Domestic," chap. 5 in *William Appleman Williams: The Tragedy of Empire* (New York: Routledge, 1995), especially 150–57.

19. Polonsky, "*Odd Man Out*," 406–07.

20. It may be noted that future blacklistees wrote or directed all of these films except *They Live By Night*. The lone exception, director Nicholas Ray, often described himself as close enough to the Left to have been blacklisted, if not under the protection of Howard Hughes. Ray's other outstanding film of the era, *Knock On Any Door*, was taken from the novel of a left-wing African-American writer, Willard Motley. See the valuable study, Bernard Eisenschitz, *Nicholas Ray: An American Journey* (London: Faber & Faber, 1995), translated by Tom Milne.

21. Edgar G. Ulmer, the sole notable director on the Left (if outside the Communist Party's orbit) in this period who made a similar effort, fled the studio system after the success of *The Black Cat* (1934). He produced independently, with small companies, a series of ethnic films in the late 1930s and early 1940s, including one of the finest ever made in Yiddish, *Gruene Felder* (Green Fields, 1937). Ulmer continued to make small and foreign-release films with minuscule budgets on his own terms, producing at least two noir classics, *Detour* (1945) and *Ruthless* (1948), and many oddly beautiful "little" films in his own gothic style. Several of his outstanding later films, including *Ruthless*, were written by blacklistees. See John Belton, *The Hollywood Professionals: Howard Hawks, Frank Borzage, Edgar G. Ulmer* (London: The Tantivy Press, 1974), 149–80.

22. See Polonsky, in *Tender Comrades*, 484–85; and Allen Eyles, "Films of Enterprise: A Studio History," *Films in Focus*, no. 35 (1970): 35–36.

23. Polonsky, in *Tender Comrades*, 486.

24. Rossen has no proper biography, but for a useful if brief treatment see Alan Casty, *The Films of Robert Rossen* (New York: The Museum of Modern Art, 1969).

25. See Bernstein, in *Tender Comrades*, 45–48, for the screenwriter's late 1940s recollections of Rossen; and Polonsky's accurate if rather cruel comments about Rossen in *Tender Comrades*, 485–86.

26. Abraham Polonsky, interview by J. D. Pasternak and F. W. Howton, in *The Image Maker*, ed. Ron Henderson (Richmond, Va.: John Knox Press, 1971), 26.

27. William Pechter, "Abraham Polonsky and *Force of Evil*," *Film Quarterly* 15 (Spring 1962): 48–49.

28. Abraham Polonsky, *Season of Fear* (New York: Cameron Associates, 1956), 165.

29. Ironically, Rossen the screenwriter in his earliest years had actually been known for his optimistic final scenes. Alan Casty could even write of *Body and Soul*, "This sudden shift to affirmation and growth at the close [was] typical of many of Rossen's films" (Casty, *The Films of Robert Rossen*, 16).

30. Quoted in Casty, *The Films of Robert Rossen*, 18.

31. "Among '48 Unity Award Winners," and "Film Unity . . . In a Changing World," flyers in Albert Maltz Papers; Polonsky, in *Tender Comrades*, 484–85.

32. Jim Cook and Kingsley Canham, *Screen* 2 (Summer 1970): 68.

33. Michel Delahaye, "Entretien avec Abraham Polonsky," *Cahiers du cinéma*, Sept. 1969, 33.

34. Bosley Crowther, "The Screen in Review," *New York Times*, Nov. 21, 1947. James Agee awarded it for "a sense of meanness to match the meanness of the world they are showing . . . and a general quality of tension and of pleasure in good workmanship" grown rare in Hollywood, in "Films," *Nation*, Nov. 8, 1947, 511. See also the illustrated puff piece in "Movie of the Week," *Life*, Sept. 29, 1947, 141–42), and reviews in *Time* ("The New Pictures," Oct. 20, 1947, 101) and *Newsweek* ("Prize-Money Bums," Sept. 29, 1947, 94).

35. Ed Sullivan, quoted in Stefan Kanfer, *A Journal of the Plague Years* (New York: Atheneum, 1973), 178.

36. Sklar, *City Boys*, 207.

37. See the appendix for the text of this transcription.

38. Sklar, *City Boys*, 210.

39. B. C. [Bosley Crowther], "At Loew's State," *New York Times*, Dec. 27, 1948.

40. "Fair to Maudlin," *New Republic*, Jan. 10, 1949, 120.

41. "Cinema," *Time*, Jan. 10, 1949, 84.

42. See, for example, Ado Kyrou, *Le Surréalisme au cinéma* (Paris: Le Terrain vague, 1963), 162.

43. See, for example, Kingsley Canham, "Polonsky: Back Into the Light," *Film* (Spring 1970): 12–15.

44. Pechter, "Abraham Polonsky and *Force of Evil*," 48.

45. Pechter, "Abraham Polonsky and *Force of Evil*," 49.

46. Pechter, "Abraham Polonsky and *Force of Evil*," 50.

47. Richard Corliss, *Talking Pictures: Screenwriters in the American Cinema* (Woodstock: Overlook Press, 1974), xxvi. Corliss was evidently responding to Andrew Sarris's "Pantheon" in the latter's *The American Cinema: Directors and*

Directions, 1929–1968. Not listing Polonsky in his Pantheon, Sarris calls Polonsky, along with Chaplin and Losey, "one of the great casualties of the anticommunist hysteria of the 1950s" and says that *Force of Evil,* upon repeated viewings, stands as "one of the great films of the modern American cinema" (Andrew Sarris, *The American Cinema: Directors and Directions, 1929–1968* [New York: E. P. Dutton, 1968], 220).

48. See "Lyric Poetry," in *The Concise Oxford Companion to Classical Literature,* ed. M. C. Howatson and Ian Chilvers (New York: Oxford University Press, 1993), 324.

49. Dorothy B. Jones, "Communism and the Movies: A Study of Film Comment," in John Cogley, *Report on Blacklisting,* vol. 1 (Washington, D.C.: The Fund for the Republic, Inc., 1956), 197.

50. Cook and Canham, "Abraham Polonsky," 57.

51. Cook and Canham, "Abraham Polonsky," 58.

52. Jones, "Communism and the Movies," 197; see also 196–233.

53. Brian Neve, *Film and Politics in America,* 91.

54. See, for example, Jack Shadoin, *Dreams and Dead Ends: The American Gangster/Crime Film* (Cambridge: MIT University Press, 1977), 134–147; Terence Butler, "Polonsky and Kazan: HUAC and the Violation of Personality," *Sight and Sound* 57 (Autumn 1988): 263–67. For a warm, if belated, U.S. academic treatment, see also Christine Noll Brinckman, "The Politics of *Force of Evil*: An Analysis of Abraham Polonsky's Preblacklist Film," in *Prospects: The Annual of American Cultural Studies,* vol. 6, ed. Jack Salzman (New York: Burt Franklin, 1981), 357–86.

55. *Martin Scorsese Presents Force of Evil* (1996).

56. Nora Sayre, *Running Time: Films of the Cold War* (New York: The Dial Press, 1978), 33; Keith Kelly, "Abraham Polonsky," *Dictionary of Literary Biography,* vol. 26, *American Screenwriters,* 8th ed. (Detroit: Gale Research, 1984), 244–48.

57. Pechter, "Abraham Polonsky and *Force of Evil,*" 48.

58. A nice overview of Odets's work is Norma Jenckes, "Clifford Odets," in *The American Radical,* ed. Mari Jo Buhle et al., (New York: Routledge, 1994), 229–35.

59. Polonsky, *Creative Differences,* 81.

60. See Paul Buhle, "The Jewish Left in the United States," in *The Immigrant Left in the United States,* ed. Paul Buhle and Dan Georgakas (Albany: SUNY Press, 1997); and the classic treatment, Sol Liptzin, *A History of Yiddish Literature* (Middle Village, N.Y.: Jonathan David, 1972).

61. Abraham Polonsky, introduction to Howard Gelman, *The Films of John Garfield* (New York: Lyle Stuart, 1974), 8.

62. Polonsky, introduction to *The Films of John Garfield,* 8.

63. Polonsky, introduction to *The Films of John Garfield,* 9.

64. Pechter, "Abraham Polonsky and *Force of Evil,*" 50.

65. See Edward Dmytryk's autobiographical *It's a Hell of a Life but Not a Bad Living* (New York: Times Books, 1978), which, unfortunately, lacks self-insight.

66. Weiler, "Report."

67. Weiler, "Report."

68. FBI Document MBB-15732, A. H. Belmont to D. M. Ladd, "Communist Infiltration in the Motion Picture Industry—C," 36, elicited from allegations by Drew Pearson against Congressman John S. Wood for supposedly failing to con-

duct hearings in 1945–46 "as a result of activities by Louis B. Mayer." The FBI had, of course, its own reasons for the investigation.

69. FBI Document LA-200365, [1951?], 7–8.

70. FBI Document L.A.100–22184, [1951], 10.

71. Polonsky often observed, with others on the scene, that CSU or any other Left-led union should have fought an all-out battle only when a great moral principle was at stake; jurisdictional conflicts offered the worst possible field of combat. But when Hollywood writers loyally manned picket lines, Polonsky recalled, he had personally hurled a couple of writer-scabs onto the street.

72. Schwartz, *The Hollywood Writers' Wars*, 239–49.

73. This aspect is nicely summarized in Larry Ceplair, "Hollywood Left," in *Encyclopedia of the American Left*, ed. Mari Jo Buhle et al., 2nd ed. (New York: Oxford University Press, 1998), 327–29; and in Larry Ceplair, "The Hollywood Blacklist," in Gary Crowdus, *The Political Companion to American Film* (Chicago: Lakeview Press, 1994), 193–99.

74. Schwartz, *The Hollywood Writers' Wars*, 254.

75. The Hollywood Ten consisted of Alvah Bessie, Herbert Biberman, Lester Cole, Edward Dmytryk, Ring Lardner, Jr., John Howard Lawson, Albert Maltz, Sam Ornitz, Robert Adrian Scott (primarily a producer), and Dalton Trumbo. Berthold Brecht, the other witness to testify, left for Germany immediately afterward.

76. "Hollywood Fights Back," radio script, 1947, Albert Maltz Papers, WSHS. Among other personalities who did not speak but signed on to the statement were Ava Gardner, Geraldine Brooks, Henry Fonda, Eddie Cantor, Katharine Hepburn, Cornel Wilde, Keenan Wynn, Benny Goodman, Rita Hayworth, Canada Lee, Margo, and Gregory Peck.

77. At that, it was Alfred Levitt who pressed the issue of the pensions. We are grateful to Levitt, then suffering from the early effects of Alzheimer's Disease, for granting Paul Buhle an interview in 1991. Schwartz, *The Hollywood Writers' Wars*, 265.

Chapter 4

1. These notebooks, again scrawled, deal largely with fragmentary notions.

2. Abraham Polonsky, interview by Jim Cook and Kingley Canham, in *Screen* 11 (Summer 1970): 63.

3. U.S. Congress, House Committee Hearings, 82nd Congress, Senate Library, Vol. 1348, 1951, 396–408.

4. House Committee Hearings, 403.

5. "Dmytryk Bares Giant Red Plot to Control Screen and Unions," *Hollywood Reporter*, Apr. 26, 1951.

6. "I Can Get It For You Wholesale," *Variety*, March 14, 1951. See also *"Tales of Hoffman* Arrives," *New York Times*, Apr. 5, 1951, which credits Polonsky with "crisp, double-edged dialogue" but complains that the setting is inadequately explored, leaving the film "average" rather than "exciting."

7. We quote below from the version of the screenplay (inconsistently paged) in the Polonsky Collection, WSHS. Polonsky considered Oscar Saul's rewrite (done while Polonsky was in France) competent, although definitely softened in tone.

8. The scene is excerpted in full, for example, in the 1995 documentary *Red Hollywood*. Although completed in 1995, *Red Hollywood* has been shown only

in film festivals; it remains a fundamental piece of work in the field and, like the rest of Thom Andersen's efforts, too little appreciated.

9. Elizabeth Cowie, "Film Noir and Women," in *Shades of Noir*, ed. Joan Copjec (London: Verso 1993), 134 ff.

10. Jerome Weidman, *Praying for Rain* (New York: Harper & Row, 1986), 134. This apparently is the only account of the incident.

11. Weidman, *Praying for Rain*, 136.

12. F. Scott Fitzgerald, *The Letters of F. Scott Fitzgerald*, ed. Anthony Turnbull (New York: Scribner's, 1963), 583, quoted in Weidman, *Praying for Rain*, 149.

13. Weidman, *Praying for Rain*, 117.

14. This is a private reminiscence made by Polonsky to Buhle and Wagner in a 1998 interview.

15. "Danger" manuscript loaned to us by John Schultheiss.

16. Thomas Mann, "Mario and the Magician," in *Stories of Three Decades*, trans. H. T. Lowe-Porter (New York: Knopf, 1936), 529.

17. Several of Mann's letters to friends about the story, some of them written in 1947 from Pacific Palisades, where he knew and met with Polonsky, can be found in Gert Sautermeister, ed., *Thomas Mann: "Mario und der Zauberer"* (Munich: Wilhelm Fink Verlag, 1981), 135–36.

18. Abraham Polonsky, "Mario and the Magician," n.d., 47, manuscript copy supplied by Abraham Polonsky.

19. Polonsky, "Mario and the Magician," 108.

20. Polonsky, "The Most Dangerous Man in America," 252.

21. Published by Little, Brown in 1951, *The World Above* was reprinted with an introduction by Paul Buhle and Dave Wagner in the University of Illinois's Radical Novel Reconsidered series in 1999. Thanks go to Alan Wald, editor of the series, for making this reprint possible. Asked about the title, Polonsky replied jocularly that he had intended it to be "The Darkness Below," a psychoanalytic commentary. When the publisher dropped that title, Polonsky substituted one that amused him—as a subtle reference to Marxist understanding.

22. See Mari Jo Buhle, *Feminism and Its Discontents: A Century of Struggle with Psychoanalysis* (Cambridge: Harvard University, 1998), 206–16.

23. Polonsky, *The World Above*, 127.

24. Polonsky, *The World Above*, 195.

25. Polonsky, *The World Above*, 376.

26. Quoted from the back cover of Abraham Polonsky, *Season of Fear* (New York: Cameron Associates, 1956).

27. Polonsky, *The World Above*, 64.

28. Polonsky, *The World Above*, 353.

29. Polonsky, *The World Above*, 353.

30. Polonsky, *The World Above*, 464.

31. Interview with Schultheiss, quoted in *Force of Evil: The Critical Edition*, 179.

32. Abraham Polonsky, "How the Blacklist Worked," *Film Culture* 3 (Fall-Winter 1970): 48. This monologue is taken from an interview by James Pasternak, who is described as a former production assistant with Otto Preminger, a producer who used blacklistees as often as possible during that era.

33. Most of the detail is discussed in various interviews (or footnotes) in McGilligan and Buhle, *Tender Comrades*. *The Naked Dawn* (1955), written by Julian Zimet and directed by Edgar Ulmer, may be the best of the unfamous and low-budget films; Bernard Gordon's *Zombies of Mora Tau* (1957) is easily the

worst. See the forthcoming volumes by Buhle and Wagner, detailing each of these films and rather over a thousand others.

34. Polonsky, "How the Blacklist Worked," 42.

35. Michael Wreszin, "Arthur Schlesinger, Jr.: Scholar-Activist in Cold War America, 1946–1956," *Salmagundi* 64–65 (Spring-Summer 1984): 265–85.

36. Polonsky, *A Season of Fear*, 5.

37. Polonsky, *A Season of Fear*, 74–75.

38. This character was clearly drawn from friendly witness Richard Collins, who had divorced the blacklisted actress Dorothy Comingore and taken their son; in later decades, Collins expressed regret at informing, a career adjustment that he had been compelled to make.

39. Polonsky, *A Season of Fear*, 224.

40. Helen Davis, "Books in Review," *Mainstream* 10 (February 1957): 57–58.

41. Edwin Berry Burgham, "We Are Pleased to Announce . . . ," *Contemporary Reader* 1 (March 1953): 5. Burgham was a prominent editor of *Science & Society*, a scholarly journal of Popular Front origin that had recently broken its informal but historic attachment to the Communist Party over the issue of "Lysenkoism," Stalin's application of ideological rules to science. The journal continued to grow more independent-minded and remains at the beginning of a new century the eldest Marxist journal in the world. See David Goldway, "*Science & Society*," in *Encyclopedia of the American Left*, 723–24. Had it survived, the *Reader* certainly would have taken the same path.

42. Properly speaking, *Freedom* (1951–55), Paul Robeson's tabloid published in Harlem, was a contemporary counterpart of the *Contemporary Reader*, issued by the Committee for Negroes in the Arts. These sister publications' contributors lists overlapped, notably in John Killens, later to figure in *Odds Against Tomorrow*. Pressed by government investigations and the threatened blacklisting of its contributors, *Freedom* folded, and with it, Robeson's last public voice.

43. Abraham Polonsky, "A Slight Disturbance," *The Contemporary Reader* 1 (August 1953): 57.

44. Polonsky, "A Slight Disturbance," 44.

45. Madeline Gilford, remarks in a panel presided over by Paul Buhle at the Socialist Scholars Conference, New York City, May 1999; see also Rita Morley Harvey's history of union struggles against the blacklist, *Those Wonderful, Terrible Years: George Heller and the American Federation of Television and Radio Artists* (Carbondale: Southern Illinois University Press, 1996), especially 140–41 for the Gilfords' case.

46. The following year veteran editor Charles Humbolt would preside over a renamed *Mainstream,* and until 1960 he would maintain a nearly nonpartisan Left quarterly, with a heavier emphasis on Latin American literature than any U.S. publication theretofore. When American Communist leaders cracked down again, they ended the final experiment of literary note in their circles. Annette Rubinstein, "*Mainstream*," *Encyclopedia of the American Left*, 469–70. *Mainstream*'s sister journal, *Freedomways* (1961–85), the last and, in many ways, most successful spinoff of Popular Front constituencies, provided a cultural and strategic voice to the civil rights movement and Pan-Africanism, with contributors that included Ossie Davis, Nikki Giovanni, Ron Dellums, Lorraine Hansberry, Ruby Dee, Angela Davis, Alice Walker, Jack O'Dell (Martin Luther King, Jr.'s, major letfward political advisor, later Jesse Jackson's Rainbow Coalition advisor), and of course, Polonsky's friend Harry Belafonte. See E. Ethelbert

Miller and Paul Buhle, "*Freedomways*," *Encyclopedia of the American Left*, 241–42.

47. This pen name was erroneously explained as that "of a prominent progressive writer who because of the threat of blacklisting cannot sign his name" (Timon [Abraham Polonsky], "The Troubled Mandarins," *Masses and Mainstream* 9 [August 1956]: 35 n). Polonsky was, of course, already blacklisted.

48. "The Troubled Mandarins," 35.

49. "The Troubled Mandarins," 37–38.

50. "The Troubled Mandarins," 42.

51. "The Troubled Mandarins," 45.

52. "The Troubled Mandarins," 46.

53. Walter Bernstein, *Inside Out: A Memoir of the Blacklist* (New York: Knopf, 1966), 153–86. Bernstein's willingness to be interviewed by Paul Buhle and to answer questions by phone is also gratefully acknowledged.

54. Bernstein, *Inside Out*, 175–80, and Bernstein's comments about the noir quality of the *Danger* episodes in "Bad Art Makes Bad Politics," interview by Dan Georgakas, *New Labor Forum*, no. 4 (Spring-Summer 1999): 143. See also a comprehensive listing, "The Blacklisted Writers and their Fronts," for *Danger* and *You Are There*, in appendix 1, John Schultheiss and Mark Schaubert, eds., *To Illuminate Our Time: The Blacklisted Teleplays of Abraham Polonsky* (Los Angeles: Sadanlaur Publications, 1993), 39–46.

55. See Paul Jarrico, Ring Lardner, Jr., Robert Lees, Alfred Lewis Levitt, Joan LaCour Scott, and Frank Tarloff, interviews in *Tender Comrades*. The most successful, by a long stretch, was Tarloff, who worked for several sitcoms including *The Dick Van Dyke Show* but mainly the *Danny Thomas Show*; the most notable project was the British-made *Robin Hood* (1955–58), upon which several blacklisted writers worked. Lees, Scott, and others provided individual scripts for *Lassie, Flipper,* and *Daktari.*

56. Despite his talent, Manoff had perpetual bad luck and died in his early fifties of a heart attack. His daughter Dinah Manoff, the television actress, has performed some of his works. Our thanks to actress (and activist) Lee Grant, Manoff's widow, for extended comments about the writer's disappointments.

57. John Schultheiss very kindly loaned us this manuscript.

58. *You Are There* had been broadcast on radio by CBS from 1947 to 1953 with John Daley as host.

59. Indeed, these productions, most on kinescope and for that reason still unavailable at the end of the century, compare favorably to the high-toned British and Commonwealth docudramas of the 1980s–90s and to the dynamic if often overacted *Roots.*

60. Abraham Polonsky, interview by John Schultheiss, 1989, quoted in the introduction to *To Illuminate Our Time: The Blacklisted Teleplays of Abraham Polonsky* (Los Angeles: Sadanlaur Publications, 1993), 10.

61. "Premiere Telecast, February 1, 1937," manuscript made available by John Schultheiss.

62. All *You Are There* shows but the Scopes trial excerpt are taken from *To Illuminate Our Time;* John Schultheiss loaned us a manuscript for the latter.

63. "The Great Adventures of Marco Polo," manuscript loaned by John Schultheiss.

64. "The Liberation of Paris," manuscript loaned by John Schultheiss.

65. "The Torment of Beethoven," in *To Illuminate Our Time*, 320, 322.

66. "The Emergence of Jazz," in *To Illuminate Our Time*, 281–82.

67. "The Secret of Sigmund Freud," in *To Illuminate Our Time*, 176.

68. "The Conquest of Mexico," in *To Illuminate Our Time*, 71.

69. "The Vindication of Savonarola," in *To Illuminate Our Time*, 235–36.

70. Quoted in the introduction to *You Are There Teleplays: The Critical Edition* (Northridge: University of California Center for Telecommunication Studies, 1997), 8–9. This volume is a slightly reworked version of *To Illuminate Our Time*, with a statement by Lumet and a few other items added.

71. *To Illuminate Our Time*, 345. During the production of Polonsky's half-hour teleplay on Freud, Russell received a phone call from a person who identified himself as Dr. Freud and indeed turned out to be the great man's nephew, also an analyst. He more or less ordered Russell to his office, where he expressed his concern about the word *secret* in the title. When Russell told him it was nothing more than a dramatic effect, Freud responded, "When I receive the script and read it I will determine whether I will file suit against your network. Good night."

Russell concluded, "Sigmund Freud's nephew did not consider it necessary to file suit against the network. He actually liked the script and at my invitation came to the studio on Sunday with Ernest Jones, author of *The Life and Works of Sigmund Freud*. They posed together, in one of the sets, with Walter Cronkite" (quoted in *To Illuminate Our Time*, 151–52).

72. A copy of the *Oedipus Rex* script is nevertheless in the Polonsky Collection, WSHS, and he may have made other contributions which he modestly declined to acknowledge. Polonsky must have found the Lenin-inspired lyrics in Pasolini's version curious indeed.

73. If his fellow blacklistees refused, during the 1970s–80s, to talk about their old Communist Party politics, this was Polonsky's equivalent, a silence to which he jocularly referred even while seeking, in every other respect, to be the helpful subject of a frank biography.

74. Robert Wise, interview by George Hickenlooper, in George Hickenlooper, ed., *Reel Conversations: Candid Interviews with Film's Foremost Directors and Critics* (New York: Citadel Books, 1991), 173.

75. Wise, in *Reel Conversations*, 166–68. This is not to ignore Wise's noted "straight" films, from *The Curse of the Cat People* (1944) to *Somebody Up There Likes Me* (1956), to *West Side Story* (1961) and *The Sound of Music* (1965), to *Star Trek* (1980). It is also interesting that Wise worked comfortably with two notable (and personally regretful) friendly witnesses, choreographer Jerome Robbins in *West Side Story* and scripter Isobel Lennart in *Two For the Seesaw*.

76. Most like the 1940s in style and feeling might be not the the film's noir plot and cinematography, but the placement of veteran character actress Gloria Grahame as the neurotic neighbor who wants to know how Ryan felt when murdering someone and who leaves her baby upstairs as she cheats on her husband with Ryan.

77. Quoted in *Odds Against Tomorrow: The Critical Edition* (Northridge: Center for Telecommunications, California State University, Northridge, 1999), 238.

78. Quoted in *Odds Against Tomorrow: The Critical Edition*, 239.

79. *Odds Against Tomorrow: The Critical Edition* 245.

80. William P. McGivern, *Odds Against Tomorrow* (New York: Dodd, Mead and Company, 1957), 45.

81. Ryan devoted an essay to explaining why he had been eager to play a racist, exploring values that he detested. He concluded that Slater was a "man who hates the whole human race," a foil to Ingram, who "emerges as the most

dignified, intelligent and superior person in the drama" ("I Didn't Want to Play a Bigot," *Ebony*, Nov., 1959, quoted in *Odds Against Tomorrow: The Critical Edition*, 153).

82. *Odds Against Tomorrow: The Critical Edition*, 133–34.

83. Nearly forty years later, the Writers Guild conferred Polonsky's credit, and he and Belafonte were on hand to take questions at a prestige reshowing at the Lincoln Center in 1999.

84. Martin C. Myrick, "John Lewis & the Film Score for *Odds Against Tomorrow*, I," and Michelle Best, "John Lewis & the Film Score for *Odds Against Tomorrow*, II," both in *Odds Against Tomorrow: The Critical Edition*, 299–307 and 309–313.

85. Bosley Crowther, "Screen: *Odds Against Tomorrow*," *New York Times*, Oct.16, 1959; "High-Minded Films," *New York Times*, Oct. 25, 1959; "*Odds Against Tomorrow*," *Variety*, Oct. 7. 1959; "Sharp, Stark, and Salty," *Newsweek*, Oct. 19, 1959, 108; "Films," *Nation*, Nov. 28, 1959, 408; "The New Pictures," *Time*, Oct. 26, 1959, 59. Special thanks to John Schultheiss for this observation, which plays a large role in his *Odds Against Tomorrow: The Critical Edition*, 191.

86. Quoted in *Odds Against Tomorrow: The Critical Edition*, 235, 252. The first two quotations are from a retrospective interview in 1998; the third from a *New York Times* interview in 1959.

87. "John Berry," in *Tender Comrades*, 82. Actually, *Tamango* finally made money in a late U.S. release, one of the first mainly black-acted pictures that actually crossed over to white audiences, but the damage had already been done to Berry's career in France. After another commercially unsuccessful film, Berry gave up moviemaking there. He had already made *The Hollywood Ten*, the first documentary on the subject, and several noir films including Garfield's final feature, *He Ran All the Way*.

88. Abraham Polonsky, interview by John Schultheiss, quoted in *Odds Against Tomorrow: The Critical Edition*, 174–175.

Chapter 5

1. Charles W. Russell, "In the Worst of Times It Was the Best of Times," Polonsky Collection, Radio-TV-Film Department, California State University, Northridge.

2. See Walter Bernstein, "Bad Art Makes for Bad Politics," interview by Dan Georgakas, in *New Labor Forum*, no. 4 (Spring-Summer 1999): 138–44. Bernstein discusses some of his most recent work, which like most of the work of the scriptwriter children of blacklistees is in made-for-television films.

3. "Sweetland," Polonsky Collection, WSHS, inconsistently paged.

4. The colonel adds, "You tell me the morality of employing and cheating children in our Northern mills. You tell me the morality of the English friends of abolition, weeping in houses heated by coal dug from mile deep mines by boys and girls chained to the wall, in darkness and in damp, like gnomes and devils. Little white children, sir, blonde hair, blue eyes, blood of their blood and bone of their bone."

5. *The Chase*, scripted by Lillian Hellman, was unfortunately a dramatic mishmash; *Black Like Me*, scripted in part by blacklisted film editor Carl Lerner but mostly by future women's history notable Gerda Lerner, was far better, but underfunded for the possibilities inherent in the theme of a reporter who dyes his

skin and experiences racism in a deeply personal way. The authors' gratitude goes to Gerda Lerner for her extended memories of filmmaking in the blacklist era.

6. "Calypso," Polonsky Collection, WSHS, inconsistently paged.

7. Abraham Polonsky, "Une expérience utopique," *Présence du cinéma*, no. 14 (June 1962): 5–7. This appeared in English for the first time in *Force of Evil: The Critical Edition* (Northridge: Center for Telecommunication Studies, California State University, Northridge, 1996), 186–88, thanks to the interventions of John Schultheiss in acquiring the original from Polonsky (the WSHS collection lacks a copy).

8. Polonsky, interview by Buhle and Wagner.

9. Richard Dougherty, *The Commissioner* (London: Rupert Hart-Davis, 1963), 16–28.

10. Dougherty, *The Commissioner*, especially 184–86, a close description that compares favorably to Tom Wolfe's throwing around Irish stereotypes in *Bonfire of the Vanities*. *Madigan* was the most notable of the three revolving elements in NBC's *Wednesday Mystery Movie* for the 1972–73 season, along with *Banacek* and *Cool Million*. Last broadcast originally in August 1973, the *Madigan* episodes have since been reshown occasionally, thanks no doubt to Widmark's following.

11. Doughtery, *The Commissioner*, 255.

12. Dougherty, *The Commissioner*, 256.

13. The comissioner's mistress is played by actress Susan Clark, who would play the Brahmin headmistress in *Tell Them Willie Boy Is Here*.

14. Dougherty, *The Commissioner*, 355–68.

15. Howard Thompson, "Screen: Widmark Hunting a Killer," *New York Times*, Mar. 30, 1968; see also "*Madigan*," *Variety*, Mar. 27, 1968, which pronounced it a "good solid big-city adventure yarn" and called Polonsky's screenplay "tough and to the point."

16. On *Dirty Harry*'s "fascism" in its disregard for the Bill of Rights, see Roger Ebert, "*Dirty Harry*," in *Roger Ebert's Video Companion*, 14th ed. (Kansas City: Andrews and McMeel, 1996), 193–94.

17. Abraham Polonsky, interview by Jim Cook and Kingsley Canham, in *Screen* 11 (Summer 1970): 69.

18. Pauline Kael, "Tell Them Willie Boy Is Here," in *5001 Nights at the Movies* (New York: Holt, Rinehart and Winston), 582. Originally published in "The Current Cinema," *The New Yorker*, Dec. 27, 1969, 47–48.

19. Roger Greenspun, "Screen: *Willie Boy Is Here* Opens," *New York Times*, Dec. 19, 1969; Robert Hatch, "Films," *Nation*, Jan. 12, 1970, 28–29; "Cinema," *Time*, Dec. 19, 1969, 76–77; Joseph Morgenstern, "Movies: Requiem for a Red Man," *Newsweek*, Dec. 8, 1969, 121–22.

20. "*Tell Them Willie Boy Is Here*," *Variety*, Oct. 22, 1969.

21. Most unfortunately, the video of the Carson show was destroyed, reportedly for legal reasons, with others from that same season. Polonsky later commented on his Carson Show appearance, "they asked me about the continued existence of blacklisting. . . . We discussed it for fifteen minutes. . . . I assume that the blacklisting [of peace activists from scientific jobs] exists widely. The only difference is that magazines and newspapers are exposing the blacklisting and getting out the information on it" (Abraham Polonsky, "How the Blacklist Worked in Hollywood," *Film Culture*, 50–51 [Fall-Winter, 1970]: 48).

22. Abraham Polonsky, interview by Eric Sherman and Martin Rubin, in Eric Sherman and Martin Rubin, eds., *The Director's Event: Interviews with Five American Film-Makers* (New York: Atheneum, 1969), 33–34.

23. Polonsky, in *The Director's Event,* 33.

24. Something of an oddity is James A. Sandos and Larry E. Burgess, eds., *The Hunt for Willie Boy: Indian-Hating and Popular Culture* (Norman: University of Oklahoma Press, 1994). The book contains a number of interesting insights into the Chemehuevi view of the historical Willie Boy and some valuable research on how accounts by a member of one of the original posses distorted the white view of the story. But the book's challenges to the script are frequently inaccurate, even though the authors show a familiarity with several of its drafts. The book is also confused in larger matters: the introduction asserts that the film is "a cautionary story about the 'other' designed to show the superiority of the white teller." But the discussion of the film that follows not only fails to offer any evidence for this remarkable statement, it drops the issue altogether. In fact, the discussion, which is generally appreciative of the film, repudiates that earlier assertion.

25. Polonsky, in *The Director's Event,* 41.

26. Published hard bound in Joseph Opatoshu, *A Roman fun a Ferd-Gonef un Andere Ertzehlungen* (New York: Literaturer Ferlag, 1917), a volume illustrated by Zuni Maud, cofounder of the Modikut theater, the first puppet theater of Yiddish plays. Thanks to Edward Portnoy for loaning this rare and delightful volume.

27. Charles Madison, *Yiddish Literature: Its Scope and Major Writers from Mendele and Sholem Aleichem to Isaac Bashevis Singer* (New York: Schocken, 1971), 326–47.

28. Perl was a member of the same early-1950s Manhattan communist group as Walter Bernstein. He wrote for television and was the principal writer of the original script for *Malcolm X* (1992), which Spike Lee lightly rewrote and lavishly produced a decade after Perl's death. Next to nothing has been written about him. His papers are in the State Historical Society of Wisconsin. We gladly acknowledge the useful information given us by his daughter, Rebecca Perl, in a summer 1998 telephone interview.

29. Eric Sherman, "Abraham Polonsky," in *American Directors,* vol. 2, ed. Jean Pierre Cousedon (New York: McGraw-Hill, 1983), 290–94.

30. Abraham Polonsky, "Making Movies," *Sight and Sound* 40 (Spring 1971): 101.

31. Roger Greenspun, "Cossacks and Jews," *New York Times,* Aug. 19, 1971; "*Romance of a Horsethief,*" *Variety,* July 21, 1971.

32. Polonsky, "Making Movies," 101.

33. Polonsky, *Zenia's Way,* 196.

34. See Edwin T. Arnold and Eugene L. Miller, *The Films and Career of Robert Aldrich* (Knoxville: University of Tennessee Press, 1986), spiced with references to and quotations from Polonsky.

35. The critical literature on Ritt is fairly abundant, including the interesting biography by Carlton Jackson, *Picking up the Tab: The Life and Movies of Martin Ritt* (Bowling Green, Ky.: Bowling Green State University Popular Press, 1994), but we wish to thank Adele Ritt for valuable reflections on her late husband's work in a 1993 Los Angeles interview.

36. Most of this work is discussed in *Tender Comrades;* most was done under conditions that precluded serious artistic intervention and encouraged cynicism by the now "graylisted" writers, no longer explicitly blacklisted by the 1960s but not offered work either.

37. Polonsky did contribute two episodes to the Canadian-made and heavily Left-influenced television series *Seaway* in 1955–56, focusing on the antifascist

tradition. He also had one major U.S. television credit, scripting "The Last Clear Chance" for NBC's *Kraft Suspense Theater.*

38. Arthur C. Clarke, *Childhood's End* (New York: Harcourt, Brace, 1953).

39. Abraham Polonsky, "Childhood's End," script, Polonsky Collection, WSHS, inconsistently paged.

40. Clarke, *Childhood's End,* 216.

41. The reviews were murderous. See Vincent Canby, "Film: *Avalanche Express,*" *New York Times,* Oct. 19, 1979; Richard Schickel, "Flat Country," *Time,* Nov. 5, 1979; and Simo, *"Avalanche Express," Variety,* July 25, 1979. Only the last seemed to appreciate the dilemma created by Robson's and Shaw's sudden deaths. Schickel bore quite a grudge against Polonsky and the black-listees, which he revealed in defenses of Elia Kazan's friendly testimony, during the controversy over Kazan's Academy Award in 1999.

42. Copy provided by Polonsky. This unpaged script is not in the State Historical Society of Wisconsin collection.

43. See Saul Landau, "From the Labor Youth League to the Cuban Revolution," in Paul Buhle, ed., *History and the New Left: Madison, Wisconsin, 1950–70* (Philadelphia: Temple University Press, 1990), 107–12. This autobiographical essay, mainly covering Landau's college days and slightly after, originated in an interview by Paul Buhle at IPS offices in Washington with Isabel Letelier in a nearby office and her daughter playing in the hallway outside.

44. John Dinges and Saul Landau, *Assassination on Embassy Row* (New York: Pantheon Books, 1980).

45. In the frame of the docudrama, even a fictional Joan Baez sings a cappella, and Bishop James Rasch pronounces the funeral service in a New York cathedral.

46. Polonsky, *Zenia's Way,* 94.

47. Polonsky, *Zenia's Way,* 39–42; this literary version compares well to one of the few contemporary reminiscences, *If You Don't Weaken* (originally published in 1940, reprinted in a 1983 edition by the University of Oklahoma Press at Norman), by Oscar Ameringer, a kindly socialist propagandist and opponent of the "direct action" rebels.

48. Polonsky, *Zenia's Way,* 158–66.

49. See Itche Goldberg, "I. L. Peretz: Der Gantzer Yid," in *Shriftn* (New York: Yiddishe Kultur Farband, 1985).

50. Polonsky, *Zenia's Way,* 267–68.

51. See *"Zenia's Way," Wilson Library Bulletin* 54 (June 1980): 675–66; Larry Ceplair, "Creative Forgetting," *The Nation,* June 14, 1980, 730–31; Leslie Raddatz, "A Boy among the Bronx Weeds," *Los Angeles Times,* June 1, 1980; Terry Curtis Fox, "Faith on the Left," *Village Voice,* Oct. 8 1980.

52. Jack Kroll, "The Borgias Would Blanch," *Newsweek,* Nov. 8, 1982, 90. Polonsky avoided a credit for his contribution to *Mommie Dearest* (1981), in one scene of which a tortured Faye Dunaway, as Joan Crawford, meets with a movie mogul. Frank Perry, the director, convinced Polonsky to work for a short time on the film.

53. "Monsignor" script provided by Polonsky, inconsistently paged.

54. Kroll, "The Borgias Would Blanch," 90.

55. Janet Maslin, "Movie: *Monsignor*—Dishonest Priest," *New York Times,* Oct. 22, 1982. See also Chris Chase, "At the Movies," *New York Times,* Oct. 22, 1982.

56. In an evident reference to Lucky Luciano, Cortese tells Reeve about the big fish who got back to Sicily, helped the Allied troops by clearing out the Ger-

man stragglers, and enjoyed unofficial rehabilitation in return ("one hand wipes the other"). Thereby Cortese got the connections.

57. "Father Francesco, you're a eunuch, both spiritual and temporal. . . . You brown-nose Cardinal Vinci and plot against the Pope. You search my luggage, sniff through my documents, lick my trash [flinging him back to crash among his bundles]. Your soul sits frozen in ice in the bottom circle of hell. You lust for power through betrayal."

58. "It's not love you betrayed. . . . You betrayed me, Clara. You destroyed me. All along you knew that moment would come when you'd end my life. And still you waited, and still you were kind and sweet and secret. You were about to murder me, and you didn't have the courage to finish me off. . . . You raped me. You violated my soul. You made it hope again, when all the years of my life it had never really hoped."

59. "Your intelligence and insight led me to find something in myself that I hadn't thought possible," Winkler is quoted as writing Polonsky in March 1989. "I was able to sit down and put my feelings on paper, constructing a script based on your writings and drafts that represented a character I understood, had compassion for and wanted to direct as a film" (Victor Navasky, "Did *Guilty by Suspicion* Miss the Point about Blacklisting?" *New York Times*, Mar. 31, 1991).

60. Navasky, "Did *Guilty by Suspicion* Miss the Point?"

61. Ebert, "*Guilty by Suspicion,*" *Roger Ebert's Video Companion*, 297.

62. Polonsky, *Zenia's Way*, 160.

63. Polonsky, *Zenia's Way*, 163.

64. Polonsky, *Zenia's Way*, 166.

65. Polonsky, *Zenia's Way*, 173.

66. Polonsky, *Zenia's Way*, 175.

67. Caryn James, "Critic's Notebook: A Walk Down Cinema's Mean Streets," *New York Times*, Feb. 23, 1996.

68. Anthony Lane, "The Current Cinema: Jack Be Quick," *New Yorker*, July 6, 1998, 79.

69. Abraham Polonsky, *Zenia's Way*, 180.

70. Jeff Kisseloff, "Another Award, Other Memories of McCarthyism," *New York Times*, May 30, 1999. Kisseloff himself was editor of one of the best books on television, *The Box: An Oral History of Television, 1920–1961*, which gave Polonsky, among many others, a chance to air his grievances (see especially 418–22).

71. William H. Honan, "Abraham Polonsky, 88, Dies; Director Damaged by Blacklist," *New York Times*, Oct. 29, 1999.

72. This commentary is based upon observations of the biographers. Paul Buhle was one of the speakers at the memorial. John Schultheiss, who continues work on a Polonsky film documentary, presided and also provided the dramatic film and video clips. An earlier memorial service at U.S.C., organized by Polonsky's students almost immediately after his death, featured Harry Belafonte.

BIBLIOGRAPHICAL NOTE

Until recent times, study of the Hollywood blacklistees and their work has been limited almost entirely to a discussion of the legal and ethical issues involved in the blacklisting process. Far and away the best work in this area continues to be Victor Navasky's *Naming Names* (New York: Viking Press, 1980). Eric Bentley, *Thirty Years of Treason: Excerpts from Hearings before the House Committee on Un-American Activities, 1938–1968* (New York: Viking, 1971), contains the most thorough published documentation of the process, although Polonsky's testimony was not among those included. Nor does Polonsky appear in the otherwise quite useful memoirs and biographies of some of the well-known fellow left-wing writers and directors such as Lester Cole, *Hollywood Red* (Palo Alto: Ramparts Press, 1971); Howard Koch, *As Time Goes By: Memoirs of a Writer* (New York: Harcourt Brace Jovanovich, 1979); Donald Ogden Stewart, *By a Stroke of Luck!* (London: Paddington Press, 1975); Bernard Gordon, *Hollywood Exile, or How I Learned to Love the Blacklist* (Austin: University of Texas Press, 1999); Maurice Rapf, *Back Lot: Growing Up with the Movies* (Lanham, Maryland: Scarecrow Press, 1999); Bruce Cook, *Dalton Trumbo* (New York: Scribner's, 1977); or David Caute, *Joseph Losey: A Revenge on Life* (New York: Oxford University Press, 1994).

Attention to the larger political and aesthetic issues of the Hollywood Left has for the most part remained sharply limited. Larry Ceplair and Steven Englund, *The Inquisition in Hollywood: Politics in the Film Community, 1930–1960* (New York: Doubleday/Anchor, 1980), describe mainly the labor conflicts and the struggle against the blacklist. Nancy Lynn Schwartz, *The Hollywood Writers' Wars* (New York: Knopf, 1982), deals mainly in personalities, although containing much of value gained in interviews. Bernard F. Dick, *Radical Innocence: A Critical Study of the Hollywood Ten* (Lexington: University Press of Kentucky, 1989), sticks to his immediate subjects, who are fiction writers as much as screenwriters. Ian Hamilton, *Writers in Hollywood, 1915–1951* (New York: Carroll and Graf, 1990), offers more on the subject of the left-wing writer (including Polonsky) than the title suggests, one evidence among many that the more recent the treatment, the more the interest in (and favorable evaluation of) Polonsky's work has grown. Brian Neve's acute *Film and Politics in America: A Social Tradition* (London: Routledge, 1992) anticipates this volume in a number of small ways.

Creative Differences: Profiles of Hollywood Dissidents (Boston: South End Press, 1978), by David Talbot and Barbara Zheutlin, could be considered a breakthrough in Polonsky studies because the forty-four page profile (with many quotations from the subject) outstripped the growing favorable film-journal commentary. Unfortunately, this volume remains almost unseen. Robert Sklar's *City Boys: Cagney, Bogart, Garfield* (Princeton: Princeton University Press, 1992) offered a most thoughtful interpretation of Garfield's films, especially Polonsky's contributions to *Body and Soul* and *Force of Evil*. Other close accounts of Polonsky's contributions, especially to noir, have been indirect but continue to add new insight, as in James Naremore, *More than Night: Film Noir in Its Contexts* (Berkeley and Los Angeles: University of California Press, 1998). John Schultheiss's admirable introductory essays and notes in *To Illuminate Our Time: The Blacklisted Teleplays of Abraham Polonsky* (Los Angeles: Sadanlaur Publications, 1993), edited by John Schultheiss and Mark Schaubert; *Force of Evil: The Critical Edition* (Northridge: Center for Telecommunication Studies, California State University, Northridge, 1993) and *Odds against Tomorrow: The Critical Edition* (Northridge: Center for Telecommunication Studies, California State University, Northridge, 1999), both edited by John Schultheiss, provide indispensable documentation and independent interpretation that all readers of this volume will wish to consult.

Many fine unpublished oral histories with Polonsky and his colleagues are scattered from UCLA to Southern Methodist University to Columbia University and other sites. Those that have reached print, along with one most exceptional memoir, have further marked the way toward a wider revaluation of Polonsky. Jeff Kisseloff's *The Box: An Oral History of Television, 1920–1961* (New York: Penguin, 1995), with its unabashed treatment of blacklisting and excerpts from interviews with Polonsky and friends like Lee Grant and Walter Bernstein, added much. Eric Sherman and Martin Rubin, *The Director's Event: Interviews with Five American Filmmakers* (New York: Atheneum, 1970), and Eric Sherman, *Directing the Film: Film Directors on Their Art* (Boston: Little, Brown, 1976), each contain interviews with Polonsky. Bernstein's *Inside Out: A Memoir of the Blacklist* (New York: Knopf, 1996) tells the story of the Polonsky-Manoff-Bernstein combination, close friendships, and collaboration on television scripts. *Tender Comrades: A Backstory of the Hollywood Blacklist* (New York: St. Martin's, 1997), by Patrick McGilligan and Paul Buhle, contains the fullest possible oral history of the blacklist milieu, a voluble and philosophical Polonsky emphatically included.

INDEX

Text: 10/13 Sabon
Display: Rotis Serif
Composition: BookMatters
Printing and binding: Friesens